A SANSKRIT GRA

FOR BEGINNE

CW00482137

ALSO FROM TIGER XENOPHON

An Anglo-Saxon Primer
Henry Sweet

An Anglo-Saxon Reader
Henry Sweet

Kennedy's New Latin Primer
Benjamin Hall Kennedy
(US and UK editions)

Grammaire Élémentaire de l'Ancien Français
Joseph Anglade

From Latin to Italian
Charles H. Grandgent

Grammar of the Gothic Language
Joseph Wright

A Greek Grammar
William W. Goodwin

ALSO FROM TIGER OF THE STRIPE

The Student's Dictionary of Anglo-Saxon
Henry Sweet

A Sanskrit
Grammar
for Beginners

F. MAX MÜLLER

Revised by
A. A. MACDONELL

TIGER **S** XENOPHON

This edition first published
in 2008 by
TIGER XENOPHON
50 Albert Road
Richmond
Surrey TW10 6DP

http://www.tigerxenophon.com

TIGER XENOPHON
is an imprint of
Tiger of the Stripe

ISBN 978-1-904799-29-0

Printed in the US and UK by
Lightning Source

PREFACE

TO THE NEW EDITION.

As I am growing old I begin to feel that it is difficult, if not impossible, to keep my books young, or to revive them constantly by what we call new editions. When I had revised the last edition of my Sanskrit Grammar, I bade farewell to it. What I had wished to achieve, little as it may seem, I had achieved, namely, to supply a grammatical manual, correct in all its rules and paradigms, and containing for all important matters references to Pâṇini, the highest grammatical authority, recognised as such by all post-Vedic writers of Sanskrit.

It may not seem, as I said, to be a very high aim to produce a correct grammar, and to make its correctness dependent on the authority of another grammarian. But when we examine other grammars, and see, for instance, such forms as nâman given through successive editions as a Nominative and Accusative singular, when we see such breaches of the simplest phonetic rules as in Benfey's impossible form adâktam [1], etc., matched in one of the most recent Sanskrit Grammars by Whitney (arauttam) [2], a claim to freedom from clerical errors will hardly be considered a very modest claim. Nor do I flatter myself to have always reached that standard of correctness which is represented to us in the truly marvellous work of Pâṇini.

It has been argued, not without a certain plausibility, that no grammar, not even that of Pâṇini, ought to be constituted into an infallible tribunal, but that the language itself and the literature should form the final court

---

[1] Kurze Grammatik, § 265, ix, p. 178, paradigm dah.
[2] Sanskrit Grammar, § 882, paradigm rudh.

of appeal in all questions of grammatical right or wrong.
True as this principle would be everywhere else, it is not so
in Sanskrit, at least, not with regard to that literature for
which alone my grammar is intended. The whole of Sanskrit literature, with the exception of the Vedic and the
Buddhistic, is so completely under the sway of Pânini's
rules that even a poet like Kâlidâsa would be considered
guilty of a grammatical blunder, if he used a form not recognised by Pânini. This is a state of things unknown in any
other literature, and supplies, I believe, a perfect justifica-
tion for the absolute deference paid by myself and others to
Pânini's authority.

There is, of course, some debatable land, such as the two
great epic poems, and again, some *rifaccimenti* of Vedic
works, such as Manu and other law-books, in which ancient
*kh*ândasa forms occur and in which Pânini's authority is not
completely recognised. Still even there the more ancient and
more historical forms, which contravene the rules of Pânini,
are looked upon by all native scholars as exceptions, so
much so that when I myself appealed to the authority of
Vyâsa, the reputed author of the Mahâbhârata, in support
of such a form as him*s*asva, which, in my Sanskrit trans-
lation of 'God save the Queen,' I had borrowed from the
Mahâbhârata, I was told that this form, not having the
authority of Pânini, would be offensive to the ears of native
scholars. Though the case was by no means so clear as my
friendly critics imagined, I gladly yielded to their remon-
strances, changing him*s*asva into u*kkh*inddhi.

My own opinion was, and is still, that a Sanskrit Grammar
for Beginners, such as mine was meant to be, and a grammar
that might safely be used by candidates for the Civil Service
of India, without their running the risk of being punished
for forms which they learn from well-accredited books,
should not attempt more than to give such rules as can
claim the authority of Pânini. To attempt the higher task
of writing an historical grammar of the Sanskrit language,

THE experience of some years' teaching has convinced me that Sanskrit, compared with other dead languages, is not difficult to learn. The fact that the ordinary Sanskrit verb has no subjunctive, only one imperative, one infinitive, and two optatives, altogether only thirteen moods and tenses in each voice, while Greek has upwards of thirty, would alone go far to prove the comparative simplicity of Sanskrit Accidence. Again, the absence in Sanskrit of the indirect construction, which constitutes a conspicuous difficulty of Syntax in the classical languages, is in itself a tolerably clear proof that the structure of complex sentences in Sanskrit must be far less involved than in Latin or Greek. On the other hand, though it must be admitted that the phonetic laws of Sanskrit present greater difficulties than in other languages, most of these difficulties will disappear when it is pointed out that the rules of Sandhi rest on two leading principles, the avoidance of hiatus in the case of vowels and assimilation in the case of consonants.

I feel sure that the exaggerated idea of the difficulties of Sanskrit commonly entertained is due to the fact that the amount of matter contained in the Sanskrit grammars hitherto published in England and America is far too exhaustive for elementary purposes. Beginners are not aware that a large proportion of the matter presented to them, though necessary for a minute and critical knowledge or high proficiency in composition, may be altogether dispensed with by those whose chief object is to be able to read with ease the best works of classical Sanskrit literature.

It was therefore with much pleasure that, at Professor Max Müller's request, I undertook the task of abridging his grammar,—which is by all Sanskrit scholars accepted as a standard work,—and of adapting it to the requirements of the many students who wish to obtain a good practical knowledge of Sanskrit, but have not sufficient leisure to make a special study of the grammar. I feel a confident hope that this edition will at the same time supply students of comparative philology with the essential grammatical knowledge of a language which must form the groundwork of their studies. It is chiefly for their benefit that the accent, which plays so important a part in phonetic change, has been supplied throughout in the transliteration, except where the word in question (this is mainly the case in compounds) does not occur in accentuated texts and analogy is not a safe guide. Transliterated *sentences*, however, (in the chapter on the particles and that on syntax,) have not been accented.

The principle by which I have been guided in the preparation of this new edition, is that an elementary grammar should be as short, simple, clear, and as practical as possible.

Convinced of the supreme value of *brevity*, I have made it my aim to omit rules referring to words rarely or never to be met with in the books usually read, to avoid overloading the rules actually given with unimportant exceptions or with the mention of rare optional forms, and to pass over altogether those portions of the grammar, which though of minor practical importance, it would take almost years of special study to master thoroughly, notably the rules on the insertion of the intermediate इ i. For the benefit of students desirous of obtaining a more minute knowledge of grammatical details, I have added in parentheses at the beginning of each paragraph figures referring to the corresponding portions of Professor Max Müller's large edition.

With a view to *simplicity*, I have endeavoured, on the one hand, to formulate as far as possible in the same words rules which have points in common, and, on the other, to draw together rules which, though usually given separately, may be learnt more easily if combined under one head. I think I have thus, for instance, succeeded in simplifying considerably the rules on the Sandhi of the diphthongs (24, 25), of the interjections (27, note), and of अः a*h* and आः â*h* (51), as well as the rules on the formation of the first aorist. On the same ground, the terminations of the first and the second conjugations for the special forms have, instead of being separated, been given in a single table (142).

For the sake of *clearness*, I have added many explanations, without which learners would find a difficulty in understanding the application of the rule, for instance, those in 75 and 76 on the change of the dental nasal and sibilant to the lingual. To the same motive are due the observations on the grouping of the various moods and tenses (133) and on the differences between the first and the second conjugations (142). I have also given a number of notes calling attention to distinctions of forms which are otherwise almost certain to be confused, as, for example, the declension of perfect participles like kritavân and rurudvân (101, note 2), or drawing useful generalizations from paradigms of declension and conjugation, which it would take much time and observation on the part of the student to make for himself, e. g. as to the instances in which the vocative differs from the nominative (82, note 1), or as to the form of the nom. and voc. sing. of changeable bases (105).

In order to give this edition a thoroughly *practical* character, I have thought it worth while to appeal to the eye of the learner by printing in thick type any important point, or, in transliterated words, any phonetic peculiarity otherwise likely to escape his attention. With the same end in view, I have arranged in alphabetical order, the prepositions, the interjections, and the particles of common occurrence, devoting special attention to the meanings and uses of the latter as being of considerable practical importance to those who are beginning to read Sanskrit. For the sake of easy reference I have given the list of verbs (altogether 206) alphabetically also, omitting both verbs and verbal forms which occur only in the grammarians. I may here remark in passing that I have throughout the grammar refrained from quoting, in exemplification of the rules given, forms not occurring in the literature, except in the comparatively few cases where the opposite course seemed necessary on pedagogic grounds.

In order to supplement what is omitted in it, the student should use the list of verbs in connection with the paradigms of the various tenses and with the list of irregularities given after each of the latter. I have appended a chapter on syntax, which, though short, I think will be found to contain all that the beginner wants, together with a brief sketch of the metres most commonly to be met with in the classical literature.

In conclusion, I must express my obligations to Prof. Stenzler's elementary Sanskrit book for suggesting to me the advisability of either retaining or omitting various rules. To Mr. Apte's excellent Guide to Sanskrit Composition I am indebted for much of the matter contained both in the section on the use of the particles and in the chapter on syntax. In preparing the list of verbs, I have derived much assistance from Prof. Whitney's valuable new work, 'Sanskrit Roots, Verb-Forms, and Primary Derivatives.' For the sketch of Sanskrit metres I have found very serviceable Prof. Oldenberg's article on the Śloka, in vol. xxxv of the Journal of the German Oriental Society, as well as Prof. Jacobi's more recent article, 'Zur Lehre vom Śloka.' From Prof. Edgren's Sanskrit Grammar I have derived some suggestions as to arrangement, and some valuable hints from Prof. Whitney's article on the Study of Sanskrit in the American Journal of Philology (vol. v, No. 3). To Professor Max Müller, above all, are due my sincere thanks for the advice and help he has always given me in this as well as in all other work I have undertaken in Sanskrit.

A. A. M.

INVERGARRY, N. B., September, 1885.

CONTENTS.

CHAPTER I. The Alphabet (1-15).

SECT.   PAGE

The Devanâgarî letters . 2
1. Sanskrit and modern
    Indian dialects . . . 3
2. Characters in which San-
    skrit is written . . . 3
3. Number of letters in the
    alphabet. 3
4. The vowels 3
5. Classified table of letters . 4
6. How to write the letters . 4
7. Marks and signs 4
8. The sibilants 5

SECT.   PAGE

9. The nasals 5
10. The three nasal semivowels 5
11. Consonants without cor-
    responding nasals . . 5
12. Anusvâra before s, sh, s, h 5
13. Combination of consonants 6
14. Peculiarities of letters in
    combination 6
15. List of compound consonants 6
16. Numerical figures . . . 8
17. Rules of pronunciation. . 8
18. The accent 9

CHAPTER II. Rules of Sandhi (19-79).

19. Meaning and use of Sandhi 10
20. Classification of vowels . 10
21. Vowels meeting vowels
    (21-27) . .   . 11
22. a and â followed other
    vowels and by diphthongs 11
23. Liquid vowels followed by
    other vowels 11
24. e and o followed by vowels 11
25. ai and au followed by vowels
26. Unchangeable vowels . . 12
27. Irregular Sandhi; preposi-
    tions ending in a or â
    followed by e, o, or ri . 12
28. The eleven final consonants 13
29. No word ends in two conso-
    nants. 13
30. Classification of consonants,
    according to their organ 14
31. According to their quality 15
32. Changes of organ and of
    quality 15
33. Changes of organ affect
    dentals, Anusvâra, and
    Visarga only 15

34. Final t before palatals (ex-
    cept k, kh) 16
35. Final n before palatals . 16
36. Final t before the linguals
    (except sh) 16
37. Final n before d, dh, n . . 16
38. Changes of quality . . . 17
39. Final k, t, t, p before nasals 18
40. Final t before l 18
41. Final n before l 18
42. Doubling of final ṅ, n, n . 18
43. Final n before firsts and
    seconds 18
44. Final ṅ and n before s, sh, s 19
45. Final n before s or s (not sh) 19
46. Final t before s 19
47. Anusvâra and final m . . 20
48. Final m in pausâ . . . 21
49. Visarga for final s and r . 21
50. Visarga before soft letters. 22
51. ah and âh before soft letters 22
52. Final radical r 22
53. Final r before initial r . . 23
54. Pronouns sah and eshah . 23
55. Bhoh, bhagoh, aghoh . . 23

SECT. PAGE
56. Nouns ending in radical r . 24
57. Initial *kh* and medial *kh* . 24
58. Initial *s* changeable to *kh* . 24
59. Initial h after k, *t*, t, p . . 25
60. Final aspiration thrown back on initial . . . 25
61. Internal Sandhi (61-79) 25
62. î, û, *ri* before vowels . . 25
63. *ri* before consonants . . 26
64. e, ai, o, au before vowels . 26
65. i and u before radical r or v 26
66. Two final consonants impossible 26
67. Consonants remain unchanged before vowels, nasals, and semivowels . 27

SECT. PAGE
68. Aspirates losing their aspiration 27
69. Soft aspirates followed by t or th 27
70. Dentals after linguals . . 28
71. n after k and *g* 28
72. n before sibilants. . . . 28
73. n before semivowels. . . 28
74. m changed to n; unchanged before y, r, l 28
75. n changed to *n* 28
76. s changed to sh 30
77. *s* before t 31
78. s changed to t before s . . 31
79. h before s is treated like gh 31

CHAPTER III. Declension (80-130).

80. I. Nouns. II. Numerals. III. Pronouns . . . 32
81. Gender, number, and case . 32
82. Case-terminations . . . 32
83. Nouns with changeable bases 33
84. Strong cases 33
85. 1. Consonant stems and 2. vowel stems . . . 34
86. A. Unchangeable bases (86-95) 34
87. Bases in gutturals, linguals, dentals, and labials (87-91) 35
88. *kitralikh* 35
89. harit, agnimath, suh*ri*d, budh, gup, kakubh . . 36
90. Bases in palatals . . . 36
91. Bases in nasals 38
92. Bases in semivowels . . 38
93. Bases in sibilants and h . 39
94. Exceptional cases in sibilants and h 39
95. Bases in s 41-43
96. B. Changeable bases (96-106) 43
97. Nouns with two bases (97-100)—1. in at . . . 43
98. Bases in mat and vat . . 44
99. 2. Bases in in 45

100. 3. Bases in *iyas* 45
101. Nouns with three bases (101-104)—1. vas . . 46
102. 2. Bases in an (man, van) 47
103. Irregular bases in an . . 49
104. 3. Bases in a*k* 50
105. Practical hints on the declension of changeable bases 52
106. Irregular nouns with changeable bases . . . 53
107. Vowel bases (107-113): a and â 54
108. Bases in radical â . . . 55
109. Bases in i and u 55
110. Irregularities: pati, sakhi, akshi, asthi, dadhi, sakthi 57
111. Bases in î and û 57
112. Bases in *ri* 60
113. Bases in ai, o, au . . . 61
114. Degrees of comparison: -tara, -tama 62
115. Primary suffixes: -îyas, -ish*tha* 62
116. Numerals (116-120): Cardinals 62
117. 118. } Declension of cardinals . 64
119. Ordinals 65
120. Numerical adverbs . . . 66

Pronouns (121–130).

SECT.	PAGE	SECT.	PAGE
121. Personal pronouns . . . 67		126. Reflexive pronouns . . . 70	
122. Demonstr. pronouns: tad . 68		127. Compound pronouns . . 70	
123. idam 68		128. Pronouns of quantity in yat	
124. adas 69		and vat 71	
125. tyad, etad; interrogative		129. Indefinite pronouns . . . 71	
kim; relative yad . . 69		130. Pronominal adjectives . . 72	

CHAPTER IV. Conjugation (131–206).

131. Active, middle, and passive	73	158. First aor.: first and second	
132. Singular, dual, and plural	73	forms: irregularities 104–6	
133. Nine tenses and moods .	73	159. Third form 106	
134. Special and general forms	74	160. Fourth form 107	
135. Two conjugations, ten		161. Second aorist: first form . 108	
classes	75	162. Irregularities 108	
136. Formation of pres. stem:		163. Second form . . . 109	
first conjugation . .	75	164. Third or reduplicated form 109	
137. Second conj.: strong forms	76	165. Metrical rhythm in redu-	
138. Ad, Hu, Su, Rudh, Tan,		plicated aorist . . . 109	
and Krî classes . . .	76	166. Special rule of redupl. . 110	
139. The augment	77	167. Irregularity 110	
140. Redupl.: general rules .	78	168. Simple future 110	
141. Special rule for Class III	79	169. Periphrastic future . . 111	
142. Terminations: table and		170. Conditional 112	
notes. 79–81		171. Benedictive (precative) . 112	
143. Paradigms 81–93		172. Modification of root in	
144. Irregularities of present		benedictive; paradigm 113	
stems 94–98		173. Passive: terminations . 113	
145. General or unmodified		174. Special forms 113	
tenses	98	175. Changes of root before	
146. Redupl. perfect: special		passive ya 113	
rules of reduplication .	98	176. Paradigm of passive . . 114	
147. Only formed from primary		177. General forms of passive. 114	
verbs	99	178. Periphrastic perfect . . 115	
148. Terminations . . .	99	179. Aorist passive, 3rd sing.. 115	
149. Peculiarity of roots in â.	99	180. How formed 115	
150. Guṇa and Vṛiddhi in sing.		181. Irregularities 115	
Parasmaipada . . .	100	182. Pres. and fut. participle . 115	
151. Weakening of root before		183. Redupl. perf. participle . 116	
accented terminations .	100	184. Pres. and fut. Âtmanepada	
152. Final vowels before vowel		and passive participle. 116	
terminations	101	185. Perf. Âtm. participle . . 117	
153. Irregularities	101	186. Perf. passive participle . 117	
154. Paradigms	102	187. Fut. passive participle . 118	
155. Periphrastic perfect, when		188. Gerund or indecl. part. . 119	
formed	103	189. Gerund suffix -ya and -tya 119	
156. Irregularities	104	190. Indeclinable part. in -am . 119	
157. Two kinds of aorists . .	104	191. Infinitive 119	

xvi

Derivative Verbs (192–206).

SECT.   PAGE

192. Causatives, formation of . 120
193. Causatives in -paya . . 120
194. Irregular causatives . . 120
195. -aya retained in general forms 120
196. Passive of causatives . . 121
197. Desideratives 121
198. Special rules of redupl. . 121
199. Irregularities 122

SECT.   PAGE

200. Intensives: not formed by all verbs 122
201. Two forms of the intensive 122
202. Base modified before intensive -ya 122
203. Conjugation of intensives 122
204. Special rules of redupl. . 123
205. Irregular intensives . . 123
206. Denominatives, formation 124

Chapter V. Indeclinable Words (207–211).

207. Prepositions 125
208. Cases governed by them . 125
209. Prepositional adverbs. . 125

210. Conjunctions and other particles . . . 126–133
211. Interjections . . . 133-4

Chapter VI. Compound Words (212–219).

212. Importance of compounds in Sanskrit . . . 134
213. Three kinds : determinatives, copulatives, and possessives 134
214. Dependent determinatives 135

215. Descriptive determinatives 136
216. Copulative compounds . 137
217. Peculiarities of copulative compounds 137
218. Possessive compounds . 137
219. Peculiarities of possessives 138

Chapter VII. Syntax (220–250).

220. Characteristics of Sanskrit syntax 139
221. Order of words . . . 139
222. Order of clauses . . . 140
223. The article 140
224. Number 140
225. Concord 141
226. Pronouns 141
227. Nominative case . . . 142
228. Accusative case. . . . 143
229. Double accusative . . . 143
230. Instrumental 144
231. Dative 146
232. Ablative 147
233. Genitive 148
234. Locative 149
235. Loc. and gen. absolute . 151
236. Time and distance . . . 152
237. Present participle . . . 152

238. Act. and pass. past part. . 152
239. Future passive participle 152
240. Indeclinable participle . 153
241. Infinitive : two kinds . 153
242. Infinitive with adjectives and nouns 154
243. No passive form of the infinitive 154
244. The present 155
245. Imperfect, perfect, aorist 155
246. Simple and periphrastic future 156
247. Imperative 156
248. Optative 156
249. Benedictive (precative) . 157
250. Conditional 157
Appendix I. List of Verbs 158–177
Appendix II. Metre . . 178–181
Sanskrit Index . . . 182–192

SANSKRIT GRAMMAR.

THE DEVANÂGARÎ LETTERS.

VOWELS.			CONSONANTS.			
Initial.	Medial.	Equivalent.		Equivalent.		Equivalent.
अ	–	a	क	k	प	p
आ	ा	â	ख	kh	फ	ph
इ	ि	i	ग	g	ब	b
ई	ी	î	घ	gh	भ	bh
उ	ॖ	u	ङ	ṅ	म	m
ऊ	ॗ	û	च	*k* (or ch)	य	y
ऋ	ॆ	ri (or ṛi)	छ	*kh* (or chh)	र	r
			ज	*g* (or j)	ल	l
			झ	*gh* (or jh)	व	v
ॠ	ॄ	rî (or ṛî)	ञ	*ñ* (or ñ)		
ऌ	ॢ	li (or ḷi)	ट	*t* (or ṭ)	श	s (or ś)
ॡ	ॣ	lî (or ḷî)	ठ	*th* (or ṭh)	ष	sh
ए	े	e	ड	*d* (or ḍ)	स	s
ऐ	ै	ai	ढ	*dh* (or ḍh)	ह	h
ओ	ो	o	ण	*n* (or ṇ)		
औ	ौ	au	त	t	·	*m* (or ṁ)
			थ	th	ँ	*m̆* (or m̆)
			द	d	ः	*h* (or ḥ)
			ध	dh	⤬	(*G*ihvâmûlîya), χ
			न	n	⤬	(Upadhmânîya), φ

CHAPTER I.

THE ALPHABET.

1 (1). The Sanskrit, or sacred language, is the ancient *literary* language of the Hindûs. From the ancient *popular* dialects, called Prâkrit, are descended most of the dialects of modern India, 'Bengâlî, Hindî, Marâthî, Gujarâtî, and Hindûstânî.

2 (2). Sanskrit is written in Devanâgarî character from left to right., Bengâlî, Grantha, Telugu, and other modern Indian characters are also commonly employed for writing Sanskrit in their respective provinces.

3 (5). The Devanâgarî alphabet consists of forty-eight letters, thirteen vowels and thirty-five consonants. These represent every sound of the Sanskrit language.

4 (13). The vowels are written differently according as they are initial or follow a consonant. They are :—

(a) Simple vowels: अ (-)[1] a, इ (f) i[2], उ (ृ) u, ऋ (ृ) ri[3], ऌ (ृ) li.

        आ (ा) â, ई (ी) î, ऊ (ू) û, ॠ (ृ) rî.

(b) Diphthongs : ए (ॆ) e, ऐ (ॆ) ai, ओ (ॊ) o, औ (ॊ) au.

Note 1. There is no sign for medial (or final) ă, as this vowel is considered to be inherent in every consonant, e. g. क = ka.

Note 2. Medial (or final) ĭ is written before the consonant after which it is pronounced, e. g. कि ki.

Note 3. If ऋ ri follows the consonant र r it retains its initial form, and the r is written over it; thus निर्ऋतिः nirritih (cp. 14).

5 (4). The following table contains a complete classification of all the letters of the Devanâgarî alphabet according to the organs with which they are pronounced (see 30).

	Hard, (tenues.)	Hard, and aspirated, (tenues aspiratæ.)	Soft, (mediæ.)	Soft, and aspirated, (mediæ aspiratæ.)	Na-sals.	Liquids.	Sibilants.	Vowels. Short, Long.	Diphthongs.
Gutturals	क k	ख kh	ग g	घ gh	ङ ṅ	ह h[2]	⤬³(χ)	अ a आ â	
Palatals	च k	छ kh	ज g	झ gh[1]	ञ ñ	य y	श s	इ i ई î	ए e ऐ ai
Linguals	ट t	ठ th	ड d	ढ dh	ण n	र r	ष sh	ऋ ri ॠ rî	ओ o औ au
Dentals	त t	थ th	द d	ध dh	न n	ल l	स s	ऌ li ॡ lî	
Labials	प p	फ ph	ब b	भ bh	म m	व v	⤬³(φ)	उ u ऊ û	

Unmodified Nasal or Anusvâra, ˙ m, or ⌣ m̐, e. g. कं kam, or कँ kam̐.
Unmodified Sibilant or Visarga, : h.

Note—In the above table, the first, second, and seventh (sibilants) columns contain hard sounds; the remaining consonants and all vowels are soft.

6 (3). In writing the Devanâgarî alphabet, the distinctive portion of each letter is written first, then the perpendicular, and lastly the horizontal line, e. g. र, त, त ta.

7 (18–20). Consonants to be pronounced without any vowel after them are marked with Virâma (ॖ). Thus ak must be written अक्.

At the end of a sentence or of a half-verse, the sign । is used as a stop; at the end of a verse or longer sentence, the sign ॥ is employed.

---

[1] The palatals, being derived from gutturals, are best transliterated by italicised gutturals.

[2] ह h is not properly a liquid, but a soft (sonant) breathing.

[3] The signs for the guttural and labial sibilants have become obsolete, and are replaced by Visarga (:).

Avagraha (ऽ) marks in our editions the elision of अ a at the beginning of a word, e. g. तेऽपि te ऽ pi for ते अपि te api.

° marks an abbreviation : thus, गतम् gatam, °तेन (ga)tena.

8 (7). There were originally five distinct signs for the sibilants; but the signs for the guttural and labial sibilants having become obsolete, their place is supplied by Visarga, the sign of the unmodified sibilant.

9 (8). There are five distinct letters for the five nasals. When these nasals are followed by consonants of their own class, they are often, for the sake of more expeditious writing, replaced by the sign of Anusvâra. Thus we may write संकिता aṃkitâ for अङ्किता aṅkitâ, संचिता aṃkitâ for अञ्चिता añkitâ; कुंडिता kuṃditâ for कुण्डिता kuṇditâ; नंदिता naṃditâ for नन्दिता nanditâ; कंपिता kaṃpitâ for कम्पिता kampitâ. The pronunciation remains unaffected by the change.

The same applies to final म् m, at the end of a sentence. Thus अहं may be written for अहम्, but it is really an m, and to be pronounced as such.

10 (9). Besides the five regular nasals, there are three nasalized letters, यँ, लँ, वँ, or यं, लं, वं, य़ँ, ल़ँ, व़ँ, which are used to represent a final म् m, if followed by an initial य y, ल l, व v; e. g. तय्ँयाति taỹ yâti for तं याति taṃ yâti; तल्ँभते tal̐ labhate for तं लभते taṃ labhate; तव्ँहति taṽ vahati for तं वहति taṃ vahati.

11 (10). The only consonants which have no corresponding nasals are र r, श s, ष sh, स s, ह h. A final म् m, therefore, before any of these letters at the beginning of words, can only be represented by Anusvâra, the natural or unmodified nasal; e. g. तं रक्षति taṃ rakshati, तं हरति taṃ harati.

12 (11). In the body of a word the only letters which can be preceded by Anusvâra are श s, ष sh, स s, ह h. Before the semi-vowels य y, र r, ल l, व v, the म् m in the body of a word is never changed into Anusvâra; e. g. गम्यते gamyate, नम्रः namraḥ.

13 (16). If a consonant is followed immediately by one or more consonants, they are all written in a group. Thus atka is written खत्क; kârtsnya, कार्त्स्न्यं. The general principle followed in the formation of these compound consonants, is to drop the perpendicular and horizontal lines except in the last letter.

14 (17). The most noticeable peculiarities in the formation of compound consonants are the following :—

The ऋ r following a consonant is written by a short transverse stroke at the foot of the letter; as क् + र = क्र or क्र kra; ग् + र = ग्र gra; त् + र = त्र or त्र tra; द् + र = द्र dra; ष् + ट् + र = ष्ट्र sh*t*ra.

The ऋ r preceding a consonant is written by ॔ placed at the top of the consonant before which it is to be sounded. Thus अर् + क = अर्क arka; वर् + ष् + म = वर्ष्म varshma. This sign for ऋ r is placed to the right (while Anusvâra is placed to the left) of any other marks at the top of the same letter; e. g. अर्केंदू arkendû.

क्ष ksha = क् + ष; क्त्व ktva = क् + त् + व.

ज्ञ g*ñ*a = ज् + ञ.

ह्न *gh*a is sometimes written न्ह.

रु ru = र् + उ; रू rû = र् + ऊ.

श् s is frequently written ग्; e. g. सु su, सू sû, स्र sra, स्क ska.

List of Compound Consonants.

15 (20). क्क k-ka, क्ख k-kha, क्व k-*k*a, क्त **k-ta**, क्त्य k-t-ya, क्त्र k-t-ra, क्त्र्य k-t-r-ya, क्त्व **k-t-va**, क्न k-na, क्न्य k-n-ya, क्म k-ma, क्य k-ya, क्र or क्र **k-ra**, क्र्य or क्र्य k-r-ya, क्ल k-la, क्व k-va, क्व्य k-v-ya, क्ष k-sha, क्ष्म k-sh-ma, क्ष्य k-sh-ya, क्ष्व k-sh-va;— ख्य kh-ya, ख्र kh-ra;—ग्य g-ya, ग्र g-ra, ग्र्य g-r-ya;—घ्न gh-na, घ्न्य gh-n-ya, घ्म gh-ma, घ्य gh-ya, घ्र gh-ra;—ङ्क ṅ-ka, ङ्क्त ṅ-k-ta, ङ्क्त्य ṅ-k-t-ya, ङ्क्य ṅ-k-ya, ङ्क्ष ṅ-k-sha, ङ्क्ष्व ṅ-k-sh-va, ङ्ख ṅ-kha,

ङ्ख *n̄-kh-ya*, ङ्ग *n̄-ga*, ङ्ग्य *n̄-g-ya*, ङ्घ *n̄-gha*, ङ्घ्य *n̄-gh-ya*, ङ्घ्र *n̄-gh-ra*, ङ्ङ *n̄-n̄a*, ङ्म *n̄-ma*, ङ्य *n̄-ya*.

च *k-ka*, च्छ *k-kha*, च्छ्र *k-kh-ra*, च्ञ *k-ña*, च्म *k-ma*, च्य *k-ya*;— ख्य *kh-ya*, ख्र *kh-ra*;—ग्ग *g-ga*, ग्घ *g-gha*, ग्ञ *g-ña*, ग्ञ्य *g-ñ-ya*, ग्म *g-ma*, ग्य *g-ya*, ग्र *g-ra*, ग्व *g-va*;—ञ्क *ñ-ka*, ञ्म *ñ-k-ma*, ञ्क्य *ñ-k-ya*, ञ्ख *ñ-kha*, ञ्ग *ñ-ga*, ञ्ञ *ñ-ña*, ञ्य *ñ-ya*.

ट्ट *t-ta*, ट्य *t-ya*;—थ्य *th-ya*, ठ्र *th-ra*;—ड्ग *d-ga*, ड्ग्य *d-g-ya*, ड्घ *d-gha*, ड्घ्र *d-gh-ra*, ड्म *d-ma*, ड्य *d-ya*;—ढ्य *dh-ya*, ढ्र *dh-ra*;— ण्ट *n-ta*, ण्ठ *n-tha*, ण्ड *n-da*, ण्ड्य *n-d-ya*, ण्ड्र *n-d-ra*, ण्ड्र्य *n-d-r-ya*, ण्ढ *n-dha*, ण्ण *n-na*, ण्म *n-ma*, ण्य *n-ya*, ण्व *n-va*.

त्क *t-ka*, त्क्र *t-k-ra*, त्त **t-ta**, त्त्य *t-t-ya*, त्त्र *t-t-ra*, त्त्व *t-t-va*, त्थ *t-tha*, त्न *t-na*, त्न्य *t-n-ya*, त्प *t-pa*, त्प्र *t-p-ra*, त्म *t-ma*, त्म्य *t-m-ya*, त्य *t-ya*, त्र or त्र **t-ra**, त्र्य *t-r-ya*, त्व *t-va*, त्स *t-sa*, त्स्न *t-s-na*, त्स्न्य *t-s-n-ya*;—थ्य *th-ya*;—द्ग *d-ga*, द्घ *d-gha*, द्घ्र *d-gh-ra*, द्द **d-da**, द्द्य *d-d-ya*, द्ध **d-dha**, द्ध्य *d-dh-ya*, द्न *d-na*, द्ब *d-ba*, द्भ **d-bha**, द्भ्य *d-bh-ya*, द्म *d-ma*, द्य *d-ya*, द्र *d-ra*, द्र्य *d-r-ya*, द्व *d-va*, द्व्य *d-v-ya*;—ध्न *dh-na*, ध्न्य *dh-n-ya*, ध्म *dh-ma*, ध्य *dh-ya*, ध्र *dh-ra*, ध्र्य *dh-r-ya*, ध्व *dh-va*;—न्त *n-ta*, न्त्य *n-t-ya*, न्त्र *n-t-ra*, न्द *n-da*, न्द्र *n-d-ra*, न्ध *n-dha*, न्ध्र *n-dh-ra*, न्न *n-na*, न्प *n-pa*, न्प्र *n-p-ra*, न्म *n-ma*, न्य *n-ya*, न्र *n-ra*, न्स *n-sa*.

प्त *p-ta*, प्त्य *p-t-ya*, प्न *p-na*, प्प *p-pa*, प्म *p-ma*, प्य *p-ya*, प्र *p-ra*, प्ल *p-la*, प्व *p-va*, प्स *p-sa*, प्स्व *p-s-va*;—ब्घ *b-gha*, ब्ग *b-ga*, ब्द *b-da*, ब्ध *b-dha*, ब्न *b-na*, ब्ब *b-ba*, ब्भ *b-bha*, ब्भ्य *b-bh-ya*, ब्य *b-ya*, ब्र *b-ra*, ब्व *b-va*;—भ्न *bh-na*, भ्य *bh-ya*, भ्र *bh-ra*, भ्व *bh-va*;—म्न *m-na*, म्प *m-pa*, म्प्र *m-p-ra*, म्ब *m-ba*, म्भ *m-bha*, म्म *m-ma*, म्य *m-ya*, म्र *m-ra*, म्ल *m-la*, म्व *m-va*.

य्य *y-ya*, य्व *y-va*;—ल्क *l-ka*, ल्प *l-pa*, ल्म *l-ma*, ल्य *l-ya*, ल्ल *l-la*, ल्व *l-va*;—व्न *v-na*, व्य *v-ya*, व्र *v-ra*, व्व *v-va*.

श्क *s-ka*, श्क्य *s-k-ya*, श्न *s-na*, श्य *s-ya*, श्र *s-ra*, श्र्य *s-r-ya*, श्ल *s-la*, श्व *s-va*, श्व्य *s-v-ya*, श्श *s-sa*;—ष्ट *sh-ta*, ष्ट्य *sh-t-ya*, ष्ट्र *sh-t-ra*, ष्ट्र्य *sh-t-r-ya*, ष्ट्व *sh-t-va*, ष्ठ *sh-tha*, ष्ण *sh-na*, ष्ण्य *sh-n-ya*, ष्प *sh-pa*, ष्प्र *sh-p-ra*, ष्म *sh-ma*, ष्य *sh-ya*, ष्व *sh-va*;—स्क *s-ka*, स्ख *s-kha*,

स्त s-ta, स्त्य s-t-ya, स्त्र s-t-ra, स्त्व s-t-va, स्थ s-tha, स्न s-na,
स्न्य s-n-ya, स्प s-pa, स्फ s-pha, स्म s-ma, स्म्य s-m-ya, स्य s-ya,
स्र s-ra, स्व s-va, स्स s-sa.

ह्न h-*na*, ह्न h-na, ह्म **h-ma**, ह्र h-ra, ह्ल h-la, ह्व h-va.

16 (21). The numerical figures in Sanskrit are :—

१	२	३	४	५	६	७	८	९	०
1	2	·3	4	5	6	7	8	9	0

These figures were adopted by the Arabs, who introduced them into Europe.

Pronunciation.

17 (22). The following rules should be noted :—

1. The vowels should be pronounced like the vowels in Italian. The short अ a, however, has rather the sound of the so-called neutral vowel in English, as the u in but.

2. The aspiration of the consonants should be heard distinctly. Thus ख kh = kh in inkhorn ; थ th like th in pothouse ; फ ph like ph in topheavy ; घ gh like gh in loghouse ; ध dh like dh in madhouse ; भ bh like bh in Hobhouse.

3. The guttural ङ ṅ has the sound of ng in king.

4. The palatals च and ज (transliterated *k* and *g* because they are derived from the gutturals) have the sound of ch in church and of j in join.

5. The linguals are pronounced similarly to the so-called dentals d, t, n in English, the tongue being turned rather further back against the roof of the palate. The dentals in Sanskrit are produced by bringing the tip of the tongue against the very edge of the upper front teeth. The English t, d, n sound like the Sanskrit linguals rather than like the Sanskrit dentals.

6. The Visarga, which is a final h sound, is a hard breathing.

7. The dental स s sounds like s in sin; the lingual ष sh like sh in shun, the palatal श s like ss in session; the difference being that in pronouncing the lingual the tongue is turned further back than in the case of the palatal.

8. The real Anusvâra is sounded as a very slight nasal, like n in the French bon.

Accent.

18 (Appendix II). The Sanskrit accent, which is marked in works belonging to the Vedic period only, but not in classical Sanskrit, is a musical accent dependent on pitch and not on stress only. It does not depend on quantity, and is not, as in the classical languages, limited to particular syllables. In this grammar it is marked in the transliterated words, in order that the student may see clearly how strong syllables are dependent on the accent and are weakened by the loss of it.

The three principal accents are: the udâtta, or acute, pronounced by raising the voice; the svarita, or circumflex, pronounced by a combined rise and fall of the voice; and the anudâtta (i. e. without udâtta), which may be marked in transliterated words by the *gravis,* and which belongs to all vowels having neither of the other two accents.

The anudâtta immediately preceding an udâtta or svarita vowel is called anudâttatara.

The anudâtta immediately following an udâtta is changed into what is called the dependent svarita.

In Sanskrit the svarita and the anudâttatara only are indicated, the former by $'$, the latter by $_$. Whenever we find a syllable marked by $_$, we know that the next syllable, if left without any mark, is udâtta, if marked by $'$, is svarita; e. g. अग्निः agníḥ, कन्या kanyā̃; अग्निना agnínâ (ag, anudâttatara; ní, udâtta; nâ, dependent svarita).

CHAPTER II.

RULES OF SANDHI OR THE COMBINATION
OF LETTERS.

19 (23). In Sanskrit every sentence is considered as one unbroken chain of syllables. The coalescence of final and initial letters is called Sandhi (putting together). The rules of Sandhi are based chiefly on the avoidance of hiatus and on assimilation.

The absence of Sandhi is in many cases sufficient to mark the stops which in other languages have to be marked by punctuation.

Though both are based on the same phonetic principles, it is essential, in order to avoid confusion, to distinguish **external Sandhi,** which determines the changes of final and initial letters of *words*, from **internal Sandhi,** which applies to the final letters of *verbal roots* and *nominal bases* when followed by certain terminations or suffixes.

Note—The rules of external Sandhi apply, with few exceptions, to words forming compounds, and to the final letters of nominal bases before the Pada or middle terminations भ्याम् bhyâm, भिः bhi*h*, भ्यः bhya*h*, सु su (see 85), or before secondary suffixes beginning with any consonant except य y.

External Sandhi.
Classification of Vowels.

20 (30-33). Vowels are divided into :—

A. 1. Simple vowels: अ a, आ â; इ i, ई î; उ u, ऊ û; ऋ ri, ॠ rî; ऌ li.

   2. Gu*n*a vowels : अ a; ए e; ओ o; अर् ar; अल् al.

   3. V*ri*ddhi vowels: आ â; ऐ ai; औ au; आर् âr; आल् âl.

Guṇa is the strengthening of the simple vowels by a preceding अ a (अ a itself remains unchanged); Vriddhi is
the further strengthening of Guṇa vowels by means of
another अ a.

B. 1. Vowels which are liable to be changed into semivowels: इ i,
ई î; उ u, ऊ û; ऋ ri, ॠ rî; also the diphthongs (the latter
half of which is इ i or उ u): *liquid* vowels.

2. Those which are not: अ a, आ â.

Combination of Final and Initial Vowels.

21 (33). If the same simple vowel (long or short) occurs at the
end and beginning of words, the result is a long vowel; e. g. सा
अपि ईक्षते sâ api îkshate becomes सापीक्षते sâpîkshate; किंतु
उदेति kintu udeti becomes किंतूदेति kintûdeti; कर्तॄ ऋजु kartri rigu
becomes कर्तॄजु kartrigu.

22 (34, 35). अ a and आ â coalesce with a following simple
liquid vowel to Guṇa; e.g. तव इंद्रः tava indrah = तवेंद्रः tavendrah;
सा उक्त्वा sâ uktvâ = सोक्त्वा soktvâ; सा ऋद्धिः sâ *riddhih* = सर्द्धिः
sarddhih: with diphthongs to Vriddhi; e. g. तव एव tava eva =
तवैव tavaiva; सा ओषधिः sâ oshadhih = सौषधिः saushadhih; सा
औत्सुक्यवती sâ autsukyavatî = सौत्सुक्यवती sautsukyavatî.

23 (36). A simple liquid vowel followed by any *other* vowel or
by a diphthong is changed into its semivowel; e. g. दधि अत्र dadhi atra = दध्यत्र dadhyatra; कर्तॄ उत kartri uta = कर्त्रुत kartruta;
मधु इव madhu iva = मध्विव madhviva; नदी अर्थम् nadî artham =
नद्यर्थम् nadyartham.

24 (37). The Guṇa vowels ए e and ओ o—

(a) if followed by अ a, remain unchanged, the अ a being dropped:
ते अपि te api = तेऽपि teⲭpi; सो अपि so api = सोऽपि
soⲭpi.

(b) if followed by any other vowel, are changed to अ a (through

अय् ay and अव् av, the semivowels being dropped): सखे
इह sakhe iha = सख इह sakha iha; प्रभो एहि prabho ehi =
प्रभ एहि prabha ehi.

25 (38). The V*riddhi* vowel ऐ ai becomes आ â (through आय् ây),
औ au becomes आव् âv (the semivowel not being dropped in this
case) before *all* vowels and diphthongs: श्रियै अर्थ: sriyai arthah =
श्रिया अर्थ: sriyâ artha*h*; but तौ इति tau iti = ताविति tâv iti.

Note—The hiatus occasioned by the dropping of य् y and व् v
in the above three cases (24, 25) remains, no further coalescence
taking place.

26 (42). **Exception**—If the vowels ई î, ऊ û, ए e are the terminations of the dual, whether of nouns, adjectives, pronouns, or
verbs, they *remain unchanged* before vowels; also the ई î of अमी
amî, nom. *plural* of the pronoun अदस् adas. अ a *is not elided*
after this dual ए e. These vowels are called Pragrihya.

Ex. कवी इमौ kavî imau, these two poets; साधू इमौ sâdhû
imau, these two merchants; विद्ये इमे vidye ime, these two sciences;
याचेते अर्थम् yâkete artham, they two ask for money; अमू अर्भकौ
amû arbhakau, these two children; अमी अश्वा: amî a*s*vâ*h*, these
horses.

Irregular Vowel Sandhi.

27 (43, 44). 1. When a preposition ending in अ a or आ â is
followed by a verb beginning with ए e or ओ o, the result of the
coalescence of the vowels is ए e or ओ o, not ऐ ai or औ au.

Ex. प्र + एजते = प्रेजते pra + e*j*ate = pre*j*ate; परा + ओहति =
परोहति parâ + ohati = parohati.

Exception—The two verbs एध् edh, to grow, and इ i, to go, if
raised by Gu*n*a to ए e, are regular.

उप + एधते = उपैधते upa + edhate = upaidhate; अव + एति =
अवैति ava + eti = avaiti.

2. When a preposition ending in अ a or आ â is followed by a

verb beginning with ऋ *ri,* the two vowels coalesce into आर् âr
instead of अर् ar.

Ex. अप + ऋच्छति = अपार्च्छति apa + *rikkh*ati = apârkkhati ; परा
+ ऋषति = परार्षति parâ + *r*ishati = parârshati.

Note (47–50)—Interjectional particles consisting of or ending
in vowels are not liable to Sandhi ; e. g. इ इंद्र i indra, Oh Indra ;
आ एवम् â evam, is it so indeed ? हे इंद्र he indra, Oh Indra ; अहो
अपेहि aho apehi, halloo, go away.

Combination of Final and Initial Consonants.

28 (54). The rules concerning the changes of final consonants
will be considerably simplified by remembering that *eleven* only
out of the thirty-five consonants can ever stand in Sanskrit at the
end of a word ; viz.

क् k, द् *t,* त् t, प् p, } ल् l, : (Visarga), (Anusvâra).
ङ् ṅ, ण् *n,* न् n, म् m, }

Because 1. final aspirates must be replaced by their corresponding unaspirated letters ;

2. final soft letters must be replaced by their corresponding hard
letters ;

3. palatals must be replaced by gutturals (छ *kh* is *always,* and
ज *g* sometimes, replaced by द् *t*);

4. of the semivowels only ल् l can be final ; final र् r is replaced
by Visarga ;

5. final ह् h is replaced by द् *t* (sometimes by त् t or क् k);

6. of the sibilants, ष sh and श *s* are replaced by द् *t* (sometimes
by क् k), स् s by Visarga, which is the only sibilant tolerated
at the end of a word.

Besides these ten, Anusvâra is the only other letter which can
stand at the end of a word.

29 (55). No word in Sanskrit ever ends in more than one consonant, except when र् r precedes a final क् k, द् *t,* त् t, प् p, which

is radical or substituted for a radical. In the case of all other combinations the final letter or letters must be dropped till only one remains, which is allowable as a final. Thus अबिभर् + त् = अबिभः abibhar + t = abibha*h*, 3 p. sg. impf. of भृ bh*ri*, to carry; सुवल्ग् + स् = सुवल् suvalg + s = suval, nom. sing., well jumping.

But ऊर्क् û*rk*, strength, nom. sing. of ऊर्ज् û*rg* : अवरिवर्त् avari-vart, 3 p. sg. impf. intens. of वृत् v*ri*t or वृध् v*ri*dh ; अमार्ट् amâr*t* from मृज् m*rig*.

The nom. sing. of चिकीर्ष् *k*ikîrsh (from the desiderative of कृ k*ri*, to do) is चिकी: kikî*h*, the final ष् sh, which would other-wise become ट् *t*, being dropped because it is a derivative suffix.

Classification of Consonants.

30 (56). **Place or organ of consonants :—**

1. The throat, the palate, the roof of the palate, the teeth, the lips, and the nose are called the places or organs of the letters.

2. By contact between the tongue and the four places,—throat, palate, roof, teeth,—the guttural, palatal, lingual, and dental consonants are formed. Labial consonants are formed by contact between the lips.

3. In forming the nasals of the five classes, the breath partially passes through the nose, while the real Anusvâra is formed in the nose only.

4. The Visarga is said by native grammarians to be pronounced in the chest; it is now pronounced by the natives like an h followed by a very short vowel, e. g. कः ka*h* sounds like kahă. The three sibilants श् *s*, ष् sh, स् s are produced by an incipient contact of the tongue with the palate, the roof, and the teeth respectively.

5. ह् h is guttural; the semivowels य् y, र् r, ल् l, व् v are palatal,

lingual, dental[1], and labial. य y, ळ l, व v can be nasalized, and are then written य़ँ, ऴँ, व़ँ, or यं, ळं, वं, य̈, l̈, v̈. र r cannot be nasalized.

31 (57). Quality of consonants.

Consonants are :—

1. Either **hard** (surd): the first, second, and seventh (sibilants) columns in the table in § 5.

   Or **soft** (sonant): all the remaining consonants, the semivowels (columns 3, 4, 5, 6), and Anusvâra (besides all the vowels and diphthongs).

2. Either **aspirated :** columns 2, 4, 7, ह h, and Anusvâra.

   Or **unaspirated :** all the rest.

It will appear from the above that the change of क् k to क़ k is a change of place, and that of क् k to ग g is a change of quality; while in the transition of क् k to ग् g, or of त् t to न् n, there is a change both of place and of quality.

32 (60). The changes which take place by the combination of the eleven final consonants with initial vowels or consonants may therefore conveniently be treated under two heads.

Final letters are changed :

    I. With regard to their places or organs.

    II. With regard to their quality.

I. Changes of Place.

33 (61). The only final consonants which are liable to change of place are the **Dentals, Anusvâra,** and **Visarga.**

a. The dentals become palatal and lingual before palatals and linguals.

b. Anusvâra and Visarga adapt themselves as much as possible to the organ of the letter by which they are followed.

---

[1] ळ l, however, is practically treated as a lingual, being derived from र r.

All other changes of final consonants are merely changes of quality; these in the case of dentals, Anusvâra, and Visarga being superadded to the changes of place.

The Dentals: त् t and न् n.

34 (62). Final त् t before palatals (च k, छ kh, ज g, झ gh, ञ ñ, श s) is changed to a palatal.

Ex. तत् + च = तच tat + ka = ta*kk*a, and this; तत् + छिनत्ति = तच्छिनत्ति tat + *kh*inatti = ta*kkh*inatti, he cuts this; तत् + शृणोति = तच्छृणोति[1] tat + *s*rinoti = ta*ks*rinoti, he hears this; तत् + जायते = तज्जायते tat + *g*âyate = ta*gg*âyate, this is born.

In the last example the final त् t is changed to च k, and then to ज g (38): the same change would take place before an initial झ gh; and before an initial ञ ñ, त् t might become either ज g or ञ ñ.

35 (63). Final न् n before ज g, झ gh, ञ ñ, and श s is changed to palatal ञ ñ.

Ex. तान् + जयति = ताञ्जयति tân + *g*ayati = tâ*ñg*ayati, he conquers them.

Note—Rules on the change of final न् n before च k, छ kh, and श s will be given in 43 and 45.

36 (64). Final त् t before ट t, ठ th, ड d, ढ dh, ण n (not ष sh) is changed to a lingual.

Ex. एतत् + ठक्कुर: = एतट्ठक्कुर: etat + *th*akkura*h* = eta*tth*akkura*h*, the idol of him; तत् + डयते = तड्डयते tat + *d*ayate = ta*dd*ayate: here the final त् t is changed to ट t and then to ड d (38): the same change would take place before an initial ढ dh; before an initial ण n, त् t might become either ड d or ण n (39).

37 (65). Final न् n before ड d, ढ dh, ण n (not ष sh) is changed to ण n.

---

[1] श s in this case is generally changed to छ kh: तच्छृणोति ta*kkh*rinoti.

Ex. महान् + डामर: = महाड्डामर: mahân + *d*âmara*h* = mahân*d*â-marah, a great uproar.

Note 1—Rules on the changes of न् n before ट् t and ठ् *th* (not ष् sh) will be given in 43.

Note 2—The changes of place with regard to final Anusvâra (*m*) and Visarga (*h*) will be explained, together with the changes of quality to which these letters are liable, in 47-52.

II. Changes of Quality.

38 (66). Final consonants must be soft before soft initials and hard before hard initials.

Note—As the nasals have no corresponding hard letters, they remain unchanged in quality before hard letters, unless the contact can be avoided by inserting sibilants, or, if the following letters are sibilants, by inserting k, *k*, *t*, or t (44, 45).

Accordingly final क् k, ट् *t*, त् t, प् p before sonants become ग् g, ड् *d*, द् d, ब् b respectively.

Note—त् t before sonant palatals and linguals will of course become ज् *g* and ड् *d* respectively by 34 and 36.

Examples :—

क् k: सम्यक् + उक्तम् = सम्यगुक्तम् samyak + uktam = samyaguktam, well said; दिक् + गज: = दिग्गज: dik + ga*g*a*h* = digga*g*a*h*, an elephant supporting the globe.

ट् *t*: परिव्राट् + अयम् = परिव्राडयम् parivrâ*t* + ayam = parivrâ*d*ayam, he is a mendicant; परिव्राट् + मित्रम् = परिव्राड्मित्रम् parivrâ*t* + mitram = parivrâ*d*mitram.

त् t: सरित् + अत्र = सरिदत्र sarit + atra = saridatra, the river there; महत् + धनु: = महद्धनु: mahat + dhanu*h* = mahaddhanu*h*, a large bow.

प् p: ककुप् + अत्र = ककुबत्र kakup + atra = kakubatra, a region there (inflectional base ककुभ् kakubh); अप् + जय: = अब्जय: ap + *g*aya*h* = ab*g*aya*h*, obtaining water.

But सरित् + जलम् = सरिज्जलम् sarit + galam = sariggalam (34),
water of the river; एतत् + डामर: = एतड्डामर: etat + dâmara*h*
= etaddâmara*h*, the uproar of them.

39 (67). क् k, ट् *t*, त् t, प् p, when followed by initial nasals,
chiefly न् n and म् m, *may*, after becoming ग् g, ड् *d*, द् d, and ब् b,
be further assimilated to the nasal, and be written ङ् ṅ, ण् *n*,
न् n, म् m.

Ex. दिक् + नाग: = दिग्नाग: or दिङ्नाग: dik + nâga*h* = dignâga*h*
or diṅnâga*h*, a world elephant; जगत् + नाथ: = जगन्नाथ: or
जगन्नाथ: gagat + nâtha*h* = gagadnâtha*h* or gagannâtha*h*, lord of
the world; अप् + नदी = अब्नदी or अम्नदी ap + nadî = abnadî or
amnadî, water-river; प्राक् + मुख: = प्राग्मुख: or प्राङ्मुख: prâk +
mukha*h* = prâgmukha*h* or prâṅmukha*h*, facing the east.

40 (70). Final त् t before ल् l becomes ल् l (not द् d).

Ex. तत् + लब्धम् = तल्लब्धम् tat + labdham = tallabdham, this is
taken.

41 (71). Final न् n before ल् l also becomes ल् l; but this ल् l,
being pronounced through the nose, is written with Anusvâra,
which in this case is usually written as a half-moon.

Ex. महान् + लाभ: = महाँल्लाभ: mahân + lâbha*h* = mahẫllâbha*h*,
large gain.

42 (72). Final ङ् ṅ, ण् *n*, and न् n, preceded by a **short** vowel
and followed by *any* vowel, are doubled.

Ex. धावन् + अश्व: = धावन्नश्व: dhâvan + asva*h* = dhâvannasva*h*,
a running horse; प्रत्यङ् + आस्ते = प्रत्यङ्ङास्ते pratyaṅ + âste = pra-
tyaṅṅâste, he sits turned towards the west; सुगण् + आस्ते =
सुगण्णास्ते sugan + âste = sugannâste, he sits counting well.

But कवीन् + आह्वयस्व kavîn + âhvayasva (call the poets) remains unchanged.

43 (73). Final न् n before initial क् k, ख् kh, and प् p, फ् ph,
remains unchanged.

Final न् n before क् k, ख् kh, requires the intercession of श् s[1].
Final न् n before ट् t, ठ् th, requires the intercession of ष् sh[1].
Final न् n before त् t, थ् th, requires the intercession of स् s[1].

Before these inserted sibilants the original न् n is changed to Anusvâra.

Ex. हसन् + चकार = हसंश्चकार hasan + kakâra = hasanskakâra, he did it laughing; चलन् + टिट्टिभः = चलंष्टिट्टिभः kalan + tittibhah = kalamshtittibhah, a moving tittibha-bird; पतन् + तरुः = पतंस्तरुः patan + taruh = patamstaruh, a falling tree.

44 (74). Final ङ् ṅ and ण् n may remain unchanged before the sibilants श् s, ष् sh, स् s; but क् k may optionally be inserted after the ङ् ṅ, and ट् t after the ण् n.

Ex. प्राङ् + शेते = प्राङ्शेते or प्राङ्क्शेते (or प्राङ्क्खेते) prâṅ + sete = prâṅsete or prâṅksete (or prâṅkkhete); सुगण् + सरति = सुगण्स-रति or सुगण्ट्सरति sugan + sarati = sugansarati or sugantsarati.

45 (75). Final न् n before ष् sh remains unchanged; before स् s it may remain unchanged or त् t is inserted; before श् s it must be changed to the palatal nasal (35) ञ् ñ; श् ñs may further be changed to श्क् ñks, श्क्ख् ñkkh, or श्ख् ñkh.

Ex. तान् + षट् = तान्षट् tân + shat = tânshat, those six; तान् + सहते = तान्सहते or तान्त्सहते tân + sahate = tânsahate or tântsa-hate, he bears them; तान् + शार्दूलान् = ताञ्शार्दूलान् or ताञ्क्शार्दू-लान् or ताञ्क्ख्शार्दूलान् or ताञ्ख्शार्दूलान् tân + sârdûlân = tâñsârdûlân or tâñksârdûlân or tâñkkhârdûlân or tâñkhârdûlân, those tigers.

46 (76). A final ट् t before स् s must remain unchanged, but त् t may be inserted.

Ex. षट् + सरितः = षट्सरितः or षट्त्सरितः shat + saritah = shatsaritah or shattsaritah, six rivers.

---

[1] This intercession is owing to the analogy of acc. pl. masc. of vowel stems and of nom. sing. of n-stems, which originally ended in ns.

Final म् m and Anusvâra.

47 (77). 1. Final म् m followed by an initial vowel remains unchanged.

Ex. किम् + अत्र = किमत्र kim + atra = kimatra, what is there?

2. Final म् m before consonants *may*, without exception, be changed to Anusvâra.

a. Before र r, श् *s*, ष् sh, स् s, and ह् h, final म् m *must* be changed to Anusvâra, as these five consonants have no corresponding nasal class-letter.

b. Before all the five letters in each of the five classes final म् m *may* be changed to the corresponding nasal of the class to which the letter belongs.

c. Before य् y, ल् l, व् v, final म् m may become यँ ँ, लँ ँ, वँ ँ (cp. 30. 5).

Examples:—1. Before र r, श् *s*, ष् sh, स् s, ह् h:—

करुणम् + रोदिति = करुणां रोदिति karu*n*am + roditi = karu*n*am roditi, he cries piteously; शय्यायाम् + शेते = शय्यायां शेते sayyâyâm + sete = sayyâyâm sete, he lies on the couch; मोक्षम् + सेवेत = मोक्षं सेवेत moksham + seveta = moksha*m* seveta, let a man cultivate religious freedom; मधुरम् + हसति = मधुरं हसति madhuram + hasati = madhuram hasati, he laughs sweetly.

2. Before letters of the five classes:—

किम् + करोषि = किं करोषि (or किङ्करोषि) kim + karoshi = kim karoshi (or kiṅ karoshi), what doest thou? शत्रुम् + जहि = शत्रुं जहि (or शत्रुञ्जहि) satrum + gahi = satru*m* gahi (or satruñ gahi), kill the enemy; गुरुम् + नमति = गुरुं नमति (or गुरुन्नमति) gurum + namati = gurum namati (or gurun namati), he salutes the teacher; किम् + फलम् = किं फलम्(or किम्फलम्) kim + phalam = ki*m* phalam (or kim phalam), what is the use? शास्त्रम् + मीमांसते = शास्त्रं मीमांसते (or शास्त्रम्मीमांसते) sâstram + mîmâmsate = sâstra*m* mîmâmsate (or sâstram mîmâmsate), he studies the book.

3. Before य् y, ल् l, व् v:—

सत्वरम् + याति = सत्वरं याति (or सत्वरय्ँयाति) satvaram + yâti = satvaram yâti (or satvaray̐ yâti), he walks quickly; विद्याम् + लभते = विद्यां लभते (or विद्याल्ँभते) vidyâm + labhate = vidyâm labhate (or vidyâl̐ labhate), he acquires wisdom; तम् + वेद = तं वेद (or तव्ँवेद) tam + veda = tam veda (or tav̐ veda), I know him.

48 (78). म् m at the end of a word *in pausâ*, i. e. at the end of a sentence, remains unchanged. It is, however, allowable to write it with the simple dot, for the sake of brevity. Ex. एवं evam, thus, instead of एवम् evam.

Visarga for final स् s and र् r.

49 (82). Visarga is the only sibilant which can be final *in pausâ*. It (as well as the other sibilants) is hard, the corresponding soft letter being र् r.

If Visarga is followed by—

1. a hard palatal, lingual, or dental, च् k, छ् kh, ट् t, ठ् th, त् t, थ् th, it is changed to the sibilant of the class to which the following letter belongs (श् s, ष् sh, स् s);

2. a hard guttural or labial, क् k, ख् kh, प् p, फ् ph, it remains unchanged;

3. a sibilant, it remains or it may be assimilated.

Examples:—

1. पूर्णः + चंद्रः = पूर्णश्चंद्रः pûrnah + kandrah = pûrnas kandrah, the full moon; नद्याः + तीरम् = नद्यास्तीरम् nadyâh + tîram = nadyâs tîram, the border of the river.

2. ततः + कामः = ततः कामः tatah + kâmah = tatah kâmah, hence love; नद्याः + पारम् = नद्याः पारम् nadyâh + pâram = nadyâh pâram, the opposite shore of the river.

3. सुप्तः + शिशुः = सुप्तश्शिशुः or सुप्तः शिशुः suptah + sisuh = suptas sisuh or suptah sisuh, the child sleeps; प्रथमः + सर्गः =

प्रथमस्सर्गे: or प्रथम: सर्ग: prathama*h* + sarga*h* = prathamas sarga*h* or prathama*h* sarga*h*, the first section.

50 (84). Visarga (except when preceded by अ a or आ â) if followed by a soft letter (consonant or vowel) is changed to र् r, this letter being the soft form of Visarga.

Ex. कवि: + अयम् = कविरयम् kavi*h* + ayam = kavirayam, this poet; गौ: + गच्छति = गौगिच्छति gau*h* + ga*kkh*ati = gaur ga*kkh*ati, the ox walks; वायु: + वाति = वायुर्वाति vâyu*h* + vâti = vâyur vâti, the wind blows.

51 (84). 1. The final syllable आः â*h* drops its Visarga before every vowel or soft consonant.

2. The final syllable अः a*h*—

(a) drops its Visarga before every *vowel* except अ a;

(b) before every soft consonant and before अ a, it is changed to ओ o, after which अ a is elided.

Examples:—1. अश्वा: + अमी = अश्वा अमी a*s*vâ*h* + amî = asvâ amî, these horses; आगता: + ऋषय: = आगता ऋषय: âgatâ*h* + *r*isha-ya*h* = âgatâ *r*ishaya*h*, the poets have arrived; हता: + गजा: = हता गजा: hatâ*h* + ga*g*â*h* = hatâ ga*g*â*h*, the elephants are killed; मा: + भि: = माभि: mâ*h* + bhi*h* = mâbhi*h*, instr. pl. of मास् mâs, moon.

2. a. कुत: + आगत: = कुत आगत: kuta*h* + âgata*h* = kuta âgata*h*, whence come? क: + एष: = क एष: ka*h* + esha*h* = ka esha*h*, who is he? क: + ऋषि: = क ऋषि: ka*h* + *r*ishi*h* = ka *r*ishi*h*, who is the poet?

b. निर्वाण: + दीप: = निर्वाणो दीप: nirvâna*h* + dîpa*h* = nirvâno dîpa*h*, the lamp is blown out; न: + भि: = नोभि: na*h* + bhi*h* = nobhi*h*, instr. pl., with the noses; नर: + अयम् = नरोऽयम् nara*h* + ayam = naro×yam, this man.

52 (85). The final syllables अः a*h* and आः â*h*, in the few instances[1] in which the Visarga represents an etymological र् r, are

---

[1] पुनर् punar, again; प्रातर् prâtar, early; अंतर् antar, within;

not subject to the exceptions of 51. In other words, सः a*h* and
आः â*h* (= original अर् ar and आर् âr) become अर् ar and आर् âr
according to the general rule (50) that Visarga before soft letters
becomes र् r.

Ex. पुनः + अपि = पुनरपि puna*h* + api = punarapi, even again;
भ्रातः + देहि = भ्रातर्देहि bhrâta*h* + dehi = bhrâtar dehi, brother,
give! द्वाः + एषा = द्वारेषा dvâ*h* + eshâ = dvâreshâ, this door.

53 (86). र् r followed by र् r is always dropped (whether it be
etymologically स् s or र् r), and a preceding short vowel is
lengthened.

Ex. विधुः + राजते = विधू राजते vidhu*h* + râ*g*ate = vidhû râ*g*ate,
the moon shines; पुनः + रोगी = पुना रोगी puna*h* + rogî = punâ
rogî, ill again.

54 (87). The two pronouns सः sa*h* and एषः esha*h*, this, retain
Visarga at the end of a sentence only, but become सो so and
एषो esho before अ a (51, 2. b).

Ex. सः + ददाति = स ददाति sa*h* + dadâti = sa dadâti, he gives;
सः + इंद्रः = स इंद्रः sa*h* + indra*h* = sa indra*h*, this Indra.

But सः + अभवत् = सोऽभवत् sa*h* + abhavat = so ＊ bhavat, he
was; मृतः सः m*rita*h sa*h*, he is dead.

55 (88). भोः bho*h*, an irregular vocative of भवत् bhavat, thou,
drops its Visarga before all vowels and soft consonants.

Ex. भोः + ईशान = भो ईशान bho*h* + îsâna = bho îsâna, Oh lord!
भोः + देवाः = भो देवाः bho*h* + devâ*h* = bho devâ*h*, Oh gods!

But भोः + छेत्तः = भोश्छेत्तः bho*h* + *kh*etta*h* = bho*s kh*etta*h*, Oh
cutter!

The same applies to the interjections भगोः bhago*h* and अघोः

स्वर् svar, heaven; अहर् ahar, day; voc. sg. of nouns in ऋ ri, e. g.
पितर् pitar, father; and some verbal forms from verbs in ऋ ri, as
अजागर् a*g*âgar, 2. 3. sg. impf. of जागृ *g*âgri, to awake.

agho*h*, really irregular vocatives of भगवत् bhagavat, God, and
अघवत् aghavat, sinner.

56 (90). Nouns ending in radical र् r, retain the र् r before the
सु su of the loc. plur., and in compounds even before nouns beginning with hard letters.

Ex. वार् + सु = वार्षु vâr + su = vârshu, in the waters; गिर् +
पति: = गीर्पति: gir + pati*h* = gîrpati*h*, lord of speech.

In compounds, however, like गीर्पति: gîrpati*h*, the optional use
of Visarga is sanctioned: गी:पति: gîhpati*h*.

57 (91). ख् *kh* at the beginning of a word, after a final short
vowel, and after the particles आ â and मा mâ, is changed to
च्छ *kkh*.

Ex. तव + छाया = तव च्छाया tava + *kh*âyâ = tava *kkh*âyâ, thy
shade; मा + छिदत् = मा च्छिदत् mâ + *kh*idat = mâ *kkh*idat, let him
not cut; आ + छादयति = आच्छादयति â + *kh*âdayati = â*kkh*âdayati, he covers.

After any other long vowel, this change is optional.

बदरीछाया or बदरीच्छाया badarî*kh*âyâ or badarî*kkh*âyâ, shade of
Badarîs.

In the body of a word the change of ख् *kh* into च्छ *kkh* is necessary after both long and short vowels.

Ex. इच्छति i*kkh*ati, he wishes; म्लेच्छ: mle*kkh*ah, a barbarian.

58 (92). Initial श् s, not followed by a hard consonant, may be
changed into ख् *kh*, if the final letter of the preceding word is a
hard consonant or ङ् *ñ* (for न् n).

Ex. वाक् + शतम् = वाक्शतम् or वाक्खतम् vâk + satam = vâk
satam or vâk *kh*atam, a hundred speeches; तत् + श्लोकेन = तच्छ्लो-
केन tat + slokena = ta*kkh*lokena, by that verse; धावन् + शश: =
धावञ्शश: or धावञ्छश: dhâvan + sasah = dhâvañ sasah or dhâvañ
*kh*asah, a running hare; अप् + शब्द: = अप्शब्द: or अप्ख्शब्द: ap +
sabdah = apsabdah or ap*kh*abdah, the sound of water.

59. Initial ह h, after softening a preceding क् k, द् t, त् t, प् p, is changed to the soft aspirate of the preceding letter.

Ex. वाक् + हि = वाग्घि vâk + hi = vâgghi, for speech; तत् + हि = तद्धि tat + hi = tad dhi, for this.

60 (93). If घ gh, द् dh, ध dh, भ bh, or ह h stand at the end of a syllable beginning with ग् g, ड् d, द् d, or ब् b, and lose their aspiration as final or otherwise, the initial consonants are aspirated by way of compensation[1].

Ex. दुह् duh, a milker, becomes धुक् dhuk; विश्वगुध् visvagudh, all attracting, becomes विश्वघुत् visvaghut; बुध् budh, wise, becomes भुत् bhut.

Internal Sandhi.

61. The rules of internal Sandhi apply to the final letters of nominal and verbal bases before all terminations of declension (except those beginning with consonants of the middle base) and conjugation, before primary suffixes, and before secondary suffixes beginning with a vowel or य् y. They are best acquired by learning paradigms of nouns and verbs first. Many of these rules agree with those of external Sandhi; the most important of those which differ from external Sandhi are here added.

Final Vowels.

62 (110). In many cases before vowels इ i and ई î are changed to इय् iy; उ u and ऊ û to उव् uv; ऋ ri to रि ri; ॠ rî to इर् ir, and after labials to उर् ur.

Ex. भी + इ = भिथि bhî + i = bhiyi; भू + इ = भुवि bhû + i = bhuvi; युयु + उः = युयुवुः yuyu + uh = yuyuvuh; मृ + अते = त्रियते

---

[1] Roots ending in a soft aspirate and beginning with ग् g, द् d, ब् b may be supposed to have had an initial aspirate also; see Grassmann in Kuhn's Zeitschrift, vol. xii, p. 111 sqq.

m*ri* + ate = mriyate; गॄ + अति = गिरति g*ri* + ati = girati; पपॄ + इ = पपुरि pap*ri* + i = papuri.

63 (111). Final ॠ *ri* before consonant terminations is changed to ईर् îr; after labials to ऊर् ûr.

Ex. गॄ g*ri*, to shout; passive गीर्यते gîryate; part. गीर्णः gîr*nah* : पॄ p*ri*, to fill; pass. पूर्यते pûryate; part. पूर्णः pûr*nah*.

64 (112). ए e, ऐ ai, ओ o, औ au are changed before suffixes beginning with vowels or य् y to अय् ay, आय् ây, अव् av, आव् âv.

Ex. ने + अन = नयन ne + ana = nayana; जे + य = जय्य ge + ya = gayya; रै + ए = राये rai + e = râye; गो + ए = गवे go + e = gave; गो + य = गव्य go + ya = gavya; नौ + अः = नावः nau + a*h* = nâva*h*.

65 (143, 144). इ i and उ u preceding radical र् r or व् v are generally lengthened when a consonant follows.

Ex. दिव् + यति = दीव्यति div + yati = dîvyati; गिर् + भिः = गीर्भिः gir + bhi*h* = gîrbhi*h*; धुर् + भिः = धूर्भिः dhur + bhi*h* = dhûrbhi*h*; गिर् + स् = गीः gir + s = gî*h*.

Final Consonants.

66 (114). Nominal or verbal bases ending in consonants and followed by terminations consisting of a single consonant, drop the termination altogether, two consonants not being tolerated at the end of a word (29). The final consonants of the base are then treated like other final consonants :—वाच् + स् = वाक् vâ*k* + s = vâk, speech: nom. sg.; प्राच् + स् = प्राङ्क् prâñ*k* + s = prân, eastern: nom. sg. masc. Here प्राङ्क् prâñk, which remains after the dropping of स् s, is, according to the same rule, reduced again to प्राङ् prâṅ, the final nasal remaining guttural, because it would have been guttural if the final क् k had remained. सुवल्ग् + स् = सुवल् suvalg + s = suval, well jumping. Here, after the dropping of स् s, there would remain सुवल्क् suvalk; but as no word can end in two

consonants, this is reduced to सुवल् suval. Before the middle
terminations सुवल्ग् suvalg assumes its middle form सुवल् suval;
hence instr. plur. सुवल्भिः suvalbhi*h*. अहन् + स् = अहन् ahan +
s = ahan, thou killedst: 2. p. sg. impf.; अद्वेष् + त् = अद्वेट् advesh
+ t = advet, he hated: 3. p. sg. impf.; अदोह् + त् = अधोक् adoh +
t = adhok, he milked: 3. p. sg. impf.

67 (115). Final consonants of verbal and nominal bases generally
remain unchanged before terminations beginning with vowels,
nasals, and semivowels. Before terminations beginning with other
letters, they follow the rules of external Sandhi, e. g. from वच् va*k*,
to speak, वच्मि va*k*mi, वाच्य vâ*k*ya, वचानि va*k*âni; but वक्ति vakti.

68 (116). Aspirates followed by terminations beginning with any
letter (except vowels, semivowels, and nasals) lose their aspiration.

Ex. मामथ् + ति = मामत्ति mâmath + ti = mâmatti, 3. p. sg. pres.
act. of the intensive मामथ् mâmath, he shakes much; रुध् + ध्वे =
रुन्द्ध्वे rundh + dhve = runddhve, 2. pl. pres. middle of रुध् rudh,
you impede; लभ् + स्ये = लप्स्ये labh + sye = lapsye, I shall take.

But युध् + इ = युधि yudh + i = yudhi, loc. sing., in battle;
लोभ् + यः = लोभ्यः lobh + ya*h* = lobhya*h*, to be desired; क्षुभ् +
नाति = क्षुभ्नाति kshubh + nâti = kshubhnâti[1], he agitates.

Note—*Two aspirates can never meet in Sanskrit.*

69 (117). The initial त् t and थ् th of suffixes are softened after
soft aspirates, and take the whole aspiration on themselves (i. e. the
final aspiration, when lost before त् t, थ् th, cannot be thrown back).

Ex. लभ् + तः = लब्धः labh + ta*h* = labdha*h*, taken; रुध् +
यः = रुद्धः rundh + tha*h* = runddha*h*, you two obstruct; अबान्ध् +
तम् = अबान्द्धम् abândh + tam = abânddham, 2. p. dual aor. 1. act.,
you two bound.

----

[1] Contrary to 75, न् n does not in this case become ण् *n* after
ष् sh, by Pâ*n*ini VIII. iv. 39.

Note (118)—If घ् gh, द् dh, ध् dh, भ् bh, ह् h, at the end of a syllable, lose their aspiration before ध्व् dhv (**not** धि dhi), भ् bh, स् s, they throw their aspiration back on ग् g, इ d, ड् d, ब् b at the beginning of the syllable (not on other letters). Cp. 60.

Ex. बुध् + स् = भुत् budh+s=bhut, knowing; भुद्भि: bhudbhi*h*, instr. plur.; भुत्सु bhutsu, loc. plur.; अभुद्ध्वम् abhuddhvam, 2. p. pl. aor. mid.

But दुग्धि dugdhi from दुह् duh, to milk, 2. sg. impv.

70 (122). Dentals after linguals become lingual.

Ex. इष् + त = इष्ट ish + ta = ish*t*a; द्विष् + धि = द्विड्ढि dvish + dhi = dvi*ddh*i ; षट् + नाम् = षण्णाम् sha*t* + nâm = sha*nn*âm.

71. न् n after क् k and ग् g becomes ञ् ñ; but remains unchanged after श् s.

Ex. यज् + न = यज्ञ ya*g* + na = yag*ñ*a; but प्रश्न: prasna*h*.

72 (133). न् n at the end of a nominal or verbal base, before sibilants (not before सु su of loc. pl.), is changed to Anusvâra.

Ex. जिघांसति *g*ighâm̐sati, he wishes to kill, from हन् han.

But सुहिन् + सु = सुहिन्सु suhin + su = suhinsu.

73 (134). न् n remains unchanged before semivowels.

Ex. हन्यते hanyate, he is killed, from हन्; तन्वन् tanvan from तन् tan, stretching.

74 (135, 136). म् m remains unchanged before य् y, र् r, ल् l; but in the nom. sg., before middle terminations, or personal terminations beginning with म् m or व् v, it is changed to न् n.

Ex. काम्य: kâmya*h* from कम् kam ; ताम्रम् tâmram from तम् tam ; अम्ल: amla*h* from अम् am.

But प्रशान् prasân, nom. sg., प्रशान्भि: prasânbhi*h*, instr. plur., प्रशान्सु prasânsu, loc. pl., from प्रशाम् prasâm ; अगन्म aganma, we went, and अगन्व aganva, we two went, from गम् gam + म ma and गम् gam + व va.

75 (96). The dental न् n, followed by a vowel or न् n, म् m, य् y,

व् v, is changed into the lingual ण् n, if it is preceded by the linguals ऋ ri, ॠ rî, र् r, or ष् sh, even though a vowel, a guttural, a labial, य् y, व् v, ह् h, or Anusvâra intervene.

Ex. नृ + नाम् = नृणाम् nri+nâm = nrinâm, of men; कर्णः karnah, ear; दूषणम् dûshanam, abuse (a vowel intervenes); वृंहणम् vrimha-nam, nourishing (Anusvâra, ह h, and a vowel intervene); अर्केण arkena, by the sun (guttural and vowel); क्षिप्णुः kshipnuh, throw-ing (vowel and labial); प्रेम्णा premnâ, by love (diphthong and labial); ब्रह्मण्यः brahmanyah, kind to Brahmans (vowel, ह h, labial, vowel, न् n followed by य् y); निषण्णः nishannah, rested (न् n followed by न् n, which is itself assimilated to ण् n); प्रायेण prâ-yena, generally (vowel, य् y, vowel); अक्षण्वत् akshanvat, having eyes (व् v follows).

But अर्चनम् arkanam, worship (palatal intervenes); अर्णवेन arna-vena, by the ocean (lingual intervenes); दर्शनम् darsanam, a system of philosophy (श् s is palatal); अर्धेन ardhena, by half (ध् dh is dental); कुर्वन्ति kurvanti, they do (न् n is followed by त् t); रामान् râmân, acc. pl., the Râmas (न् n is final).

Note—The number of intervening letters, it will be seen from the above examples, is not limited. In the word रामायण Râmâ-yana, for example, five letters (three vowels, a labial, and a semi-vowel) intervene between the र् r and the ण् n.

Table showing the Changes of न् n into ण् n.

ऋ ri,	in spite of intervening Vowels,	change	if there follow Vowels, or
ॠ rî,	Gutturals (including ह h and Anusvâra),	न् n	न् n, म् m,
र् r,	Labials (including व् v),	into	य् y,
ष् sh,	and य् y,	ण् n	व् v.

76 (100). A dental स् s [1] followed by a vowel, or by त् t, थ् th, न् n, म् m, य् y, व् v, is changed into the lingual ष् sh, if it is immediately preceded by क् k, र् r, ल् l, or by any vowel except अ a or आ â, either immediately or with Anusvâra, Visarga, or ष् sh intervening.

Ex. सर्पिः sarpi*h*, clarified butter (स् s being final does not change to ष् sh); सर्पिषा sarpishâ, inst. sg.; सर्पींषि sarpîmshi (Anusvâra intervenes); सर्पिःषु sarpi*h*shu (Visarga intervenes) or सर्पिष्षु sarpishshu (ष् sh intervenes); वाक्षु vâkshu, loc. plur. of वाच् vâ*k*, speech; गीर्षु gîrshu, loc. plur. of गिर् gir, speech; कमल्+सु = कमल्षु kamal+su=kamalshu; ध्रोक्ष्यति dhrokshyati, fut. of द्रुह् druh, to hate (here ह् h is changed, by 69, note, to क् k, the aspiration being thrown on the initial द् d).

Table showing the Changes of स् s into ष् sh.

Any Vowels except अ, आ â, (in spite of inserted Anusvâra, Visarga, or sibilant intervening,) also क् k, र् r, ल् l if immediately preceding,	change स् s into ष् sh	if there follow Vowels, or त् t, थ् th, न् n, म् m, य् y, व् v.

Note—These two rules should be thoroughly acquired, since the change from the dental n and s to the lingual must constantly be made in declension and conjugation. They are best learned by comparing them and noting the following points:—

1. स् s must be followed by the same letters as न् n, + त् t and थ् th.

---

[1] This rule applies to the स् s of suffixes and terminations, not to radical स् s. Hence सुपिसौ supisau, because the स् s belongs to the root पिस् pis.

2. The change is caused by the same lingual letters, ऋ *ri*, ॠ *rî* (included in the vowels), र् r, ष् sh (included in the intervening letters), + क् k, ळ् l, and the vowels except अ a and आ â.

3. The consonants which change the स् s must precede *immediately* (this is not necessary in the case of न् n), while the vowels admit of intervening letters in both cases.

77 (125). श् *s* before त् t becomes ष् sh.

Ex. दृश् *dris* + त ta becomes दृष्ट *drishta* (70).

श् *s* before other consonants follows the rules of external Sandhi.

78 (132). The final स् s of roots becomes त् t before the स् s of the *general* tenses (135); e. g. वस् vas, to dwell, वत्स्यति vatsyati, 3. sg. fut. act. The same change takes place in the middle cases of the suffix वस् vas (102).

79 (127). ह् h before स् s, and in roots which begin with द् d before other consonants also, is treated like घ् gh; e. g. लेह् + सि = लेक्षि leh + si = lekshi; दह् + स्यति = धक्ष्यति dah + syati = dhakshyati (69, note); दह् + त = दग्ध dah + ta = dagdha (69).

In other roots त् t, थ् th, ध् dh, following ह् h, are changed to ढ् *dh*, the ह् h is dropped, and a preceding short vowel lengthened.

Ex. लिह् + तः = लीढः lih + ta*h* = lî*dh*a*h*; रोह् + तुम् = रोढुम् roh + tum = ro*dh*um.

Note—Exceptions to this are नह् + तः = नद्धः nah + ta*h* = naddha*h*; दृह् + त = दृढ drih + ta = dri*dh*a; वह् + तुम् = वोढुम् vah + tum = vo*dh*um; सह् + तुम् = सोढुम् sah + tum = so*dh*um.

CHAPTER III.

DECLENSION.

80. Declension is most conveniently treated under three heads:—

　　1. Nouns and adjectives; 2. numerals; 3. pronouns.

81 (149). In Sanskrit there are:—

a. Three genders: masculine, feminine, and neuter.

b. Three numbers: singular, dual, and plural.

c. **Eight cases:** nominative, vocative, accusative, **instrumental,** dative, ablative, genitive, **locative.**

Note—It is important to know the cases in this order, because it is the only arrangement by which such cases as are identical in form, either in the singular, the dual, or the plural, may be grouped together.

82 (152). Declension consists in the addition of case-terminations to the stem or base.

The normal case-terminations are:—

	SINGULAR.		DUAL.		PLURAL.	
	M. F.	N.	M. F.	N.	M. F.	N.
N.	स् s	म् m				
V.[1]	—	म् m	औ au	ई î	अस् as	इ i[2]
A.	अम् am					
I.	आ â				भिस् bhis	
D.	ए e		भ्याम् bhyâm			
Ab.	अस् as				भ्यस् bhyas	
G.	अस् as		ओस् os		आम् âm	
L.	इ i				सु su	

Note 1. The vocative is the same as the nominative in all numbers *except the masc. and fem. sing.* of vowel stems generally and *the masc. sing.* of consonant stems in at, an, in, as, yas, vas.

Note 2. The nom. acc. voc. pl. neut. (which ends in इ i) inserts a nasal before a final consonant of the base. This nasal is determined by the consonant which follows it; hence ङ् ṅ before gutturals, ञ् ñ before palatals, ण् n before linguals, न् n before dentals, म् m before labials, Anusvâra before sibilants and ह h. Neuters ending in a nasal or a semivowel do not insert the nasal in the plural.

83 (179). An important distinction in nominal and adjectival bases (chiefly bases ending in consonants) is that between **strong** and **weak** cases.

If bases have *two* forms, **strong** cases and **weak** cases are distinguished.

If bases have *three* forms, **strong** (Aṅga), **middle** (Pada), and **weakest** (Bha) are distinguished.

Note—Difference of accent is the cause of the distinction. The stem always being accented in the strong cases, naturally preserved its full form, while the accent having originally rested on the terminations in the weak cases, the stem was consequently shortened. The last vowel of the base is often shortened in the vocative, because the accent is **always** on the first syllable[1].

84 (179). The strong cases are:—

> Nom. voc. acc. sing.
> Nom. voc. acc. dual ⎱ of masculine nouns[2].
> Nom. voc. (**not acc.**) plur. ⎰

Nom. voc. acc. **plural only** of **neuters.**

All the other cases are weak.

When there are *three* bases, the middle cases are those the terminations of which begin with a consonant (i. e. भ्याम् bhyâm,

---

[1] For the sake of brevity, the accent of the *nom.* sg. du. pl. only is, as a rule, given in the paradigms.

[2] Nearly all nouns with changeable bases form the feminine in ई î (105, 4).

भि: bhi*h*, भ्य: bhya*h*, सु su). The weakest are all the remaining weak cases (viz. those of which the terminations begin with vowels); e. g. प्रत्यंचौ pratya*ñk*au, nom. dual (strong base प्रत्यंच् pratya*ñk*); प्रत्यग्भिः pratyagbhi*h* (middle base प्रत्यच् pratya*k*); प्रतीचो: pratî*koh*, gen. dual (weakest base प्रतीच् pratî*k*).

In neuters with three bases the nom. voc. acc. singular is middle, the nom. voc. acc. dual weakest; e. g. nom. voc. acc. sg. प्रत्यक् pratyak, nom. voc. acc. du. प्रतीची pratîkî, nom. voc. acc. pl. प्रत्यंचि pratya*ñk*i. The other cases are as in the masculine.

NOUNS AND ADJECTIVES.

85 (153). This declension may conveniently be divided into two classes :—

    I. Bases ending in consonants.
        A. Unchangeable bases.   B. Changeable bases.
    II. Bases ending in vowels.
        A. In अ a and आ â.
        B. In इ i and उ u.
        C. In ई î and ऊ û.
        D. In ऋ *ri*.
        E. In ऐ ai, ओ o, औ au.

Note—In order to avoid confusing the minds of beginners, it is advisable to commence with the bases in consonants, because these add the case-terminations given in 82 without modification. Some grammars begin with the vowel declension in अ a (II. A), since this is the most important, containing as it does the majority of all the declined bases of the language. But the wide deviation of its endings from the normal terminations makes it objectionable to begin with them.

A. Unchangeable Bases.

86 (151, 153). These bases may end in all consonants except ङ् *ṅ*, ञ् *ñ*, य् y. The bases are liable to such changes only as are

required by the rules of Sandhi before the terminations. Masculines and feminines ending in the same consonant are inflected exactly alike. The neuters are different (as in the other declensions) in the nom. voc. acc. of all numbers.

The स् s of the nom. sing. masc. and fem. is always dropped, because no word may end in two consonants (29).

The voc. sg. m. and f. is the same as the nom. except in bases in (derivative) खस् as (95).

On the insertion of the nasal in the nom. voc. acc. pl. neut., see 82, note 2.

87. Bases in the first four letters of the guttural, the lingual, the dental, and the labial classes (see 5) end in क् k, ट् t, त् t, प् p (cp. 28) respectively in the nom. sg. and before the loc. pl. suffix सु su, and in ग् g, ड् d, द् d, ब् b respectively before the terminations beginning with भ् bh. They retain their original sound before vowel terminations.

Bases in Gutturals.

88 (156). Paradigm: चित्रलिख् ḱitralíkh, painter (चित्र ḱitra, picture, √लिख् likh, to paint).

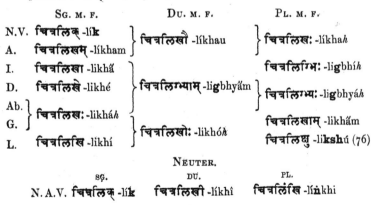

	SG. M. F.	DU. M. F.	PL. M. F.
N.V.	चित्रलिक् -lík		
		चित्रलिखौ -líkhau	चित्रलिख: -líkhaḥ
A.	चित्रलिखम् -líkham		
I.	चित्रलिखा -likhấ		चित्रलिग्भि: -ligbhíḥ
D.	चित्रलिखे -likhé	चित्रलिग्भ्याम् -ligbhyẵm	
Ab.			चित्रलिग्भ्य: -ligbhyáḥ
G.	चित्रलिख: -likháḥ		चित्रलिखाम् -likhẵm
L.	चित्रलिखि -likhí	चित्रलिखो: -likhóḥ	चित्रलिक्षु -likshú (76)

		NEUTER.	
	SG.	DU.	PL.
N. A. V.	चित्रलिक् -lík	चित्रलिखी -likhî	चित्रलिंखि -líṅkhi

Note—In the paradigms of regular nouns with unchangeable bases it will be sufficient to remember the nom. sing., nom. instr. loc. pl., and nom. pl. neut.

Bases in Dentals[1] and Labials.

89 (157). These are declined like चिचलिख kitralikh.

BASE.	NOM. SG.	NOM. PL. M. F.	INSTR. PL.	LOC. PL.	NOM. PL. N.
हरित् harít, green, m. f. n.	हरित् harít	हरितः harítaḥ	हरिद्भिः harídbhiḥ	हरित्सु harítsu	हरिंति harínti
अग्निमथ् agnimáth, fire-kindling, m.f.n.	अग्निमत् agnimát	°मथः -máthaḥ	°मद्भिः -madbhíḥ	°मत्सु -matsú	°मंथि -mánthi
सुहृद् suhŕd, friendly, m. f. n.	सुहृत् suhṛt	सुहृदः suhŕdaḥ	सुहृद्भिः suhṛdbhíḥ	सुहृत्सु suhṛtsú	सुहृंदि suhŕndi
बुध् budh, knowing, m. f. n.	भुत् bhút	बुधः búdhaḥ	भुद्भिः bhudbhíḥ	भुत्सु bhutsú	बुंधि búndhi
गुप् gup, guardian, m. f. n.	गुप् gúp	गुपः gúpaḥ	गुब्भिः gubbhíḥ	गुप्सु gupsú	गुंपि gúmpi
ककुभ् kakúbh, region, f.	ककुप् kakúp	ककुभः kakúbhaḥ	ककुब्भिः kakúbbhiḥ	ककुप्सु kakúpsu	°ककुंभि -kakúmbhi[2]

Bases in Palatals.

90 (158). The palatals (च k, छ kh, ज g, ह gh) must be treated separately from the other four classes, because they undergo a change of organ as well as of quality (30, 31) in the nom. sg. and before terminations beginning with consonants (28, 3). They are retained (except छ kh) only when followed by a vowel.

1. च k[3] is changed to क k or ग g.

Base जलमुच् galamúk, masc. cloud (water-dropping).

---

[1] There are hardly any bases ending in linguals.

[2] Used as a neuter at the end of a compound adjective.

[3] Bases ending in अच् ak are changeable (104, III).

NOM. SG.	NOM. PL.	INSTR. PL.	LOC. PL.	NOM. PL. N.
जलमुक्	जलमुच:	जलमुग्भि:	जलमुक्षु	जलमुंचि
galamúk	galamúkah	galamugbhíh	galamukshú	galamúñki

Like जलमुच् galamuk are declined वाच् vâk, f. speech; त्वच् tvak, f. skin; रुच् ruk, f. light; सुच् sruk, f. ladle.

Note (159)—The special bases कुंच् kruñk, curlew, प्रांच् prâñk, worshipping, वृश्च् vrisk, cutting, are respectively declined in the nom. sg., nom. instr. loc. pl. thus :—

कुङ् krúṅ	कुंच: krúñkah	कुङ्भि: krúṅbhih	कुंषु krúṅkshu
प्राङ् prâṅ	प्रांच: prâñkah	प्राङ्भि: prâṅbhih	प्रांषु prâṅkshu
वृट् vrit	वृश्च: vriskah	वृड्भि: vridbhíh	वृट्सु vritsú

2 (160). छ् kh is changed to ट् t when final and before consonants, but to श् s before vowels.

BASE.	NOM.SG.	NOM.PL.	INSTR.PL.	LOC.PL.	NOM.PL.N.
प्राछ् prâkh, an asker	प्राट्	प्राश:	प्राड्भि:	प्राट्सु	प्रांशि
	prât	prâsah	prâdbhíh	prâtsú	prâmsi

3 (161). ज् g is changed to क् k or ग् g.

BASE.	NOM.SG.	NOM.PL.	INSTR.PL.	LOC.PL.	NOM.PL.N.
रुज् rug, disease	रुक्	रुज:	रुग्भि:	रुक्षु	रुंजि
	rúk	rúgah	rugbhíh	rukshú	rúñgi
ऊर्ज् ûrg, strength	ऊर्क्	ऊर्ज:	ऊर्ग्भि:	ऊर्क्षु	ऊर्जि
	úrk	úrgah	úrgbhíh	úrkshú	úrgi

Like रुज् rug are declined वणिज् vanig, m. merchant; भिषज् bhishág, m. physician; ऋत्विज् ritvíg, m. priest; स्रज् srag, f. garland; असृज् ásrig, n. blood.

Note 1. Nouns derived from any of the six roots—यज् yag, to sacrifice; भ्रज्ज् bhragg, to roast; भ्राज् bhrâg, to shine; राज् râg, to shine, to rule; मृज् mrig, to clean; सृज् srig, to emit, to create; also परिव्राज् parivrâg, a mendicant—change ज् g to ट् t

or इ *d*; e. g. nom. sg. and pl. of परिव्राज् parivrâ*g* are परिव्राट्
parivrâ*t*, परिव्राज: parivrâ*gah*; सम्राज् samrâ*g*, m. sovereign:
सम्राट् samrâ*t*, सम्राज: samrâ*gah*; देवेज् devé*g* (from देव deva +
यज् ya*g*), worshipper of the gods: देवेट् devé*t*, देवेज: devé*gah*;
भृज्ज् bhr*igg*, roasting: भृट् bhr*ít*, भृज्ज: bhr*íggah*.

Note 2. अवयाज् avayâ*g*, a Vedic priest, is irregular in changing
its base to अवयस् avayas in the nom. and before consonants:—

NOM. SG.	VOC. SG.	NOM. PL.	INSTR. PL.	LOC. PL.
अवया:	अवया: or अवय:	अवयाज:	अवयोभि:	अवय:सु
avayâ*h*	ávayâ*h* or ávaya*h*	avayâ*gah*	avayó*bhih*	avayâ*hsu*

4. Bases in ह् *gh*, which are rare, change ह् *gh* to क् k or ग् g.

Bases in Nasals.

91 (154). 1. No base ends in ङ् *ṅ* or ञ् *ñ* (86).

2. Bases in ण् *n* undergo no change.

Base सुगण् sugá*n*, a ready reckoner, m. f. n. (सु su, well, and
गण gan, to count).

NOM. SG.	NOM. PL.	INSTR. PL.	LOC. PL.	NOM. PL. N.
सुगण्	सुगणा:	सुगणभि:	सुगण्सु	सुगणि
sugá*n*	sugá*nah*	sugá*nbhih*	sugá*nsu*	sugá*ni* (82, n. 2)

3. Bases in न् n are changeable, and will be treated in 99, 102.

4 (178). Bases in the labial nasal म् m change म् m to न् n in
the nom. sg. and before consonants. The म् m is retained before
vowels.

BASE.	NOM. SG.	NOM. PL.	INSTR. PL.	LOC. PL.
प्रशाम् prasâm, mild,	प्रशान्	प्रशाम:	प्रशान्भि:	प्रशान्सु
m. f.	prasá*n*	prasâ*mah*	prasâ*nbhih*	prasâ*nsú*

Bases in Semivowels.

92 (164). 1. No base ends in य् y or (practically) in व् v[1].

2. Bases in ल् l undergo no modification.

---

[1] See decl. of दिव् div, 106.

3. Bases in र r are regular, except that इ i and उ u, preceding the र r, are lengthened if the र r is final or followed by a consonant. In the loc. pl. the र r (being radical) remains unchanged before षु shu (56).

BASE.	NOM. VOC. SG.	NOM. PL.	INSTR. PL.	LOC. PL.
गिर् gir, f. voice	गी: gîʰ	गिर: giraʰ	गीर्भि: gîrbhíʰ	गीर्षु gîrshú
पुर् pur, f. town	पू: pûʰ	पुर: púraʰ	पूर्भि: pûrbhíʰ	पूर्षु pûrshú
वार् vâr, n. water	वा: vâʰ	वारि vâri	वार्भि: vârbhíʰ	वार्षु vârshú
द्वार् dvâr, f. door	द्वा: dvâʰ	द्वार: dvấraʰ	द्वार्भि: dvârbhíʰ	द्वार्षु dvârshú

Bases in Sibilants (श s, ष sh, क्ष ksh) and ह h.

93 (174). Bases in श s, ष sh, क्ष ksh, and ह h change these letters to ट t when final and before consonants (cp. 28, 5 and 6).

BASE.	NOM. SG.	NOM. PL.	NOM. PL. N.	INSTR. PL.	LOC. PL.
विश् vis, m. f. n. one who enters	विट् vít	विश: vísah	विंशि vímsi	विड्भि: vidbhíʰ	वित्सु vitsú
द्विष् dvish, m. f. n. hating	द्विट् dvít	द्विष: dvíshah	द्विंषि dvímshi	द्विड्भि: dvidbhíʰ	द्वित्सु dvitsú
तक्ष् taksh, m. f. n. paring	तट् tát	तक्ष: tákshah	तंक्षि támkshi	तड्भि: tadbhíʰ	तत्सु tatsú
गुह् guh, m. f. n. covering	घुट् ghút	गुह: gúhah	गुंहि gúmhi	घुड्भि: ghudbhíʰ	घुट्सु ghutsú

94 (174). **Exceptions.**

1. Bases in श s.

a. Bases derived from दिश् dis, to show, दृश् dris, to see, and स्पृश् spris, to touch, change श s to क् k; e. g. दिश् dis, f. a country:

NOM. SG.	NOM. PL.	NOM. PL. N.	INSTR. PL.	LOC. PL.
दिक् dík	दिश: dísah	दिंशि dímsi	दिग्भि: digbhíʰ	दिक्षु dikshú

b. Bases from नश् nas, to destroy, change श् s to ट् t or क् k; e. g. जीवनश् *gîvanás*, m. f. n. life-destroying:

NOM. SG.	INSTR. PL.	LOC. PL.
जीवनट् or °नक्	°नड्भिः or °नग्भिः	°नट्सु or °नक्षु
gîvaná*t* or -ná**k**	-na*d*bhí*h* or -na*g*bhí*h*	-na*t*sú or -na**ksh**ú

c. पुरोडाश् *purodắs*, an offering, or a priest, is irregular, being declined like अवयाज् avayâ*g* (90, 3, n. 2):

NOM. SG.	NOM. PL.	INSTR. PL.
पुरोडा: puroda̐*h*	पुरोडाशः purodắsa*h*	पुरोडोभिः purod*ó*bhi*h*

2. Bases derived from धृष् dhrish, to dare, change ष् sh to क् k; e. g. दधृष् dadhr*ísh*, bold:

NOM. SG.	NOM. PL.	NOM. PL. N.	INSTR. PL.	LOC. PL.
दधृक्	दधृषः	दधृंषि	दधृग्भिः	दधृषु
dadhr*ík*	dadhr*íshah*	dadhr*ímshi*	dadhr*íg*bhi*h*	dadhr*íkshu*

3. Bases in ह् h.

a. Bases from roots ending in ह् h, and beginning with द् d, change ह् h to क् k; also उष्णिह् ushn*íh*, a metre; e. g. दुह् duh, m. f. n. milking:

NOM. SG.	NOM. PL.	NOM. PL. N.	INSTR. PL.	LOC. PL.
धुक्dhúk	दुहः dúha*h*	दुंहि dúmhi	धुग्भिः dhug*bhíh*	धुक्षु dhukshú

b. Bases derived from the roots द्रुह् druh, to hate, मुह् muh, to confound, स्निह् snih, to love, स्नुह् snuh, to spue, change ह् h to ट् t or क् k; e. g. द्रुह् druh, m. f. n. hating:

NOM. SG.	NOM. PL.	NOM. PL. N.	INSTR. PL.	LOC. PL.
ध्रुट् or ध्रुक्	द्रुहः	द्रुंहि	ध्रुड्भिः or ध्रुग्भिः	ध्रुट्सु or ध्रुक्षु
dhrú*t* or dhrúk	drúha*h*	drúmhi	dhru*d*bhí*h* or dhrug*bhíh*	dhru*t*sú or dhrukshú

c. Bases from नह् nah, to bind, change ह् h to त् t; e. g. उपानह् upânáh, f. a shoe:

NOM. SG.	NOM. PL.	INSTR. PL.	LOC. PL.
उपानत्	उपानहः	उपानद्भिः	उपानत्सु
upânát	upânáha*h*	upânád*bhih*	upânátsu

Bases in the Dental Sibilant स् s.

95 (165). I. Bases in अस् as, इस् is, उस् us.

In these bases it is important to distinguish the **derivative** from the **radical**[1].

The following rules must be carefully noted.

1. Derivative अस् as is lengthened in the nom. (**not vocative**) sing. masc. and fem. (**not neuter**).

2. Derivative इस् is and उस् us remain unchanged.

3. Derivative अस् as, इस् is, उस् us lengthen their vowel (besides nasalizing it) in the nom. voc. acc. pl. neut.

4. Derivative इस् is and उस् us before vowels become इष् ish and उष् ush (76).

These rules are reversed in the case of **radical** अस् as, इस् is, उस् us; in other words, (1) अस् as remains unchanged in the nom. sg. masc. and fem., while (2) इस् is and उस् us are lengthened (**voc. and neut. also**); (3) the vowel of the nom. voc. acc. pl. neut. is never lengthened; (4) इस् is and उस् us remain unchanged before vowels.

Note—Rad. इस् is and उस् us (**not** अस् as) are lengthened before consonant terminations; अस् as always becomes ओ o before भ bh.

		NOM. SG.	VOC. SG.	NOM. PL.	INSTR. PL.	LOC. PL.	NOM. P
Der. सुमनस् sumánas		सुमना:	°न:	°नस:	°नोभि:	°न:सु	°नां
kind, m. f. n.		sumána*h*	-na*h*	-nasa*h*	-nobhi*h*	-na*h*su	-nâ*n*

---

[1] It is easy to recognise a radical as, is, us, by remembering that all roots being monosyllabic, only one syllable must remain after prefixes are detached; e. g. सुतुस् sutus, well-sounding, from सु su, well, and तुस् tus. But सुमनस् sumanas, well-minded, from सु su, well, and मनस् manas, mind, from मन् man, to think, + अस् as.

	N.V.SG.	NOM.PL.	INSTR.PL.	LOC.PL.	NOM.PL.N.
Rad. पिंडग्रस् pin*d*a-grás	°ग्र:	°ग्रस:	°ग्रोभि:	°ग्र:सु	°ग्रंसि
eating a mouthful, m.f.n.	-gráh	-grása*h*	-grobhí*h*	-gra*h*sú	-grámsi
Der. सुज्योतिस् su*yy*otís	°ति:	°तिष:	°तिर्भि:	°ति:षु	°तींषि
well-lighted, m. f. n.	-tí*h*	-tísha*h*	-tírbhi*h*	-tí*h*shu	-tĭmshi
Rad. सुपिस् supís	°पी:	°पिस:	°पीर्भि:	°पी:षु	°पिंसि
well-walking, m. f. n.	-pĭ*h*	-pís*a*h	-pĭrbhí*h*	-pĭ*h*shú	-pímsi
Der. दीर्घायुस् dîrghấyus	°यु:	°युष:	°युर्भि:	°यु:षु	°यूंषि
long-lived, m. f. n.	-yu*h*	-yusha*h*	-yurbhi*h*	-yu*h*shu	-yûmshi
Rad. सुतुस् sutús	°तृ:	°तुस:	°तूर्भि:	°तृ:षु	°तुंसि
well-sounding, m. f. n.	-tŭ*h*	-túsa*h*	-túrbhí*h*	-tŭ*h*shú	-túm*s*i

Note 1 (173). ध्वस् dhvas (from ध्वंस् dhvams, to fall) and स्रस् sras
(from स्रंस् srams, to fall) when used at the end of compounds
change their स् s to त् t in the nom. and voc. sg., and before
terminations beginning with consonants.

NOM. VOC.	NOM. PL.	INSTR. PL.	LOC. PL.
पर्णध्वत्	पर्णध्वस:	पर्णध्वद्भि:	पर्णध्वत्सु
parnadhvát	parnadhvása*h*	parnadhva**d**bhi*h*	parnadhva**t**sú

Note 2. Nouns derived from desideratives (197), though ending
in derivative इस् is[1], lengthen the vowel in the nom. sg. m. f. n.,
and before consonants. In the neut. pl. no nasal is inserted.

NOM. M.F.N.	NOM. PL.	INSTR. PL.	LOC. PL.	NOM. PL. N.
पिपठी:	पिपठिष:	पिपठीर्भि:	पिपठी:षु	पिपठिषि
pipa*th*ĭ*h*	pipa*th*isha*h*	pipa*th*ĭrbhi*h*	pipa*th*ĭ*h*shu	pipa*th*ishi

Note 3. आशिस् âsís, f. blessing, is declined: nom. voc. आशी:
âsĭ*h*, nom. pl. आशिष: âsísha*h*, pl.n. आशींषि âsĭmshi, instr. आशीर्भि:
âsĭrbhi*h*, loc. आशी:षु âsĭ*h*shu or आशीष्षु âsĭshshu. (This optional

---

[1] In this case the इस् is is not *one* suffix, i. e. पिपठिस् pipa*th*is =
pipa*th* + i + s. Hence, probably, the difference of treatment.

spelling applies to the loc. pl. of all unchangeable bases in स् s preceded by a vowel: मनःसु or मनस्सु; सुतूःषु or सुतूष्षु; दोःषु or दोष्षु; cp. 49, 3.)

II. Bases in स् s preceded by other vowels (very few).

BASE.	NOM. SG.	NOM. PL.	NOM. PL. N.	INSTR. PL.	LOC. PL.
चकास् kakâs, splen-did, m. f. n.	चका: kakâh	चकास: kakâsah	चकांसि kakâmsi	चकाभि: kakâbhih	चका:सु kakâhsu
दोस् dos, arm, m. (n.)	दो: dóh	दोष: dóshah	दोंषि dómshi	दोर्भि: dórbhih	दो:षु dóhshu
चिकीर्स् kikîrs, desir-ous of acting, m.f.n.	चिकी: kikîh	चिकोर्ष: kikîrshah	चिकोर्षि kikîrshi	चिकीर्भि: kikîrbhih	चिकीर्षु kikîrshu
सुहिंस् suhims, one who strikes well, m. f. n.	सुहिन् suhín	सुहिंस: suhímsah	सुहिंसि suhímsi	सुहिन्भि: suhinbhíh	सुहिन्सु suhinsú

B. Changeable Bases.

96. Regular changeable bases end in त् t, न् n, स् s, or च् k.

Those in त् t end in अत् at (मत् mat, वत् vat).

Those in न् n end in अन् an (मन् man, वन् van) or इन् in (मिन् min, विन् vin).

Those in स् s end in यस् yas (comparatives) or वस् vas (perf. participles active).

Those in च् k are derived from अच् ak, to move.

Of these bases, those in अत् at, इन् in, and यस् yas have *two* forms, i. e. strong and weak cases; those in अन् an, वस् vas, and च् k have *three* forms, i. e. strong, middle, and weakest cases (83).

97 (182). **Nouns with two Bases.**

1. **Bases in अत् at.**

a. **Present Participles** in अत् at (masc. and neut.) The strong base is in अंत् ant, the weak in अत् at.

Base अदत् adát, eating, from अद् ad, to eat.

SINGULAR.	DUAL.	PLURAL.

MASCULINE.

| N.V. | अदन् adán | अदंतौ adántau | अदंतः adántah |
| A. | अदंतम् adántam | अदंतौ adántau | अदतः adatáh |

I.	अदता adatá		अदद्भिः adádbhih
D.	अदते adaté	अदद्ग्याम् adádbhyâm	अदद्य: adádbhyah
Ab.			
G.	अदतः adatáh	अदतो: adatóh	अदताम् adatám
L.	अदति adatí		अदत्सु adátsu

NEUTER.

| N.A. | अदत् adát | अदती adatí | अदंति adánti |

Note (186)—महत् mahat, great, originally a present participle, forms its strong base in आंत् ânt.

N. महान् mahán	N.V. pl. m. °हांत:-hántah	n. °हांति-hánti
A. महांतम्-mahántam	°हत:-hatáh	
I. महता mahatá	°हद्भिः-hádbhih	
V. महन् máhan		

98 (187). b. Bases in मत् mat and वत् vat (which are adjectives, meaning 'possessed of,' 'having') differ from those in अत् at solely in lengthening the vowel in the N. sg. masc.

अग्निमत् agnimát, having fire.

N. sg. अग्निमान्-mán	N.V. pl. °मंत:-mántah	n. °मंति-mánti
A. अग्निमंतम्-mántam	°मत:-matáh	
V. अग्निमन्-man		

ज्ञानवत् *gñânavát*, having knowledge.

N. ज्ञानवान् *gñânavân*	N.V. ज्ञानवंत: *gñânavántah*
V. ज्ञानवन् *gñânavan*	A. ज्ञानवत: *gñânavatáh*

Note 1 (188)—भवत् bhávat, when it means 'Your Honour,' is declined like ज्ञानवत् *gñânavat* (the voc. is भवन् bhávan or भो: **bho***h*); when it means 'being,' pres. part. of भू bhû, it is regular (like अदत् adat).

Note 2 (190)—कियत् kíyat, how much? and इयत् íyat, so much, are declined like nouns in मत् mat: N. कियान् kíyân, V. कियन् kíyan.

99 (203). 2. **Bases in** इन् **in.**

These form their weak base by dropping the न् n (but only before consonants).

They drop the न् n in the N. sg. m. and n., and lengthen the vowel in the N. masc., lengthening it also in the N.A.V. pl. neut.

MASCULINE.

N. sg.	धनी dhanî	pl.	धनिन: dhanínah
A.	धनिनम् dhanínam		धनिन: dhanínah
I.	धनिना dhanínâ		धनिभि: dhaníbhih
V.	धनिन् dhánin		

NEUTER.

N.A.	धनि dhaní		धनीनि dhanîni
V.	धनि dhâni or धनिन् dhánin		

100 (206). 3. **Bases in** ईयस् **îyas (comparative** suffix) form their strong cases from ईयांस् îyâms. Base गरीयस् garîyas, heavier.

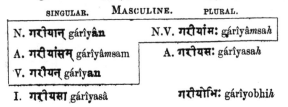

SINGULAR. MASCULINE.	PLURAL.
N. गरीयान् garîyân	N.V. गरीयांस: garîyâmsah
A. गरीयांसम् garîyâmsam	A. गरीयस: garîyasah
V. गरीयन् garîyan	
I. गरीयसा garîyasâ	गरीयोभि: garîyobhih

NEUTER.

N. A. गरीय: gárîya*h*   गरीयसी gárîyasî   गरीयांसि gárîyâmsi

Nouns with three Bases.

101 (204). 1. **Participles of the reduplicated perfect in वस् vas.** The strong base is वांस् vâ*m*s; the middle, वत् vat; the weak, उष् ush[1].

रुरुद्वस् rurudvás, having wept, from रुद् rud, to weep.

MASCULINE.

N. रुरुद्वान् rurudvá**n**	N.V. °द्वांसौ -dvá*m*sau	N.V. °द्वांस: -dvá*m*sa*h*
A. रुरुद्वांसम् rurudyá*m*sam	°द्वांसौ -dvá*m*sau	°दुष: -dúsha*h*
V. रुरुद्वन् rúrudva**n**		
I. रुरुदुषा rurudúshâ	°द्ब्याम् -dvádbhyâm	
L. रुरुदुषि rurudúshi	°दुषो: -dúsho*h*	

NEUTER.

N. रुरुद्वत् rurudvát	°दुषी -dúshî	°द्वांसि -dvá*m*si

Note 1 (205)—Participles in वस् vas, which insert an इ i between the reduplicated root and the termination, drop the इ i whenever the termination वस् vas is changed to उष् ush, but **radical** इ i or ई î is never dropped in this case. Hence the I. sg. of तस्थिवान् tasthivân, from स्था sthâ, to stand, is तस्थुषा tasthushâ, but of निनीवान् ninîvân it is निन्युषा nin**y**ushâ.

---

[1] The स् s of वस् vas is changed to त् t before स् s and भ् bh, as in वत्स्यामि vatsyâmi, future of वस् vas, to dwell (+ स्यामि syâmi). उष् ush is deduced from वस् vas. Unaccented व va commonly becomes उ u. उस् us before vowels regularly becomes उष् ush.

The following examples of reduplicated perfect participles (cp. 183) may be useful:—

MIDDLE BASE.	NOM. SG.	NOM. PL.	ACC. PL.	INSTR. PL.
शुश्रुवस् susruvás, having heard	शुश्रुवान् susruván	शुश्रुवांस: susruvā́msah	शुश्रुवुष: susruvúshah	शुश्रुवद्भि: susruvádbhih
पेचिवस् pekivás, having cooked	पेचिवान् pekiván	पेचिवांस: pekivā́msah	पेचुष: pekúshah	पेचिवद्भि: pekivádbhih
जग्मिवस् gagmivás, having gone	जग्मिवान् gagmiván	जग्मिवांस: gagmivā́msah	जग्मुष: gagmúshah	जग्मिवद्भि: gagmivádbhih
जगन्वस् gaganvás[1], having gone	जगन्वान् gaganván	जगन्वांस: gaganvā́msah	जग्मुष: gagmúshah	जगन्वद्भि: gaganvádbhih
जघ्निवस् gaghnivás, having killed	जघ्निवान् gaghniván	जघ्निवांस: gaghnivā́msah	जघ्नुष: gaghnúshah	जघ्निवद्भि: gaghnivádbhih
जघन्वस् gaghanvás, having killed	जघन्वान् gaghanván	जघन्वांस: gaghanvā́msah	जघ्नुष: gaghnúshah	जघन्वद्भि: gaghanvádbhih

Note 2. Beginners are apt to confound this *reduplicated* perf. act. participle with the active participle formed by adding the suffix वत् vat to the perf. passive participle; e. g. कृत kritá, pf. pt. pass., done, कृतवत् kritávat, having done: N. कृतवान् kritá-vân, A. कृतवंतम् kritávantam. The cause of the confusion is that both end in °वान् vân in the N. sg.

102. 2. Bases in सन् an (अन् an, मन् man, वन् van).

Their strong base is आन् ân; their weakest, न् n; and their middle base अ a.

The N. sg. masc. has आ â, neut. अ a (cp. the bases in इन् in).

If the suffixes मन् man and वन् van are immediately preceded by a consonant, they do not drop their अ a in the weakest cases. This is to avoid the concurrence of three consonants, though the rule does not apply to bases in simple सन् an. Hence आत्मना âtmánâ, but तक्ष्णा tákshnâ.

---

[1] On the change of म् m to न् n, see 74.

In all other words the ऄ a is optionally retained in the L. sg. and in the N. A.V. dual neut.

राजन् râ*g*an, m. a king.

	SING.		PLUR.
N. राजा râ*g*â		N.V. राजान: râ*g*âna*h*	
A. राजानम् râ*g*ânam		राज्ञ: râ*g*ña*h*	
V. राजन् râ*g*an			

I. राज्ञा râ*g*ñâ	राजभि: râ*g*abhi*h*
L. राज्ञि râ*g*ñi or राजनि râ*g*ani	राजसु râ*g*asu

नामन् nâman, n. name.

	SING.	DUAL.	PLUR.
N. A. नाम nâma	नाम्नी nâmnî or नामनी nâmanî	नामानि nâmâni
V. नाम nâma or नामन् nâman		

I. नाम्ना nâmnâ	नामभ्याम् nâmabhyâm	नामभि: nâmabhi*h*
L. नाम्नि nâmni or नामनि nâmani	नाम्नो: nâmno*h*	नामसु nâmasu

ब्रह्मन् brahmán, m. n. the creator (मन् man preceded by a consonant).

MASCULINE.

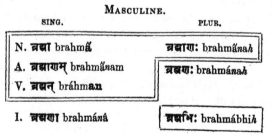

	SING.	PLUR.
N. ब्रह्मा brahmâ̂	ब्रह्माण: brahmâ*n*a*h*	
A. ब्रह्माणम् brahmâ*n*am	ब्रह्मण: brahmána*h*	
V. ब्रह्मन् bráhman		
I. ब्रह्मणा brahmá*n*â	ब्रह्मभि: brahmábhi*h*	

Irregular Bases in अन् an.

103 (195). 1. पथिन् pathín, m. path, has for its strong base
पंथान् pánthân; for its middle base पथि pathí; for its weakest
base पथ् path.

The N.V. sg. are irregular.

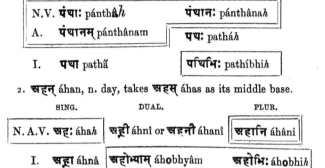

SING.	PLUR.
N.V. पंथा: pánthâ*h*	पंथान: pánthâna*h*
A. पंथानम् pánthânam	पथ: patháh
I. पथा pathâ	पथिभि: pathíbhi*h*

2. अहन् áhan, n. day, takes अहस् áhas as its middle base.

	SING.	DUAL.		PLUR.
N.A.V.	अह: áha*h*	अह्नी áhnî or अहनी áhanî		अहानि áhâni
I.	अह्ना áhnâ	अहोभ्याम् áho**bh**yâm		अहोभि: áho**bh**i*h*
L.	{ अह्नि áhni अहनि áhani	अह्नो: áhno*h*		{ अह:सु áha*h*su अहस्सु áhassu

The Visarga of the N. sg. is treated like an original र् r (52).
Hence अहरह: áharaha*h*, day by day; and, in composition, e. g.
अहर्गण: ahargàna*h*. Exception: अहोरात्र: ahorâtráh, m.[1] day
and night.

3, 4 (199). श्वन् svân, m. a dog, युवन् yúvan, m. (juven-is), young,
take शुन् sun[2], यून् yûn[3] as their weakest base. Otherwise they
are declined regularly like ब्रह्मन् brahmán, m.

---

[1] रात्री râtrî, f. night, becomes रात्र râtrá, m. (or n.) at the
end of compounds (cp. 215, 2).

[2] u = unaccented va (101, 1, foot-note). Cp. κύων = svâ(n) and
κυνός.

[3] For yu-un; u for va; cp. similar contraction in Lat. jūn-ior.

	SING.		PLUR.	

N. श्वा *svằ* (κύων) युवा *yúvâ*   श्वान: *svằnah* युवान: *yúvânah*

A. श्वानम् *svânam* युवानम् *yúvânam*   शुन: *súnah* यून: *yū́nah*

V. श्वन् *svấn* (κύον) युवन् *yúvan*   I. श्वभि: *svábhih* युवभि: *yúvabhih*

5 (202). हन् han (from √ हन् han, to kill) at the end of compounds takes हन् han (lengthening the vowel in the nom. sing.) for its strong base, ह ha for its middle, and घ्न ghn for its weakest base.

ब्रह्महन् brahmahán, a Brâhman-killer.

NOM. SG.	NOM. PL.	ACC. PL.	INSTR. PL.	NOM. PL. N.
हा hằ	हन: hánah	घ्न: ghnáh	हभि: hábhih	हानि hằni
ब्रह्महा	ब्रह्महण:	ब्रह्मघ्न:	ब्रह्महभि:	ब्रह्महाणि
brahmahẚ	brahmahánah	brahmaghnáh	brahmahábhih	brahmahẚni

Loc. sg. ब्रह्मघ्नि brahmaghní or ब्रह्महणि brahmaháni.

III. Bases in अच् a*k*.

104 (181). These form their strong base in अंच् a*ñk*, their middle in अच् a*k*, their weakest in ईच् î*k* or ऊच् û*k*[1] (according as अच् a*k* is preceded by य् y or व् v).

प्रत्यच् pratyá*k*, behind.

MASCULINE.

	SING.	DUAL.	PLUR.
N.V.	प्रत्यङ् pratyáṅ	°त्यंचौ -tyáñkau	°त्यंच: -tyáñkah
A.	प्रत्यंचम् pratyáñkam	°त्यंचौ -tyáñkau	°तीच: -tîkáh
I.	प्रतीचा pratîkẚ	°त्यग्भ्याम् -tyagbhyẚm	°त्यग्भि: -tyagbhíh
L.	प्रतीची pratîkî́	°तीचो: -tîkóh	°त्यक्षु -tyakshú

---

[1] For यच् ya*k* and वच् va*k* respectively. Unaccented य ya and व va are contracted to ई î and ऊ û in this case, though they are more commonly shortened to इ ĭ and उ ŭ.

NEUTER.

N. A. प्रत्यक् pratyák	॰ तीची -tîkî̃	॰ त्यंचि -tyáñki

Other words in अच् ak are:—

STRONG BASE.	MIDDLE BASE.	WEAKEST BASE.
सम्यंच् samyáñk, right	सम्यच् samyák	समीच् samîk
न्यंच् nyáñk, low	न्यच् nyãk	नीच् nîk
सध्रंच् sadhryáñk, accompanying	सध्र्यच् sadhryãk	सध्रीच् sadhrîk
अन्वंच् anváñk, following	अन्वच् anvák	अनूच् anûk
विष्वंच् víshvañk, all-pervading	विष्वच् víshvak	विषूच् víshûk
उदंच् údañk, upward	उदच् údak	उदीच् údîk[1]
तिर्यंच् tiryáñk, tortuous	तिर्यच् tiryák	तिरश्च् tirásk[2]

Note—प्राच् prãk, forward, eastern[3], and अवाच् ávâk, downward, south, have only two bases, प्रांच् práñk and अवांच् aváñk for the strong, and प्राच् prâk and अवाच् avâk for the weak.

MASCULINE.

N.V. sg. प्राङ् práñ[4]	pl. प्रांच: práñkah
A. प्रांचम् práñkam	प्राच: prâkah
I. प्राचा prâkâ	प्राग्भि: prãgbhih
L. प्राचि prâki	प्राक्षु prâkshu

---

[1] î, though no y precedes the a, by analogy.

[2] From tirás (Lat. trans) + ak, to go. The y in the strong and middle base is due to analogy.

[3] प्रांच् práñk, 'worshipping,' is unchangeable (90, 1, note).

[4] For प्राञ्ज् + स् práñk + s = práñk = práñ.

105. The beginner will find it useful to remember the following points with regard to changeable bases :—

1. The vowel of the suffix is lengthened in the N. sg. masc. in all changeable bases except those in अच् a*k* and अत् at.

अग्निमान् agnimân, विद्यावान् vidyâvân; राजा râgâ, ब्रह्मा brahmâ, प्रतिदिवा pratidivâ; धनी dhanî, वाग्मी vâgmî, मेधावी medhâvî; गरीयान् garîyân; रुरुड्वान् rurudvân.

But भवन् bhávan; प्रत्यङ् pratyáṅ.

2. The N. sg. masc. ends in a nasal in all changeable bases except those in अन् an (also मन् man, वन् van) and those in इन् in (also मिन् min, विन् vin).

3. All nouns with changeable bases, which lengthen the vowel in the N. sg. masc., shorten it in the vocative.

अग्निमन् ágniman, विद्यावन् vídyâvan; राजन् râgan, ब्रह्मन् bráhman, प्रतिदिवन् prátidivan; धनिन् dhánin, वाग्मिन् vâgmin, मेधाविन् médhâvin; गरीयन् garîyan; रुरुड्वन् rúrudvan.

But भवन् bhávan; प्रत्यङ् prátyaṅ.

4. The feminines of nouns with changeable bases are formed by adding ई î to the weak base (when there are two bases) or to the weakest (when there are three). They follow the vowel declension in ई î (like नदी nadî, 111).

Ex. अग्निमती agnimátî, विद्यावती vidyâvatî; राज्ञी râgñî; धनिनी dhaninî, वाग्मिनी vâgmínî, मेधाविनी medhâvínî; गरीयसी garîyasî; रुरुदुषी rurudúshî; भवती bhávatî; प्रतीची pratîkî.

Exceptions.—Bases in वन् van become वरी varî: पीवन् pîvan (πίων), fat, f. पीवरी pîvarî (πίειρα). Bases in मन् man are declined like masculines: दामन् dâman, f. rope; N. sg. दामा dâmâ, A. दामानम् dâmânam.

Irregular Nouns with changeable Bases.

106. 1. अप् ap, water, is always plural. It lengthens its अ a in the strong cases (N.V.) and substitutes त् t for प् p before भ् bh.

N. आप: ā́paḥ | A. अप: apáḥ I. अद्भि: adbhíḥ L. अप्सु apsú

2 (213). दिव् div or द्यु dyu, f. sky, uses द्यु dyu for its middle base, दिव् div everywhere else except the N. V. sg., which is irregular.

	SING.		PLUR.
N.	द्यौ: dyaúḥ (Ζεύς = Δjeυs)	N.V.	दिव: dívaḥ
A.	दिवम् dívam		दिव: diváḥ
I.	दिवा divā́		द्युभि: dyúbhiḥ
Ab.G.	दिव: diváḥ (Διϝós)		दिवाम् divā́m
L.	दिवि diví (Διϝί)		द्युषु dyúshu
V.	द्यौ: dyaúḥ (Ζεῦ)		

3 (210). अनडुत् anaḍut, an ox, has three bases: strong, अनड्वाह anaḍvā́h; middle, अनडुद् anaḍúd; weakest, अनडुह anaḍúh.

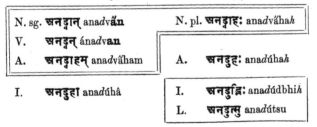

N. sg.	अनड्वान् anaḍvā́n	N. pl.	अनड्वाह: anaḍvā́haḥ
V.	अनड्वन् ánaḍvan		
A.	अनड्वाहम् anaḍvā́ham	A.	अनडुह: anaḍúhaḥ
I.	अनडुहा anaḍúhâ	I.	अनडुद्भि: anaḍúdbhiḥ
		L.	अनडुत्सु anaḍútsu

4 (212). पुम् pum, man, has three bases: strong, पुमांस् púmâms; middle, पुम् pum; weakest, पुंस् pums.

N. *sg.* पुमान् púm**ân**	N.V. *pl.* पुमांस: púmâ*m*sa*h*
V. पुमन् púm**an**	A. पुंस: pu*m*sá*h*
A. पुमांसम् púmâ*m*sam	

I. पुंसा pu*m*s**ä**	I. पुंभि: pu*m*bhí*h*
	L. पुंसु pu*m*sú

Bases ending in Vowels.

107 (238). **A. Bases in** अ a **and** आ â (अ a = Gk. -*os*, -*ov*; Lat. -us, -um : आ â = Gk. *a*, *η*; Lat. a).

	SINGULAR.	
MASC.	FEM.	NEUT.
Base कांत kântá	कांता kântấ	कांत kântá
N. कांत: kântá*h*	कांता kântấ	कांतम् kântám
A. कांतम् kântám	कांताम् kântâm	कांतम् kântám
I. कांतेन kânt**éna**	कांतया kântá**yâ**	कांतेन kânt**éna**
D. कांताय kântấ**ya**	कांतायै kântấ**yai**[1]	कांताय kântấ**ya**
Ab. कांतात् kântất	कांताया: kântấ**yâ***h*	कांतात् kântất
G. कांतस्य kântá**sya**	कांताया: kântấ**yâ***h*	कांतस्य kântá**sya**
L. कांते kânté	कांतायाम् kântấ**yâm**	कांते kânté
V. कांत kânta	कांते kắnte[2]	कांत kắnta
	DUAL.	
N. A.V. कांतौ kântaú	कांते kânté	कांते kânté
I.D.Ab. कांताभ्याम् kântấ**bhyâm**	कांताभ्याम् kântấbhyâm	कांताभ्याम् kântấ**bhyâm**
G. L. कांतयो: kântá**yo***h*	कांतयो: kântá**yo***h*	कांतयो: kântá**yo***h*

---

[1] The vowel declension (except bases in ऋ *ri* and diphthóngs) has the special endings ऐ ai, आ: â*h*, आम् âm in the dat., abl. gen., loc. sg. respectively.

[2] अंबा ambâ, mother, forms its V. in अ a : अंब amba.

PLURAL.

N.V.	कांता: kântá*h*	कांता: kântá*h*	कांतानि kântá*n*i [1]
A.	कांतान् kântá*n* [2]	कांता: kântá*h*	कांतानि kântá*n*i
I.	कांतै: kânta*íh*	कांताभि: kântábhi*h*	कांतै: kânta*íh*
D. Ab.	कांतेभ्य: kânté*bhyah*	कांताभ्य: kântá*bhyah*	कांतेभ्य: kânté*bhyah*
G.	कांतानाम् kântá*n*âm	कांतानाम् kântá*n*âm	कांतानाम् kântá*n*âm
L.	कांतेषु kânté*shu*	कांतासु kântá*su*	कांतेषु kânté*shu*

Note—Certain adjectives in ख: a*h*, खा â, खम् am follow the pronominal declension (122).

108 (239). Bases in radical खा â, declined alike in the masc. and fem., throw off the खा â in the weakest cases. In the neuter they shorten खा â to ख a and are declined like कांतम् kântám.

विश्वपा visvapâ̇, all-protecting (√पा pâ), is declined thus :—

N.V. विश्वपा: visvapá*h*	विश्वपौ visvapaú	विश्वपा: -pá*h*
A. विश्वपाम् visvapâm	विश्वपौ visvapaú	विश्वप: -pá*h*

I. विश्वपा visvap-â	विश्वपाभ्याम् -pábhyâm ° पाभि: -pábhi*h*	
L. विश्वपि visvap-í	विश्वपो: visvap-ó*h*	विश्वपासु -pâsu

B. Bases in इ i and उ u: masc., fem., neut.

109 (230). Base शुचि súki, pure ; मृदु mridú, soft.

SINGULAR.

	MASC.	FEM.	NEUT.	MASC.	FEM.	NEUT.
N.	शुचि:	शुचि:	शुचि	मृदु:	मृदु:	मृदु
	súki*h*	súki*h*	súki	mridú*h*	mridú*h*	mridú
A.	शुचिम्	शुचिम्	शुचि	मृदुम्	मृदुम्	मृदु
	súkim	súkim	súki	mridúm	mridúm	mridú

---

[1] Cp. 82, note 2.

[2] Orig. am + s: Goth. -ans, Gk. -*ovs*, Lat. -ōs.

	MASC.	FEM.	NEUT.	MASC.	FEM.	NEUT.
I.	शुचिना	शुच्या	शुचिना	मृदुना	मृद्वा	मृदुना
	súkinâ	súkyâ	súkinâ	mridúnâ	mridvá	mridúnâ
D.	शुचये	शुच्यै	शुचिने	मृदवे	मृद्वै	मृदुने
	súkaye	súkyai[1]	súkine	mridáve	mridvaí[1]	mridúne
Ab. G.	शुचेः	शुच्याः	शुचिनः	मृदोः	मृद्वाः	मृदुनः
	súkeh	súkyâh	súkinah	mridóh	mridváh	mridúnah
L.	शुचौ	शुच्याम्	शुचिनि	मृदौ	मृद्वाम्	मृदुनि
	súkau	súkyâm	súkini	mridau	mridvám	mridúni
V.	शुचे	शुचे	शुचि	मृदो	मृदो	मृदु
	súke	súke	súki	mrído	mrído	mrídu

DUAL.

N.A.V.	शुची	शुची	शुचिनी	मृदू	मृदू	मृदुनी
	súkî	súkî	súkinî	mridû	mridû	mridúnî

I.D.Ab.	शुचिभ्याम् súkibhyâm		मृदुभ्याम् mridúbhyâm		
G.L.	शुच्योः	शुच्योः	शुचिनोः मृद्वोः	मृद्वोः	मृदुनोः
	súkyoh	súkyoh	súkinoh mridvóh	mridvóh	mridúnoh

PLURAL.

	MASC.	FEM.	NEUT.	MASC.	FEM.	NEUT.
N.V.	शुचयः	शुचयः	शुचीनि	मृदवः	मृदवः	मृदूनि
	súkayah	súkayah	súkîni	mridávah	mridávah	mridûni
A.	शुचीन्	शुचीः	शुचीनि	मृदून्	मृदूः	मृदूनि
	súkîn	súkîh	súkîni	mridûn	mridûh	mridûni
I.	शुचिभिः súkibhih		मृदुभिः mridúbhih			
D.Ab.	शुचिभ्यः súkibhyah		मृदुभ्यः mridúbhyah			
G.	शुचीनाम् súkînâm		मृदूनाम् mridûnâm			
L.	शुचिषु súkishu		मृदुषु mridúshu			

Note 1. Neuter adjectives (not nouns) may be declined throughout (except N.A.V. of all numbers), and fem. adjectives

---

[1] See 107, foot-note.

and nouns in the D. Ab. G. L. sg., like masculines. Thus the L. sg.
of मति matí, thought, is मत्याम् matyám or मतौ mataú, but of वारि
vári, neut. water, only वारिणि várini.

Note 2. Bases in उ u sometimes form the fem. by lengthening
the vowel or adding ई î; e.g. कुरु: kúruh, a Kuru, fem. कुरू: kú-
rûh; लघु: laghúh, light, fem. either the same or लघ्वी laghvî.

Irregularities.

110. 1 (233). पति páti, a lord, is irregular in the weak cases of
the singular: I. पत्या pátyâ, D. पत्ये pátye, Ab. G. पत्यु: pátyuh,
L. पत्यौ pátyau. At the end of compounds it is regular (like शुचि
súki).

2 (232). सखि sákhi, a friend, has the same irregularities, but,
besides, has a special base, सखाय् sakhây, in the strong cases:
N. सखा sákhâ, A. सखायम् sákhâyam, I. सख्या sákhyâ, D. सख्ये
sákhye, Ab. G. सख्यु: sákhyuh, L. सख्यौ sákhyau, V. सखे sákhe;
du. N. A. V. सखायौ sákhâyau, pl. N. V. सखाय: sákhâyah, A.
सखीन् sákhîn. At the end of compounds सखि sakhi is regular in
the weak cases, but retains the base सखाय् sakhây in the strong.

3 (234). The neuters, अक्षि ákshi, an eye, अस्थि ásthi, bone, दधि
dádhi, curds, सक्थि sákthi, thigh, form their weakest cases from
bases in अन् án (like नामन् nâman, 102, 2); e.g. I. sg. अक्ष्णा
akshnâ, etc.

C. Bases in ई î and ऊ û: feminine[1].

111 (225). The following points, in which monosyllabic and
polysyllabic bases differ in declension, should be noted:—

1. Monosyllabic bases change ई î and ऊ û to इय् iy and उव् uv
before vowels, the polysyllabic to य् y and व् v.

---

[1] A few polysyllabic words in ई î and ऊ û, besides roots in ई î
and ऊ û at the end of compounds, are masc. as well as fem.

2. Monosyllabic bases **may** take the special fem. terminations [1], polysyllabic bases **must**.

3. Polysyllabic bases shorten ई î and ऊ û in the V. sg.

4. Polysyllabic bases in ई î have **no** स् s in the N. sg., except लक्ष्मी: lakshmî*h*, goddess of prosperity, तरी: tarî*h*, boat, तंत्री: tántrî*h*, lute.

5. Polysyllabic bases form the A. sg. in ईम् îm and ऊम् ûm, the A. pl. in ई: î*h* and ऊ: û*h*.

SINGULAR.

Base	धी dhî, thought	भू bhû, earth	नदी nadî, river	वधू vadhû, woman
N.V.	धी: dhî*h*	भू: bhû*h*	नदी nadî	वधू: vadhû*h*
A.	धियम् dhíyam	भुवम् bhúvam	नदीम् nadîm	वधूम् vadhûm
I.	धिया dhiyá	भुवा bhuvá	नद्या nadyá	वध्वा vadhvá
D.	धिये dhiyé	भुवे bhuvé	नद्यै nadyaí	वध्वै vadhvaí
Ab. G.	धिय: dhiyáh	भुव: bhuváh	नद्या:nadyá*h*	वध्वा:vadhvá*h*
L.	धियि dhiyí	भुवि bhuví	नद्याम् nadyám	वध्वाम् vadhvám
V.			नदि nádi	वधु vádhu

DUAL.

N.A.V.	धियौ dhíyau	भुवौ bhúvau	नद्यौ nadyaú	वध्वौ vadhvaú
I.D.Ab.	धीभ्याम् dhîbhyâm	भूभ्याम् bhûbhyâm	नदीभ्याम् nadîbhyâm	वधूभ्याम् vadhûbhyâm
G.L.	धियो: dhiyóh	भुवो: bhuvóh	नद्यो: nadyóh	वध्वो: vadhvóh

---

[1] 107, foot-note.

PLURAL.

N. A.V. धियः dhíya*h* भुवः bhúva*h* नद्यः nadyá*h* वध्वः vadhvá*h*

A. नदीः nadí*h* वधूः vadhú*h*

I. धीभिः भूभिः नदीभिः वधूभिः
dhíbhi*h* bhûbhí*h* nadî́bhi*h* vadhû́bhi*h*

D. Ab. धीभ्यः भूभ्यः नदीभ्यः वधूभ्यः
dhíbhyá*h* bhûbhyá*h* nadî́bhya*h* vadhû́bhya*h*

G. धियाम् भुवाम् नदीनाम् वधूनाम्
dhiyǎ́m bhuvǎ́m nadî́**n**âm vadhû́**n**âm

L. धीषु भूषु नदीषु वधूषु
dhíshú bhûshú nadî́shu vadhû́shu

Note (228)—स्त्री strî, woman, though monosyllabic, drops स् s
in N. sg., **must** take the special fem. terminations, has an optional A. sg. and pl. like नदी nadî, and shortens ई î in V.

N. sg. स्त्री N. A.V. du. स्त्रियौ N. pl. स्त्रियः
strî́ stríyau stríya*h*

A. स्त्रियम् I. D. Ab. स्त्रीभ्याम् A. स्त्रियः
stríyam strîbhyǎm stríya*h*

स्त्रीम् G. L. स्त्रियोः स्त्रीः
strî́m striyó*h* strî́*h*

I. स्त्रिया I. स्त्रीभिः
striyǎ́ strîbhí*h*

D. स्त्रियै D. Ab. स्त्रीभ्यः
striyaí strîbhyá*h*

Ab. G. स्त्रियाः G. स्त्रीणाम्
striyǎ́*h* strînǎ́m

L. स्त्रियाम् L. स्त्रीषु
striyǎ́m strîshú

V. स्त्रि strí

D. Bases in ऋ *ri*: masc., fem., neut.

112 (235). SINGULAR.

	MASC.	FEM.	NEUT.
Base	नप्तृ nápt*ri*, grandson	स्वसृ svás*ri*, sister	धातृ dhâtr*í*, providence
N.	नप्ता náptâ	स्वसा svásâ	धातृ dhâtr*í*
A.	नप्तारम् náptâram	स्वसारम् svásâram	धातृ dhâtr*í*
I.	नप्त्रा náptrâ	स्वस्रा svásrâ	°तृणा -tr*í*nâ or °त्रा -trâ
D.	नप्त्रे náptre	स्वस्रे svásre	°तृणे -tr*í*ne or °त्रे -tré
Ab.G.	नप्तु: (र्) náptu*h* (r)	स्वसु: (र्) svásu*h* (r)	°तृण: -tr*í*nah or °तु:-tu*h*
L.	नप्तरि náptari	स्वसरि svásari	°तृणि-tr*í*ni or °तरि-tári
V.	नप्त: (र्) nápta*h* (r)	स्वस: (र्) svása*h* (r)	धातृ dhâtri or °त: -ta*h*

DUAL.

N. A. V.	नप्तारौ náptârau	स्वसारौ svásârau	धातृणी dhâtr*í*nî
I. D. Ab.	नप्तृभ्याम् náptr*i*bhyâm	स्वसृभ्याम् svásr*i*bhyâm	°तृभ्याम् °tr*í*bhyâm
G. L.	नप्त्रो: náptro*h*	स्वस्रो: svásro*h*	°तृणो: °tr*í*noh

PLURAL.

N. V.	नप्तार: náptâra*h*	स्वसार: svásâra*h*	धातृणि dhâtr*î*ni
A.	नप्तॄन् náptr*î*n	स्वसॄ: svásr*î́h*	धातृणि dhâtr*î*ni
I.	नप्तृभि: náptr*i*bhi*h*	स्वसृभि: svásr*i*bhi*h*	धातृभि: dhâtr*í*bhi*h*
D. Ab.	नप्तृभ्य: náptr*i*bhya*h*	स्वसृभ्य: svásr*i*bhya*h*	धातृभ्य: dhâtr*í*bhya*h*
G.	नप्तॄणाम् náptr*î*nâm	स्वसॄणाम् svásr*î*nâm	धातॄणाम् dhâtr*î*nâm
L.	नप्तृषु náptr*i*shu	स्वसृषु svásr*i*shu	धातृषु dhâtr*í*shu

Note 1. The names of relations in ऋ *ri* (except नप्तृ náptri, स्वसृ svásri, and भर्तृ bhartri, husband) have a **short** अ a before र् r; e. g. पितृ pitr*í*, father, and मातृ mâtr*í*, mother: N. पिता pitâ, माता mâtâ; du. N. A. V. पितरौ pitárau, मातरौ mâtárau; pl. N. पितर: pitára*h*, मातर: mâtára*h*; A. पितॄन् pitr*î́*n, मातृ: mâtr*î́h*.

Note 2 (237). नृ nri, man, is declined like पितृ pitri, only the G.

pl. is नृणाम् nrīnăm or नॄणाम् nrĭnăm. N. ना nắ, A. नरम् náram,
I. ना nrắ, D. ने nré, A. G. नु: (र्) núh (r), L. नरि nári, V. न: náh.

Note 3 (236). क्रोष्टृ kroshtri, jackal, is irregular in forming its
middle base from क्रोष्टु kroshtu.

Note 4. The fem. of adjectives in ऋ ri is formed by adding ई î:
m. कर्तृ kartrí, f. कर्त्री kartrî (like नदी nadî).

E. Bases in ऐ ai, ओ o, औ au.

113 (217, 218). Base रै rai, m. wealth; गो go, m. f. bull, cow ;
नौ nau, f. ship.

SINGULAR.

N.V. रा: rắh	गौ: gaúh	नौ: naúh (ναύς)
A. रायम् rắyam	गाम् gắm	नावम् nắvam (νῆϝα)
I. राया rāyắ	गवा gávā	नावा nāvắ
D. राये rāyé	गवे gáve	नावे nāvé
Ab.G. राय: rāyáh	गो: góh	नाव: nāváh (νηϝός)
L. रायि rāyí	गवि gávi	नावि nāví (νηϝί)

DUAL.

N.A.V. रायौ rắyau	गावौ gắvau	नावौ nāvau
I.D.Ab. राभ्याम् rābhyắm	गोभ्याम् góbhyām	नौभ्याम् naubhyắm
G.L. रायो: rāyóh	गवो: gávoh	नावो: nāvóh

PLURAL.

N.V. राय: rắyah	गाव: gắvah	नाव: nắvah (νῆϝες)
A. राय: rāyáh	गा: gắh	नाव: nắvah
I. राभि: rābhíh	गोभि: góbhih	नौभि: naubhíh (ναῦφι)
D.Ab. राभ्य: rābhyáh	गोभ्य: góbhyah	नौभ्य: naubhyáh
G. रायाम् rāyắm	गवाम् gávām	नावाम् nāvắm (νηϝῶν)
L. रासु rāsú	गोषु góshu	नौषु naushú (ναυσί)

Note—द्यो dyo, f. heaven, is declined like गो go. It coincides
in N. and V. sg. with दिव् div, sky (106, 2).

Degrees of Comparison.

114 (249). The (secondary) suffix of the comparative तर tara (Gk. -τερο) and that of the superlative तम tama (Lat. -timo) are added to the weak or middle base: शुचि *súki*, शुचितर *súkitara*, शुचितम *súki-tama*; प्राच् *prák*, प्राक्तर *práktara*, प्राक्तम *práktama*; धनिन् dhanín, धनितर dhanítara, धनितम dhanítama; विद्वस् vidvás, विद्वत्तर vidváttara, विद्वत्तम vidváttama; प्रत्यच् pratyák, प्रत्यक्तर pratyák-tara, प्रत्यक्तम pratyáktama.

115 (251). Before the other (primary) suffixes of the comparative ईयस् íyas (rarely यस् yas, Gk. -ιων, Lat. -ior) and of the superlative इष्ठ ishtha (Gk. -ιστο), bases are reduced to one syllable, suffixes being dropped: मतिमान् matimán, wise, मतीयस् mátiyas, मतिष्ठ mátishtha; वृंदारक vrindáraka, beautiful, वृंदीयस् vríndiyas, वृंदिष्ठ vríndishtha. Some of these comparatives and superlatives have no corresponding positive from the same root. कनीयस् kániyas, कनिष्ठ kánishtha, and नेदीयस् nédiyas, नेदिष्ठ nédishtha, belong only in sense to अल्प álpa, small, and संतिक antiká, near, respectively.

(252). As a rule the root takes Guṇa before these two suffixes, with metathesis of अर् ar. क्षुद्र kshudrá, mean, क्षोदीयस् kshódi-yas; तृप्र triprá, त्रपीयस् trápiyas. There are, however, many irregular forms, e. g. बहुल bahulá, frequent, बंहीयस् bámhiyas.

These primary comparatives and superlatives have the acute on the first syllable.

NUMERALS.

116 (253).   **Cardinals.**

1	१	एक éka.		7	७	सप्तन् saptán (ἑπτά).
2	२	द्वि dví.		8	८	अष्टन् ashtán (ὀκτώ).
3	३	त्रि trí.		9	९	नवन् návan (ἐννέα).
4	४	चतुर् katúr.		10	१०	दशन् dásan (δέκα).
5	५	पंचन् páñkan.		11	११	एकादशन् ékâdasan.
6	६	षष् shásh.		12	१२	द्वादशन् dvâdasan.

13 १३ त्रयोदशन् tráyodasan.

14 १४ चतुदेशन् káturdasan.

15 १५ पंचदशन् páñkadasan.

16 १६ षोडशन् shódasan.

17 १७ सप्तदशन् saptádasan.

18 १८ अष्टदशन् ashtádasan.

19 १९ नवदशन् návadasan.

ऊनविंशति únavimsati.

20 २० विंशति vimsatí.

21 २१ एकविंशति ékavimsati.

22 २२ द्वाविंशति dvávimsati.

23 २३ त्रयोविंशति tráyovimsati.

28 २८ अष्टाविंशति ashtávimsati.

29 २९ नवविंशति návavimsati.

ऊनत्रिंशत् únatrimsat.

30 ३० त्रिंशत् trimsát.

39 ३९ नवत्रिंशत् návatrimsat.

ऊनचत्वारिंशत् únakatvá-
rimsat.

40 ४० चत्वारिंशत् katvârimsát.

49 ४९ नवचत्वारिंशत् návakatvá-
rimsat.

ऊनपंचाशत् únapañkásat.

50 ५० पंचाशत् pañkását.

60 ६० षष्टि shashtí.

70 ७० सप्तति saptatí.

80 ८० अशीति asîtí.

90 ९० नवति navatí.

100 १०० शतम् satám.

101 १०१ एकशतम् ékasatam.

एकाधिकम् शतम् ekâ-
dhikam satam.

102 १०२ द्विशतम् dvísatam.

द्व्यधिकम् शतम् dvya-
dhikam satam.

103 १०३ त्रिशतम् trísatam.

त्र्यधिकम् शतम् tryadhi-
kam satam.

110 ११० दशशतम् dásasatam.

दशाधिकम् शतम् dasâ-
dhikam satam.

200 २०० द्वे शते dvé saté.

द्विशतम् dvísatam.

300 ३०० त्रीणि शतानि trîni satáni.

त्रिशतम् trísatam.

1000 १००० दश शतानि dása satáni.

सहस्रम् sahásram.

Note—In order to form the numbers from 20 to 100 not
enumerated above, it is only necessary to remember that 2, 3, and
8 are द्वा dvá, त्रयस् tráyas, and अष्टा ashtá before 20 and 30 (द्वा-
विंशति dvávimsati, त्रयोविंशति tráyovimsati, अष्टात्रिंशत् ashtá-

trim*sat*), and द्वि dví, त्रि trí, अष्ट ash*tá* before 80; both forms
may be used with 40 to 70 and with 90.

Declension of Cardinals.

117 (254). Only the first four cardinals distinguish the genders.

एक: éka*h*, एका ékâ, एकम् ékam, following the declension of the
pronominal adjectives, is inflected like सर्व sarva (130, b).

द्वि dví is declined as the dual of the base द्व dva.

N. A. V. द्वौ dvaú, द्वे dvé, द्वे dvé; I. D. Ab. द्वाभ्याम् dvâbhyâm,
G. L. द्वयो: dváyo*h*.

त्रि trí, f. तिसृ tisrí, and चतुर् katúr, f. चतसृ *k*atasri, are declined
thus :—

	MASC.	NEUT.	FEM.	MASC.	NEUT.	FEM.
N.V.	त्रय:	त्रीणि	तिस्र:	चत्वार:	चत्वारि	चतस्र:
	tráya*h*	trí*n*i	tisrá*h*	kat**v**â*r*a*h*	kat**v**â*r*i	*k*átasra*h*
A.	त्रीन्	त्रीणि	तिस्र:	चतुर:	चत्वारि	चतस्र:
	tr**ín**	trí*n*i	tisrá*h*	katúra*h*	kat**v**â*r*i	*k*átasra*h*
I.	त्रिभि:	तिसृभि:		चतुर्भि:		चतसृभि:
	tribhí*h*	tisrí*bhi*h		katúrbhi*h*		*k*atasrí*bhi*h
D. Ab.	त्रिभ्य:	तिसृभ्य:		चतुर्भ्य:		चतसृभ्य:
	tribhyá*h*	tisrí*bhya*h		katúrbhya*h*		*k*atasrí*bhya*h
G.	त्रयाणाम्	तिसृणाम्		चतुर्णाम्		चतसृणाम्
	trayânâm	tis*rí*nâm		*k*aturnâm		katas*rí*nâm
L.	त्रिषु	तिसृषु		चतुर्षु		चतसृषु
	trishú	tisrí*sh*u		*k*atúrshu		*k*atasrí*sh*u

118 (257). षष् shásh: N. A. V. षट् shá*t*, I. षड्भि: sha*d*bhí*h*,
D. Ab. षड्भ्य: sha*d*bhyá*h*, G. षण्णाम् sha*nn*âm, L. षट्सु sha*t*sú.

The numerals in अन् an are all declined like पंचन् páñ*k*an :—

N. A. V. पंच páñ*k*a, I. पंचभि: pañkábhi*h*, D. Ab. पंचभ्य: pañká-
b*h*ya*h*, G. पंचानाम् pañkânâm, L. पंचसु pañkásu.

अष्टन् ashtán, however, has the following alternative forms :—

N. A. V. अष्टौ ashtaú, I. अष्टाभि: ashtábhíh, D. Ab. अष्टाभ्य: ashtábhyáh, L. अष्टासु ashtású.

Note (258). a. The numerals 3 to 19 are used as plurals agreeing with their substantives in number and case (3 and 4 in gender also).

b. The numerals 20 to 99 are sing. fem.; शत satá and सहस्र sahásra, sing. neut. (sometimes masc.), are used with nouns in the same case (in apposition) or in the G. plur.

119 (259). Ordinals.

1st प्रथम:, °मा, °मम्, prathamáh, -â, -ám.

2nd द्वितीय:, °या, °यम्, dvitíyah, -â, -am.

3rd तृतीय:, °या, °यम्, tritíyah, -â, -am.

4th चतुर्थे:, °र्थी, °र्थम्, katurtháh, -í, -ám.

तुरीय:, °या, °यम्, turíyah, -â, -am.

तुर्य:, °या, °र्यम्, túryah, -â, -am.

5th पंचम:, °मी, °मम्, pañkamáh, -í, -ám.

6th षष्ठ:, °ष्ठी, °ष्ठम्, shashtháh, -í, -ám.

7th सप्तम: saptamáh.

8th अष्टम: ashtamáh.

9th नवम: navamáh.

10th दशम: dasamáh.

11th एकादश: ekâdasáh.

19th नवदश: navadasáh.

ऊनविंश: ûnavimsáh.

ऊनविंशतितम: ûnavimsatitamáh.

20th विंश: vimsáh.

विंशतितम: vimsatitamáh.

30th त्रिंश: trimsáh.

त्रिंशत्तम: trimsattamáh.

40th चत्वारिंश: katvârimsáh.

चत्वारिंशत्तम: katvârimsattamáh.

50th पंचाश: pañkâsáh.

पंचाशत्तम: pañkâsattamáh.

60th षष्टितम: shashtitamáh.

61st एकषष्टितम: ekashashtitamáh.

एकषष्ठ: ekashashtháh.

70th सप्ततितम: saptatitamá*h*.

71st एकसप्ततितम: ekasaptati-
tamá*h*.

एकसप्तत: ekasaptatá*h*.

80th अशीतितम: asîtitamá*h*.

81st एकाशीतितम:ekâsîtitamá*h*.

एकाशीत: ekâsîtá*h*.

90th नवतितम: navatitamá*h*.

91st एकनवतितम: ekanavati-
tamá*h*.

एकनवत: ekanavatá*h*.

100th शततम: satatamá*h*.

Note—The feminine from 5 onwards is always formed with ई î.

Numerical Adverbs and other Derivatives.

120 (260). सकृत् sakrít, once.

द्वि: dvíh, twice.

त्रि: tríh, thrice.

चतु: katúh, four times.

पंचकृत्व: pañkakritváh, five times.

षट्कृत्व: shatkritváh, six times, etc.

एकधा ekadhâ, in one way.

द्विधा dvidhâ or द्वेधा dvedhâ, in two ways.

त्रिधा tridhâ or त्रेधा tredhâ, in three ways.

चतुर्धा katurdhâ, in four ways.

पंचधा pañkadhâ, in five ways.

षोढा shodhâ, in six ways, etc.

एकश: ekasáh, one-fold.

द्विश: dvisáh, two-fold.

त्रिश: trisáh, three-fold, etc.

द्वयम् dvayám or द्वितयम् dvítayam, a pair.

त्रयम् trayám or त्रितयम् trítayam or त्रयी trayî, a triad.

चतुष्टयम् kátushtayam, a tetrad.

पंचतयम् páñkatayam, a pentad, etc.

PRONOUNS AND PRONOMINAL ADJECTIVES.

121 (261).   **Personal Pronouns.**

Base (in composition) मद् mád   Base (in composition) त्वद् tvád
and असद् asmád.   and युष्मद् yushmád.

SINGULAR.

N. अहम् ahám, I.   त्वम् tvám, thou

A. माम् mǎm, me   त्वाम् tvǎm, thee

I. मया máyâ, by me   त्वया tváyâ, by thee

D. मह्यम्máhyam(mihi),to me   तुभ्यम् túbhyam (tibi), to thee

Ab. मत् mát, from me   त्वत् tvát, from thee

G. मम máma, of me   तव táva, of thee

L. मयि máyi, in me   त्वयि tváyi, in thee

DUAL.

N. A. आवाम् âvǎm   युवाम् yuvǎm

I. D. Ab. आवाभ्याम् âvǎbhyâm   युवाभ्याम् yuvǎbhyâm

G. L. आवयो: âváyoh   युवयो: yuváyoh

PLURAL.

N. वयम् vayám, we   यूयम् yûyám, you

A. अस्मान् asmǎn, us   युष्मान् yushmǎn, you

I. अस्माभि: asmábhih, by us   युष्माभि: yushmǎbhih, by you

D. अस्मभ्यम् asmábhyam, to us   युष्मभ्यम्yushmábhyam,to you

Ab. अस्मत् asmát, from us   युष्मत् yushmát, from you

G. अस्माकम् asmǎkam[1], of us   युष्माकम्yushmǎkam[1], of you

L. अस्मासु asmǎsu, in us   युष्मासु yushmǎsu, in you

---

[1] This is properly not a genitive at all, but a neuter sing. of an adjective stem formed with the suffix -ka.

The following enclitic forms are also used: Sg. A. मा mâ, त्वा tvâ; D. G. मे me, ते te. Du. A. D. G. नौ nau, वाम् vâm. Pl. A. D. G. नः nah, वः vah.

Demonstrative Pronouns.

122 (262). Base (in composition) तद् tád, that (also=he, she, it).

	SINGULAR.		PLURAL.	
	MASC.	FEM.	MASC.	FEM.
N.	सः sáh (ó)[1]	सा sắ (ý)	ते té	ताः tắh
A.	तम् tám	ताम् tắm	तान् tắn	ताः tắh
I.	तेन téna	तया táyâ	तैः taíh	ताभिः tắbhih
D.	तस्मै tásmai	तस्यै tásyai	तेभ्यः tébhyah	ताभ्यः tắbhyah
Ab.	तस्मात् tásmât	तस्याः tásyâh		
G.	तस्य tásya		तेषाम् téshâm	तासाम् tắsâm
L.	तस्मिन् tásmin	तस्याम् tásyâm	तेषु téshu	तासु tásu

Dual, m. f., N. A.V. तौ taú, ते té; I. D. Ab. ताभ्याम् tắbhyâm; G. L. तयोः táyoh.

Neuter, N. A. sg. तत् tát (Gk. τό, Lat. is-tud, Engl. **that**), du. ते té, pl. तानि tắni. The other cases are the same as in the masc.

123 (269). Base (in composition) इदम् idám, this (indefinitely).

	SINGULAR.		PLURAL.	
	MASC.	FEM.	MASC.	FEM.
N.	अयम् ayám	इयम् iyám	इमे imé	इमाः imắh
A.	इमम् imám	इमाम् imám	इमान् imắn	इमाः imắh
I.	अनेन anéna	अनया anáyâ	एभिः ebhíh	आभिः âbhíh
D.	अस्मै asmaí	अस्यै asyaí	एभ्यः ebhyáh	आभ्यः âbhyáh
Ab.	अस्मात् asmât	अस्याः asyâh		
G.	अस्य asyá		एषाम् eshám	आसाम् âsám
L.	अस्मिन् asmín	अस्याम् asyám	एषु eshú	आसु âsú

---

[1] Cp. 54.

Dual, m. f., N. A. V. इमौ imaú, इमे imé; I. D. Ab. आभ्याम् âbhyãm;
G. L. अनयोः anáyoh.

Neuter, N. A. sg. इदम् idám, du. इमे imé, pl. इमानि imãni.

124 (271). Base (in composition) अदस् adás, that.

	SINGULAR.		PLURAL.	
	MASC.	FEM.	MASC.	FEM.
N.	असौ asaú	असौ asaú	अमी amí	अमूः amúh
A.	अमुम् amúm	अमूम् amúm	अमून् amún	अमूः amúh
I.	अमुना amúnâ	अमुया amuyã	अमीभिः amíbhih	अमूभिः amúbhih
D.	अमुष्मै amúshmai	अमुष्यै amúshyai	अमीभ्यः amíbhyah	अमूभ्यः amúbhyah
Ab.	अमुष्मात् amúshmât	अमुष्याः amúshyâh		
G.	अमुष्य amúshya		अमीषाम् amíshâm	अमूषाम् amúshâm
L.	अमुष्मिन् amúshmin	अमुष्याम् amúshyâm	अमीषु amíshu	अमूषु amúshu

Dual, m. f. n., N. A. V. अमू amú; I. D. Ab. अमूभ्याम् amúbhyâm,
अमुयोः amúyoh.

Neuter, N. A. sg. अदः adáh, pl. अमूनि amúni.

125. Like तद् tád are inflected:

A. 1 (263). The demonstrative pronouns: त्यद् tyad, he, she, it;
sg. N. स्यः syáh, स्या syã, त्यत् tyát; A. त्यम् tyám, त्याम् tyãm,
त्यत् tyát, etc.

2 (268). एतद् etád, this (very near); sg. N. एषः esháh[1], एषा eshã,
एतत् etát; A. एतम् etám, एताम् etãm, एतत् etát, etc.

3 (270). एनद् enad (enclitic), he, she, it, is defective, only occurring in the A. sg. du. and pl., I. sg., and G. L. du. It is
substituted for एतद् etád and इदम् idám when these refer to an
एतद् etád or इदम् idám in a preceding sentence.

B (273). The **interrogative** pronoun किम् kím, who? sg. N.
कः káh, का kã, किम् kím; A. कम् kám, काम् kãm, किम् kím.

---

[1] Cp. 54.

C (272). The **relative** यद् yád, who, which: sg. N. यः yáh, या yấ, यत् yát; A. यम् yám, याम् yấm, यत् yát.

Reflexive Pronouns.

126. 1 (265). स्वयम् svayám, self, is indeclinable (=' of one's self'): स्वयं वृतवान् svayám vritávân, I chose it myself, thou chosest it thyself, he chose it himself; स्वयं वृतवती svayám vri-távatî, she chose it herself.

2 (266). आत्मन् âtmán, self, is declined like ब्रह्मन् brahmán (102): आत्मानमात्मना पश्य âtmấnam âtmánâ pásya, see thyself by thyself, gnosce te ipsum. It is used in the singular masc. even when referring to nouns in another gender or number.

3 (267). खः sváh, खा svâ, खम् svám is a reflexive adjective, corresponding to Latin suus, sua, suum: खं पुत्रं दृष्ट्वा svám putrám drishtvấ, having seen his own son. (On the decl. of ख sva, see 130, c.) निज nigá is used in the same sense: निजं धैर्यमदर्शयत् nigám dhaíryam ádarsayat, he showed his (own) courage.

Compound Pronouns.

127 (275). By adding दृश dris, दृश drisa, or दृक्ष driksha to certain pronominal bases, the following compound pronouns have been formed :—

तादृश tâdrís, तादृश tâdrísa, तादृक्ष tâdríksha, such like.

एतादृश etâdrís, एतादृश etâdrísa, एतादृक्ष etâdríksha, this like.

यादृश yâdrís, यादृश yâdrísa, यादृक्ष yâdríksha, what like.

ईदृश îdrís, ईदृश îdrísa, ईदृक्ष îdríksha, this like.

कीदृश kîdrís, कीदृश kîdrísa, कीदृक्ष kîdríksha, what like?

Similarly formed are मादृश mâdrísa, त्वादृश tvâdrísa, like me, like thee, etc. The feminine is formed with ई î: तादृक् tâdrík, m. n.; तादृशी tâdrísî, f.

128 (276). By adding वत् vat and यत् yat to certain pronominal bases, the following compounds, implying quantity, have been formed:—

तावत् távat, so much
एतावत् etávat, so much } declined like nouns in वत् vat (98).
यावत् yávat, as much

इयत् íyat, so much
कियत् kíyat, how much } इयान् íyân, इयती íyatî, इयत् íyat (98).

Note—कति káti, how many? तति táti, so many, and यति yáti, as many, are uninflected in the N. A., but in the other cases are declined like शुचि súki (109).

129 (277). The interrogative किम् kím, by adding चित् kit, चन kaná, or अपि ápi, is changed to an indefinite pronoun.

कश्चित् káskit, काचित् kákit, किंचित् kímkit, some one; also कच्चित् kákkit, anything.

कश्चन káskaná, काचन kákaná, किंचन kímkaná, some one.

कोऽपि kó×pi, काऽपि kápi, किमपि kímapi, some one.

In the same manner indefinite adverbs are formed: कदा kadá, when? कदाचित् kadákit, कदाचन kadákaná, once; क्व kvá, where? न क्वापि ná kvápi, not anywhere.

Sometimes the relative pronoun is prefixed to the interrogative, to render it indefinite: यः कः yáh káh, whosoever; यस्य कस्य yásya kásya, of whomsoever. Likewise यः कश्चित् yáh káskit, whosoever, or यः कश्च yáh káska, or यः कश्चन yáh káskaná.

The relative pronoun, if doubled, assumes an indefinite or rather distributive meaning: यो यः, या या, यद्यद्, yó yah, yá yá, yádyad, whosoever. Occasionally the relative and demonstrative pronouns are combined for the same purpose: यत्तद् yáttad, whatsoever.

Pronominal Adjectives.

130 (278). These are adjectives which follow the pronominal declension (तद् tád, 122) altogether or in part, but only if they are used in the senses given below.

a. अन्य anyá, other; अन्यतर anyatará, either; इतर ítara, other; एकतम ekatamá, one (of many); त्व tvá, other; and words formed with तर tara and तम tama from the pronominal stems क ka, त ta, य ya (कतर katará, which of two? कतम katamá, which of many? etc.), follow the pronominal declension throughout, taking द् d in N. A.V. sg. neut.; e. g. अन्य: anyáh, अन्या anyá, अन्यत् anyát.

b. The following differ only in taking म् m instead of द् d in N. A.V. sg. neut.: उभय ubháya, both; एक éka (117), one; एकतर ekatará, either; विश्व vísva, सम sama (enclitic), सिम simá, सर्व sárva, all; नेम néma, half.

Ex. सर्व sárva: sg. N. सर्व: sárvah, सर्वा sárvâ, सर्वम् sárvam; D. सर्वस्मै sárvasmai; Ab. सर्वस्मात् sárvasmât; G. सर्वस्य sárvasya; L. सर्वस्मिन् sárvasmin: pl. N. सर्वे sárve, सर्वा: sárvâh, सर्वाणि sárvâni.

Note—उभय ubháya has no dual, and नेम néma has optionally नेमा: némâh in the N. pl. masc.

c. The following optionally take the terminations of the nominal declension in the Ab. and L. sg. m. n., and in the N. pl. m.: अधर ádhara, inferior, west; अंतर ántara, outer (except अंतरा पू: ántarâ pûk, suburb) or lower (scil. garment); अपर ápara, other or inferior; अवर ávara, posterior, west; उत्तर úttara, subsequent, north; दक्षिण dákshina, right, south; पर pára, subsequent; पूर्व pûrva, prior, east; स्व svá, own.

Ex. पूर्व pûrva: sg. Ab. पूर्वस्मात् pûrvasmât or पूर्वात् pûrvát; L. पूर्वस्मिन् pûrvasmin or पूर्वे pûrve: pl. N. पूर्वे pûrve or पूर्वा: pûrvâh.

d (283). अर्ध ardhá, half; अल्प álpa, little; कतिपय katipayá, some; चरम karamá, last; प्रथम prathamá, first; द्वय dvayá, two-

fold (and similar words in **य** ya: **त्रय** trayá); **द्वितय** dvítaya, two-
fold (and similar words in **तय** taya: **त्रितय** trítaya), may follow the
pronominal declension in the N. pl., and **द्वितीय** dvitī́ya and **तृतीय**
trítī́ya in the whole singular.

Ex. **चरमाः** *k*aramā́*h* or **चरमे** *k*aramé: D. **द्वितीयाय** dvitī́yâya or
द्वितीयस्मै dvitī́yasmai; Ab. **द्वितीयात्** dvitī́yât or **द्वितीयस्मात्** dvitī́-
yasmât; G. **द्वितीयस्य** dvitī́yasya; L. **द्वितीये** dvitī́ye or **द्वितीयस्मिन्**
dvitī́yasmin: N. pl. **द्वितीयाः** dvitī́yâ*h*.

Note—At the end of possessive compounds (218) these pronominal adjectives are treated like ordinary words.

CHAPTER IV.

CONJUGATION.

131 (286). Sanskrit verbs are inflected with either active or
middle terminations.

The **active** voice is called **Parasmai-pada**, i. e. transitive
(lit. ' word for another,' from **परस्मै** párasmai, D. sg. of **पर** pára,
another, i. e. a verb the action of which refers to another).

The **middle** voice is called **Âtmane-pada**, i. e. intransitive
(from **आत्मने** âtmáne, D. sg. of **आत्मन्** âtmán, self, i. e. a verb the
action of which refers to the agent).

The **passive** takes the terminations of the Âtmanepada, pre-
fixing **य** ya to them in the four special or modified forms. In the
other forms the passive, with two exceptions (178, 179), coincides
with the Âtmanepada.

132. The Sanskrit verb has in each tense and mood three
numbers, Singular, Dual, and Plural, with three persons in each.

133 (290). There are in Sanskrit forms for nine moods and

tenses: 1. Present (indicative); 2. Imperfect (indicative); 3. Imperative; 4. Optative (potential); 5. Perfect (reduplicated and periphrastic); 6. Aorist (first and second); 7. Future (simple and periphrastic); 8. Conditional; 9. Benedictive or Precative (a kind of aorist optative).

The above forms contain two principal groups, the present group (present, imperfect, imperative, optative) and the sibilant group (simple future, conditional, first aorist, benedictive). Of the remaining forms, two are reduplicated (perfect and second aorist, 3 : see 164), two are periphrastic (perfect and future), and one a root-preterite (second aorist, 1 and 2 : see 161 and 163).

Besides these forms, there is *one* infinitive (191), unconnected with any tense-stem ; and participles connected with three tenses, present, simple future, and perfect, active, middle, and passive.

There is neither a pluperfect nor a subjunctive in classical Sanskrit, nor is there an optative or imperative of any tense except the present. There are therefore far fewer verbal forms in non-Vedic Sanskrit than in Greek.

Special and General Forms.

134 (294). The four first of the above-mentioned forms, which may be called the Special or Modified Forms, belong to the present stem (cp. Gk. τύπτ-ω, ἔ-τυπτ-ον, τύπτ-οιμι, τύπτ-ε with aor. ἔ-τυπ-ον). This present stem is formed from the root in ten different ways. Hence Sanskrit grammarians have divided all verbs into ten classes, a division which may conveniently be retained. In the other five forms, which may be called General or Unmodified Forms, the terminations are added immediately (or after inserting a sibilant) to the root. In the tenth class, however (nearly all the verbs of which are secondary), the present stem is used in most of the general forms, as in the other secondary verbs (causatives, desideratives, intensives, and denominatives, which will be treated in 192–206).

The Ten Classes.

135 (295). The ten classes are divided into **two conjugations.** In the first, comprising the 1st, 4th, 6th, and 10th classes, the present stem ends in श a, and remains unchanged throughout.

In the second conjugation, which comprises all the remaining classes, the terminations are added directly to the root or to the suffixes उ u, नु nu, or नी nî in the **present stem,** which **is changeable,** being **either strong or weak.**

Formation of the Present Stem.

136 (296).   **A. First Conjugation.**

1. The first or Bhû class adds श a to the last letter of the root, which takes Guna of a final vowel (short or long) and of a short medial vowel followed by *one* consonant.

भू bhû, to be: present stem भव bháv-a; बुध् budh, to know: बोध bódh-a.

2. The sixth or Tud class adds an accented श a to the root, which (not having the accent) does not take Guna. Before the श a, final इ i and ई î are changed to इय् iy, उ u and ऊ û to उव् uv, ऋ ri to रिय् riy, and ॠ rî to इर् ir.

तुद् tud, to strike: present stem तुद tud-á. रि ri, to go: रिय riy-á. नू nû, to praise: नुव nuv-á. मृ mri, to die: मिय mriy-á. कृ krî, to scatter: किर kir-á.

3. The fourth or Div class adds य ya to the last letter of the root (this य ya having been accented originally, some roots of this class are shortened: व्यध् vyadh, विध्य vídh-ya).

नह् nah, to bind: नह्य náh-ya. दिव् div, to play: दीव्य dív-ya (65).

4. The tenth or Kur class adds शय áya to the last letter of the root.

A final vowel takes Vriddhi; a short medial vowel followed by *one* consonant takes Guna.

श a and ऋ rî followed by one consonant become आ â and ईर्

ír respectively: मी mî, to walk: मायय mây-áya. चुर् kur, to steal: चोरय kor-áya. दल् dal, to cut: दालय dâl-áya. कृत् krít, to praise: कीर्तय kírt-áya.

137 (321). **B. Second Conjugation.**

The **strong forms** are:—

(1) The singular present and imperfect active.

(2) All first persons imperative **active and middle.**

(3) Third singular imperative active.

The strong forms have Gu*n*a of the radical vowel or the affix (the terminations being unaccented or weak). नी nî, however, is represented by ना nâ (9th class), and न् n by न na (7th class).

Note 1. The vowel of the root or affix is shortened in the weak forms owing to the terminations being accented (or strong).

Note 2. Among the general forms (134) the reduplicated perfect alone has a changeable base, the singular active being strong (see 151).

138 (299). 1. The **second** or Ad class adds the terminations directly to the root, which in the strong forms takes Gu*n*a if possible (136, 1).

Note—This and the seventh are the most difficult classes, because so many rules of internal Sandhi have to be observed, the various initials of the terminations coming into direct contact with the final of the root.

अद् ad, to eat: अग्मि ád-mi, अत्सि át-si, अत्ति át-ti. इ i, to go: एमि émi, एषि éshi, एति éti. लिह् lih, to lick: लेग्मि léh-mi, लेक्षि lé**k-sh**i, लेढि lé-*dh*i (79).

2. The **third** or Hu class adds the terminations directly to the reduplicated root, which in the strong forms takes Gu*n*a if possible.

हु hu, to sacrifice: जुहोमि *g*u-hó-mi, I sacrifice; जुहुम: *g*u-hu-má*h*, we sacrifice.

Note—The intensive verbs conjugated in the Parasmaipada (201) follow this class.

3. The **seventh** or Rudh class adds the terminations directly to the final consonant, before which न् n is inserted in the weak, and न na in the strong forms.

युज् yug, to join: युंज्मः yu*ñg*-má*h*, we join; युनज्मि yu-ná-*g*-mi, I join.

4. The **fifth** or Su class adds नु nu, which takes Gu*n*a in the strong forms, to the root.

सु su, to squeeze out: सुनुमः su-nu-má*h*, 1st pl. pres.; सुनोमि su-nó-mi, 1st sg. pres.

5. The **eighth** or Tan class adds उ u, which in the strong forms becomes ओ o, to the root.

तन् tan, to stretch: तनुमः tan-u-má*h*, 1st pl. pres.; तनोमि tan-ó-mi, 1st sg. pres.

Note—All verbs belonging to this class end in न् n, except कृ k*ri*: करोमि kar-ó-mi, I do.

6. The **ninth** or Krî class adds to the root the syllable नी nî, which becomes ना nâ in the strong forms and is shortened to न् n before vowels in the weak forms.

क्री krî, to buy: क्रीणीमः krî-*n*î-má*h*, 1st pl.; क्रीणामि krî-*n*ắ-mi, 1st sing.; क्रीणंति krî*n*-ánti, 3rd pl.

The Augment.

139 (301). The imperfect, the aorist, and the conditional take अ a (which is accented) as their augment. **This अ a forms Vr*i*ddhi with an initial vowel.**

बुध् budh: pres. बोधामि bódhâmi; impf. अबोधम् ábodham. उंद् und: उनत्ति unátti, he wets; impf. औनत् aúnat. ऋ r*i*: ऋच्छति r*í*kk*h*ati, he goes; impf. आर्च्छत् ắrkk*h*at.

The augment of the impf. and aor. (which are then used imperatively) is dropped after the prohibitive particle मा mắ (μή): मा भवान् कार्षीत् mắ bhávân kârshît, Let not your Honour do this! or मा स्म करोत् mắ sma karot, May he not do it!

Reduplication.

140 (302). Five verbal forms take reduplication in Sanskrit, viz. the present stem of the third conjugational class, the perfect, the reduplicated aorist, the desiderative, and the intensive. Each of these five has certain peculiarities, which must be treated separately under the special rules of reduplication (141, 146, 166, 198, 204). Common to all are the following.

General Rules of Reduplication.

1 (303). The first syllable of a root (i. e. that portion of it which ends with a vowel) is reduplicated; e. g. बुध् budh=बुबुध् bu-budh.

2 (304). Aspirated letters are represented by their corresponding unaspirated letters; e. g. भिद् bhid, to cut, = बिभिद् bibhid; धू dhû, to shake, =दुधू dudhû.

3 (305). Gutturals are represented by the corresponding pala-tals, ह h by ज् g; e. g. कुट् kuṭ, to sever, =चुकुट् kukuṭ; खन् khan, to dig, = चखन् kakhan; गम् gam, to go, = जगम् gagam; हस् has, to laugh, = जहस् gahas.

4 (306). If the root begins with more than one consonant, the first only is reduplicated; e. g. क्रुश् krus, to shout, =चुक्रुश् kukrus; क्षिप् kship, to throw, = चिक्षिप् kikship.

5 (307). If a root begins with a sibilant followed by a hard consonant, the latter is reduplicated; e. g. स्तु stu, to praise, = तुष्टु tushtu; स्था sthâ, to stand, = तस्था tasthâ; स्युत् skyut, to drop, = चुष्युत् kuskyut; स्कंद् skand, to approach, = चस्कंद् kaskand. But स्मृ smri, to pine, = सस्मृ sasmri (m is soft).

6 (308). If the radical vowel, whether final or medial, is long, it is shortened in the reduplicative syllable; e. g. गाह् gâh, to enter, = जगाह् gagâh; क्री krî, to buy, = चिक्री kikrî; सूद् sûd, to strike, = सुषूद् sushûd.

7 (309). If the radical (not final) vowel is ए e or ऐ ai, it becomes

इ i; if it is ओ o or औ au, it becomes उ u: e. g. सेव् sev, to worship, = सिषेव् sishev; ढौक् dhauk, to approach, = दुढौक् dudhauk.

8 (310). Roots with final ए e, ऐ ai, ओ o are treated like roots ending in आ â, taking अ a in the reduplicative syllable; e. g. धे dhe, to feed, = दधौ dadhau; गै gai, to sing, = जगौ gagau; शो so, to sharpen, = शशौ sasau.

Special Rule of Reduplication for the Third Class.

141 (316). ऋ ri and ॠ rí are represented in reduplication by इ i; e. g. भृ bhri, to bear, = बिभर्ति bibhárti; पृ prí, to fill, = पिपर्ति píparti.

Terminations.

142 (321). The following table gives the terminations, which are on the whole the same for all verbs, of the four modified forms. The chief difference is in the optative, which is characterised by ए e in the first, and या yâ and ई î in the second conjugation. It will prevent confusion to remember that the present has the primary (mi, si, ti, etc.), while the impf., opt., and impv. (the latter with some variations) have the secondary terminations (m, s, t, etc.)

Of the five general forms (133) the Future and, for the most part (especially in the middle), the Perfect take the primary, while the Conditional, the Aorist, and the Benedictive take the secondary, terminations.

In order to understand the difference between the two conjugations, it is worth noting that, as in the a-declension, so in the a-conjugation, the accent never falls on the terminations, but always on the same syllable of the base (on the root in the first and fourth, on the affix in the sixth and tenth classes), which therefore remains unchanged. On the other hand, as in the declension of changeable bases, so in the second conjugation, the strong base has the accent, and is shortened in the weak forms by the shifting of the accent to the terminations. **In the second**

conjugation, therefore, **the terminations are accented** except in the strong forms (137) and in the imperfect (the augment always being accented).

PARASMAIPADA.

Present.	Imperfect.	Optative. 1st conj.	Optative. 2nd conj.	Imperative.
1. मि mi[1]	अम् am[2]	एयम् eyam[3]	याम् yâm	आनि âni
2. सि si	स् s	एस् es	यास् yâs	— (1) हि hi[4] (2)
3. ति ti	त् t	एत् et	यात् yât	तु tu
1. व: vah	व va	एव eva	याव yâva	आव âva
2. थ: thah	तम् tam	एतम् etam	यातम् yâtam	तम् tam
3. त: tah	ताम् tâm	एताम् etâm	याताम् yâtâm	ताम् tâm
1. म: mah	म ma	एम ema	याम yâma	आम âma
2. थ tha	त ta	एत eta	यात yâta	त ta
3. अन्ति anti[5]	अन् an[6]	एयुस् eyus	युस् yus	अन्तु antu[5]

ÂTMANEPADA.

Present.	Imperfect.	Optative.	Optative.	Imperative.
1. ए e	ए e (1) इ i (2)	एय eya	ई îya	ऐ ai
2. से se	थास् thâs	एथास् ethâs	ईथास् îthâs	स्व sva
3. ते te	त t..	एत eta	ईत îta	ताम् tâm
1. वहे vahe	वहि vahi	एवहि evahi	ईवहि îvahi	आवहै âvahai
2. एथे ethe(1)	एथाम् ethâm(1)	एयाथाम् eyâthâm	ईयाथाम् îyâthâm	एथाम् ethâm(1)
आथे âthe(2)	आथाम् âthâm(2)		îyâthâm	आथाम् âthâm(2)
3. एते ete(1)	एताम् etâm(1)	एयाताम् eyâtâm	ईयाताम् îyâtâm	एताम् etâm(1)
आते âte(2)	आताम् âtâm(2)	eyâtâm	îyâtâm	आताम् âtâm(2)
1. महे mahe	महि mahi	एमहि emahi	ईमहि îmahi	आमहै âmahai
2. ध्वे dhve	ध्वम् dhvam	एध्वम् edhvam	ईध्वम् îdhvam	ध्वम् dhvam
3. अन्ते ante(1)	अन्त anta(1)	एरन् eran	ईरन् îran	अन्ताम् antâm(1)
अते ate(2)	अत ata(2)			अताम् atâm(2)

Note 1—The final श a of the first conjugation is lengthened before म् m or व् v; e. g. भवामि bhávâ-mi, भवाव: bhávâ-va*h*.

Note 2—Terminations beginning with vowels should be added in the first conjugation after dropping the final श a. Thus भव bháva + एत् et = भवेत् bháv-et.

Note 3—The terminations of the first conjugation given in the above table as beginning with ए e really contain the final श a of the base + इ i ; but on practical grounds it is preferable to assume that they begin with ए e.

Note 4—Verbs of the first conjugation take no termination in the 2nd sg. impv. Par. Those of the second generally take हि hi, which becomes धि dhi (= Gk. -θι) after a consonant (in 2, 3, 7). Verbs of the fifth and eighth drop हि hi, unless the उ u is preceded by a conjunct consonant : चिनु *k*i-nú, but आप्नुहि âp-nu-hí; Verbs of the ninth class, if ending in a consonant, take आन âna instead of हि hi : मथ् math, मथान math-ắna ; but क्री krî, क्रीणीहि krî-*n*î-hí.

Note 5—Verbs of the third class, and reduplicated bases (cp. 145, cl. II, 5 ; also 203), take अति ati and अतु atu in the 3rd pl. pres. and impv. Par. In the **Âtm.** of the whole **second conjugation** the न् n of the **3rd pl.** pres., impf., and impv. **is rejected.**

Note 6—Verbs of the third class, reduplicated bases, and विद् vid (cl. II), to know, in the 3rd pl. impf. Par., instead of अन् an, take उ: u*h*, before which a final vowel requires Gu*n*a. उ: u*h* may also be added to द्विष् dvish and to roots in आ â : अद्विषन् ádvish-an or अद्विषु: ádvish-u*h* ; या yâ (cl. II), to go, अयान् áyân or अयु: áy-u*h*.

Paradigms.

143 (322). As the four classes of the first conjugation are inflected exactly alike, one paradigm will suffice for them. The same applies to the fifth and eighth classes. In the second class, द्विष् dvish has been used, instead of अद् ad, for the paradigm, because it illustrates better than अद् ad both the rules of internal Sandhi and the difference between strong and weak forms.

FIRST CONJUGATION.

First Class : √भू bhû, to be; Present stem भव bháv-a.

	PARASMAIPADA.			ÂTMANEPADA.		
	SINGULAR.	DUAL.	PLURAL.	SINGULAR.	DUAL.	PLURAL.

Present.

	PARASMAIPADA			ÂTMANEPADA		
	SINGULAR	DUAL	PLURAL	SINGULAR	DUAL	PLURAL
1.	भवामि bhávâ-mi	भवावः bhávâ-vah	भवामः bhávâ-mah	भवे bháv-e	भवावहे bhávâ-vahe	भवामहे bhávâ-mahe
2.	भवसि bháva-si	भवथः bháva-thah	भवथ bháva-ta	भवसे bháva-se	भवेथे bháv-ethe	भवध्वे bháva-dhve
3.	भवति bháva-ti	भवतः bháva-tah	भवन्ति bháv-anti	भवते bháva-te	भवेते bháv-ete	भवन्ते bháv-ante

Imperfect.

	PARASMAIPADA			ÂTMANEPADA		
	SINGULAR	DUAL	PLURAL	SINGULAR	DUAL	PLURAL
1.	अभवम् ábhav-am	अभवाव ábhavâ-va	अभवाम ábhavâ-ma	अभवे ábhav-e	अभवावहि ábhavâ-vahi	अभवामहि ábhavâ-mahi
2.	अभवः ábhava-h	अभवतम् ábhava-tam	अभवत ábhava-ta	अभवथाः ábhava-thâh	अभवेथाम् ábhav-ethâm	अभवध्वम् ábhava-dhvam
3.	अभवत् ábhava-t	अभवताम् ábhava-tâm	अभवन् ábhav-an	अभवत ábhava-ta	अभवेताम् ábhav-etâm	अभवन्त ábhav-anta

Imperative.

1. भवानि bháv-âni	भवाव bháv-âva	भवाम bháv-âma	भवै bháv-ai	भवावहै bháv-âvahai	भवामहै bháv-âmahai
2. भव bháva	भवतम् bháva-tam	भवत bháva-ta	भवस्व bháva-sva	भवेथाम् bháv-ethâm	भवध्वम् bháva-dhvam
3. भवतु bháva-tu	भवताम् bháva-tâm	भवन्तु bháv-antu	भवताम् bháva-tâm	भवेताम् bháv-etâm	भवन्ताम् bháv-antâm

Optative.

1. भवेयम् bháv-eyam	भवेव bháv-eva	भवेम bháv-ema	भवेय bháv-eya	भवेवहि bháv-evahi	भवेमहि bháv-emahi
2. भवेः bháv-eḥ	भवेतम् bháv-etam	भवेत bháv-eta	भवेथाः bháv-ethâḥ	भवेयाथाम् bháv-eyâthâm	भवेध्वम् bháv-edhvam
3. भवेत् bháv-et	भवेताम् bháv-etâm	भवेयुः bháv-eyuḥ	भवेत bháv-eta	भवेयाताम् bháv-eyâtâm	भवेरन् bháv-eran

SECOND CONJUGATION.

Second Class: √द्विष् (dvish, to hate; Present stem द्विष dvish, द्वेष dvésh.

Present.

	PARASMAIPADA.			ÂTMANEPADA.		
	SINGULAR.	DUAL.	PLURAL.	SINGULAR.	DUAL.	PLURAL.
1.	द्वेषि dvésh-mi	द्विष्वः dvish-váh	द्विष्म: dvish-máh	द्विषे dvish-é	द्विष्वहे dvish-váhe	द्विष्महे dvish-máhe
2.	द्वेषि dvék-shi	द्विष्ठ: dvish-tháh	द्विष्ठ dvish-thá	द्विक्षे dvik-shé	द्विषाथे dvish-áthe	द्विड्ढ्वे dvid-dhvé
3.	द्वेषि dvésh-ti	द्विष्ट: dvish-táh	द्विषंति dvish-ánti	द्विष्टे dvish-té	द्विषाते dvish-áte	द्विषते dvish-áte

Imperfect.

	PARASMAIPADA.			ÂTMANEPADA.		
	SINGULAR.	DUAL.	PLURAL.	SINGULAR.	DUAL.	PLURAL.
1.	अद्वेषम् ádvesh-am	अद्विष्व ádvish-va	अद्विष्म ádvish-ma	अद्विषि ádvish-i	अद्विष्वहि ádvish-vahi	अद्विष्महि ádvish-mahi
2.	अद्वेट् ádvet	अद्विष्टम् ádvish-tam	अद्विष्ट ádvish-ta	अद्विष्ठाः ádvish-thâh	अद्विषाथाम् ádvish-âthâm	अद्विड्ढ्वम् ádvid-dhvam
3.	अद्वेट् ádvet	अद्विष्टाम् ádvish-tâm	अद्विषन् ádvish-an	अद्विष्ट ádvish-ta	अद्विषाताम् ádvish-âtâm	अद्विषत ádvish-ata

Imperative.

	Parasmaipada Sing.	Dual	Plural	Ātmanepada Sing.	Dual	Plural
1.	द्वेषाणि dvésh-âni	द्वेषाव dvésh-âva	द्वेषाम dvésh-âma	द्वेषै dvésh-ai	द्वेषावहै dvésh-âvahai	द्वेषामहै dvésh-âmahai
2.	द्विड्ढि dvid-*dhi*	द्विड्ढम् dvish-*t*âm	द्विड्ढ dvish-*t*á	द्विक्ष्व dvik-**shvá**	द्विषाथाम् dvish-âthâm	द्विड्ढ्वम् dvid-*dhvám*
3.	द्वेष्टु dvésh-*t*u	द्विष्टाम् dvish-*t*âm	द्विषन्तु dvish-ántu	द्विष्टाम् dvish-*t*âm	द्विषाताम् dvish-âtâm	द्विषताम् dvish-átâm

Optative.

	Parasmaipada Sing.	Dual	Plural	Ātmanepada Sing.	Dual	Plural
1.	द्विष्याम् dvish-yâm	द्विष्याव dvish-yâva	द्विष्याम dvish-yâma	द्विषीय dvish-îyá	द्विषीवहि dvish-îváhi	द्विषीमहि dvish-îmáhi
2.	द्विष्याः dvish-yâh	द्विष्यातम् dvish-yâtam	द्विष्यात dvish-yâta	द्विषीथाः dvish-îthâ*h*	द्विषीयाथाम् dvish-îyâthâm	द्विषीध्वम् dvish-îdhvám
3.	द्विष्यात् dvish-yât	द्विष्याताम् dvish-yâtâm	द्विष्युः dvish-yúh	द्विषीत dvish-îtá	द्विषीयाताम् dvish-îyâtâm	द्विषीरन् dvish-îrân

Third Class : √हु hu, to sacrifice; Present stem जुहु guhu, जुहो guhó.

PARASMAIPADA.

Present.

	SINGULAR.	DUAL.	PLURAL.
1.	जुहोमि guhó-mi	जुहुवः guhu-váh	जुहुमः guhu-máh
2.	जुहोषि guhó-shi	जुहुथः guhu-tháh	जुहुथ guhu-thá
3.	जुहोति guhó-ti	जुहुतः guhu-táh	जुह्वति gúhv-ati

Imperfect.

	SINGULAR.	DUAL.	PLURAL.
1.	अजुहवम् águhav-am	अजुहुव águhu-va	अजुहुम águhu-ma
2.	अजुहोः águho-h	अजुहुतम् águhu-tam	अजुहुत águhu-ta
3.	अजुहोत् águho-t	अजुहुताम् águhu-tâm	अजुहवुः águhav-uh

ÂTMANEPADA.

Present.

	SINGULAR.	DUAL.	PLURAL.
1.	जुह्वे gúhv-e	जुहुवहे guhu-váhe	जुहुमहे guhu-máhe
2.	जुहुषे guhu-shé	जुह्वाथे gúhv-áthe	जुहुध्वे guhu-dhvé
3.	जुहुते guhu-té	जुह्वाते gúhv-áte	जुह्वते gúhv-ate

Imperfect.

	SINGULAR.	DUAL.	PLURAL.
1.	अजुह्वि águhv-i	अजुहुवहि águhu-vahi	अजुहुमहि águhu-mahi
2.	अजुहुथाः águhu-tháh	अजुह्वाथाम् águhv-âthâm	अजुहुध्वम् águhu-dhvam
3.	अजुहुत águhu-ta	अजुह्वाताम् águhv-âtâm	अजुह्वत águhv-ata

Imperative.

1.	जुहवानि guháv-âni	जुहवाव guháv-âva	जुहवाम guháv-âma	जुहवै guháv-ai	जुहवावहै guháv-âvahai	जुहवामहै guháv-âmahai
2.	जुहुधि guhu-**dhí**	जुहुताम् guhu-tâm	जुहुत guhu-tá	जुहुष्व guhu-shvá	जुहाथाम् guhu-âthâm	जुहुध्वम् guhu-dhvâm
3.	जुहोतु guhótu	जुहुताम् guhu-tấm	जुह्वतु gúhv-**atu**	जुहुताम् guhu-tâm	जुह्वाताम् gúhv-**âtâm**	जुह्वताम् gúhv-**atâm**

Optative.

1.	जुहुयाम् guhu-yấm	जुहुयाव guhu-yấva	जुहुयाम guhu-yấma	जुह्वीय guhv-îyá	जुह्वीवहि guhv-îváhi	जुह्वीमहि guhv-îmáhi
2.	जुहुयाः guhu-yấh	जुहुयातम् guhu-yấtam	जुहुयात guhu-yấta	जुह्वीथाः guhv-îthấh	जुह्वीयाथाम् guhv-îyấthâm	जुह्वीध्वम् guhv-îdhvâm
3.	जुहुयात् guhu-yất	जुहुयाताम् guhu-yấtâm	जुहुयुः guhu-yúh	जुह्वीत guhv-îtá	जुह्वीयाताम् guhv-îyấtâm	जुह्वीरन् guhv-îrán

Fifth Class : √ सु su, to distil; Present stem सुनु sunu, सुनो sunó.

Present.

	PARASMAIPADA.			ÂTMANEPADA.		
	SINGULAR.	DUAL.	PLURAL.	SINGULAR.	DUAL.	PLURAL.
1.	सुनोमि sunó-mi	सुनुवः sunu-váḥ	सुनुमः sunu-máḥ	सुन्वे sunv-é	सुनुवहे sunu-váhe	सुनुमहे sunu-máhe
2.	सुनोषि sunó-shi	सुनुथः sunu-tháḥ	सुनुथ sunu-thá	सुनुषे sunu-shé	सुन्वाथे sunv-åthe	सुनुध्वे sunu-dhvé
3.	सुनोति sunó-ti	सुनुतः sunu-táḥ	सुन्वन्ति sunv-ánti	सुनुते sunu-té	सुन्वाते sunv-åte	सुन्वते sunv-åte

Imperfect.

	PARASMAIPADA.			ÂTMANEPADA.		
	SINGULAR.	DUAL.	PLURAL.	SINGULAR.	DUAL.	PLURAL.
1.	असुनवम् ásunav-am	असुनुव ásunu-va	असुनुम ásunu-ma	असुन्वि ásunv-i	असुनुवहि ásunu-vahi	असुनुमहि ásunu-mahi
2.	असुनोः ásuno-ḥ	असुनुतम् ásunu-tam	असुनुत ásunu-ta	असुनुथाः ásunu-tháḥ	असुन्वाथाम् ásunv-âthâm	असुनुध्वम् ásunu-dhvam
3.	असुनोत् ásuno-t	असुनुताम् ásunu-tâm	असुन्वन् ásunv-an	असुनुत ásunu-ta	असुन्वाताम् ásunv-âtâm	असुन्वत ásunv-ata

Imperative.

1. सुनवानि sunáv-āni	सुनवाव sunáv-āva	सुनवाम sunáv-āma	सुनवै sunáv-ai	सुनवावहै sunáv-āvahai	सुनवामहै sunáv-āmahai
2. सुनु sunú	सुनुतम् sunu-tám	सुनुत sunu-tá	सुनुष्व sunu-shvá	सुन्वाथाम् sunv-āthām	सुनुध्वम् sunu-dhvám
3. सुनोतु sunó-tu	सुनुताम् sunu-tām	सुन्वन्तु sunv-ántu	सुनुताम् sunu-tām	सुन्वाताम् sunv-ātām	सुन्वताम् sunv-átām

Optative.

1. सुनुयाम् sunu-yām	सुनुयाव sunu-yāva	सुनुयाम sunu-yāma	सुन्वीय sunv-íya	सुन्वीवहि sunv-ívåhi	सुन्वीमहि sunv-ímåhi
2. सुनुयाः sunu-yáh	सुनुयातम् sunu-yátam	सुनुयात sunu-yáta	सुन्वीथाः sunv-íthåh	सुन्वीयाथाम् sunv-íyåthåm	सुन्वीध्वम् sunv-ídhvám
3. सुनुयात् sunu-yát	सुनुयाताम् sunu-yátām	सुनुयुः sunu-yúh	सुन्वीत sunv-ítá	सुन्वीयाताम् sunv-íyátám	सुन्वीरन् sunv-írán

Seventh Class: √ रुध् rudh, to obstruct; Present stem रुन्ध् rundh, रुणध् ruṇádh.

Present.

	PARASMAIPADA.			ÂTMANEPADA.		
	SINGULAR.	DUAL.	PLURAL.	SINGULAR.	DUAL.	PLURAL.
1.	रुणिम्म ruṇádh-mi	रुन्ध्वः rundh-váḥ	रुन्ध्मः rundh-máḥ	रुन्धे rundh-é	रुन्ध्वहे rundh-váhe	रुन्ध्महे rundh-máhe
2.	रुणत्सि runát-si	रुन्द्धः rund-dháḥ	रुन्द्ध rund-dhá	रुन्त्से runt-sé	रुन्धाथे rundh-áthe	रुन्द्ध्वे rund-dhvé
3.	रुणत्ति runát-ti	रुन्द्धः rund-dháḥ	रुन्धन्ति rundh-ánti	रुन्द्धे rund-dhé	रुन्धाते rundh-áte	रुन्धते rundh-áte

Imperfect.

	PARASMAIPADA.			ÂTMANEPADA.		
1.	अरुणधम् áruṇadh-am	अरुन्ध्व árundh-va	अरुन्ध्म árundh-ma	अरुन्धि árundh-i	अरुन्ध्वहि árundh-vahi	अरुन्ध्महि árundh-mahi
2.	अरुणत् árunat	अरुन्द्धम् árund-dham	अरुन्द्ध árund-dha	अरुन्द्धाः árund-dháḥ	अरुन्धाथाम् árund-áthám	अरुन्ध्वम् árund-dhvam
3.	अरुणत् árunat	अरुन्द्धाम् árund-dhám	अरुन्धन् árundh-an	अरुन्द्ध árund-dha	अरुन्धाताम् árund-átám	अरुन्धत árundh-ata

Imperative.

1. रुणधानि ruṇádh-âni	रुणधाव ruṇádh-âva	रुणधाम ruṇádh-âma	रुणधै ruṇádh-ai	रुणधावहै ruṇádh-âvahai	रुणधामहै ruṇádh-âmahai
2. रुन्धि rund-dhí	रुन्द्धम् rund-dhâm	रुन्द्ध rund-dhá	रुन्त्स्व runt-svá	रुन्धाथाम् rundh-âthâm	रुन्द्ध्वम् rund-dhvám
3. रुणद्धु ruṇád-dhu	रुन्द्धाम् rund-dhâm	रुन्धन्तु rundh-ántu	रुन्द्धाम् rund-dhâm	रुन्धाताम् rundh-âtâm	रुन्धाताम् rundh-âtâm

Optative.

1. रुन्ध्याम् rundh-yâm	रुन्ध्याव rundh-yâva	रुन्ध्याम rundh-yâma	रुन्धीय rundh-îyá	रुन्धीवहि rundh-îváhi	रुन्धीमहि rundh-îmáhi
2. रुन्ध्याः rundh-yâḥ	रुन्ध्यातम् rundh-yâtam	रुन्ध्यात rundh-yâta	रुन्धीथाः rundh-îthâḥ	रुन्धीयाथाम् rundh-îyâthâm	रुन्धीध्वम् rundh-îdhvám
3. रुन्ध्यात् rundh-yât	रुन्ध्याताम् rundh-yâtâm	रुन्ध्युः rundh-yúḥ	रुन्धीत rundh-îtá	रुन्धीयाताम् rundh-îyâtâm	रुन्धीरन् rundh-îrán

Ninth Class : √क्री krî, to buy ; Present stem क्रीणी krînî, क्रीणा krînâ, क्रीण् krin.

Present.

PARASMAIPADA.

	SINGULAR.	DUAL.	PLURAL.
1.	क्रीणामि krînấ-mi	क्रीणीवः krînî-vấh	क्रीणीमः krînî-mấh
2.	क्रीणासि krînấ-si	क्रीणीथः krînî-thấh	क्रीणीथ krînî-thấ
3.	क्रीणाति krînấ-ti	क्रीणीतः krînî-tấh	क्रीणन्ति krîn-ánti

ÂTMANEPADA.

	SINGULAR.	DUAL.	PLURAL.
1.	क्रीणे krîn-é	क्रीणीवहे krînî-váhe	क्रीणीमहे krînî-máhe
2.	क्रीणीषे krînî-shé	क्रीणाथे krîn-áthe	क्रीणीध्वे krînî-dhvé
3.	क्रीणीते krînî-té	क्रीणाते krîn-áte	क्रीणाते krîn-âte

Imperfect.

PARASMAIPADA.

	SINGULAR.	DUAL.	PLURAL.
1.	अक्रीणाम् ákrînấ-m	अक्रीणीव ákrînî-va	अक्रीणीम ákrînî-ma
2.	अक्रीणाः ákrînấ-h	अक्रीणीतम् ákrînî-tam	अक्रीणीत ákrînî-ta
3.	अक्रीणात् ákrînấ-t	अक्रीणीताम् ákrînî-tâm	अक्रीणन् ákrîn-an

ÂTMANEPADA.

	SINGULAR.	DUAL.	PLURAL.
1.	अक्रीणि ákrîn-i	अक्रीणीवहि ákrînî-vahi	अक्रीणीमहि ákrînî-mahi
2.	अक्रीणीथाः ákrînî-thâh	अक्रीणीथाम् ákrînî-âthâm	अक्रीणीध्वम् ákrînî-dhvam
3.	अक्रीणीत ákrînî-ta	अक्रीणाताम् ákrîn-âtâm	अक्रीणात ákrîn-ata

Imperative.

1.	क्रीणानि krînâni	क्रीणाव krînâ-va	क्रीणाम krînâ-ma	क्रीणै krînaí	क्रीणावहै krînâ-vahai	क्रीणामहै krînâ-mahai
2.	क्रीणीहि krînî-hí	क्रीणीतम् krînî-tám	क्रीणीत krînî-tá	क्रीणीष्व krînî-shvá	क्रीणाथाम् krîn-âthâm	क्रीणीध्वम् krînî-dhvâm
3.	क्रीणातु krînâ-tu	क्रीणीताम् krînî-tâm	क्रीणन्तु krîn-ântu	क्रीणीताम् krînî-tâm	क्रीणाताम् krîn-âtâm	क्रीणाताम् krîn-âtâm

Optative.

1.	क्रीणीयाम् krînî-yâm	क्रीणीयाव krînî-yâva	क्रीणीयाम krînî-yâma	क्रीणीय krîn-îyá	क्रीणीवहि krîn-îvâhi	क्रीणीमहि krîn-îmâhi
2.	क्रीणीयाः krînî-yâh	क्रीणीयातम् krînî-yâta	क्रीणीयात krînî-yâta	क्रीणीथाः krîn-îthâh	क्रीणीयाथाम् krîn-îyâthâm	क्रीणीध्वम् krîn-îdhvâm
3.	क्रीणीयात् krînî-yât	क्रीणीयाताम् krînî-yâtâm	क्रीणीयुः krînî-yúh	क्रीणीत krîn-îtá	क्रीणीयाताम् krîn-îyâtâm	क्रीणीरन् krîn-îrán

Irregularities.

First Conjugation.

144. **First or Bhû Class.** 1. क्रम् kram, to step, आ-चम्
â-*k*am, to sip, गुह् guh, to conceal, ष्ठिव् sh*th*iv, to spit, lengthen
their vowel in the present base: क्राम krắma, आचाम â-*k*ắma, गूह
gúha, ष्ठीव sh*th*îva; मृज् m*rig*, to cleanse, takes V*ri*ddhi: मार्ज्
mắr*g*a; सद् sad, to sink, takes ई î: सीद sî́da (Lat. sîdo).

2. ऋ *ri*, to go, गम् gam, to go, यम् yam, to restrain, form the
present base with च्छ *kkh*a (=Gk. σκ): ऋच्छ *rí*k*kh*a, गच्छ gá*kkh*a,
यच्छ yá*kkh*a (also इष् ish, to wish, in the 6th cl.: इच्छ i*kkh*ắ).

3. घ्रा ghrâ, to smell, पा pâ, to drink, स्था sthâ, to stand, have
a reduplicated present base: जिघ्र *g*íghra, पिब píba (Lat. bibo),
तिष्ठ tísh*th*a (Gk. ἵστη-, Lat. sisto).

4. दंश् da*m*s, to bite, मंथ् manth, to churn, रंज् ra*ñg*, to tinge,
संज् sa*ñg*, to adhere, खंज् sva*ñg*, to embrace, drop the nasal: दश
dá*sa*, etc.

5. दृश् d*ri*s, to see, ध्मा dhmâ, to blow, म्ना mnâ, to study, substitute पश्य pá*sy*a, धम dháma, मन mána.

6. गुप् gup, to protect, धूप् dhûp, to warm, take आय âya:
गोपाय gopấya, धूपाय dhûpấya; कम् kam takes अय aya with
V*ri*ddhi: कामय kâmáya (properly causative).

Fourth or Div Class. 1. तम् tam, to languish, दम् dam, to
tame, भ्रम् bhram, to roam, मद् mad, to rejoice, शम् sam, to cease,
श्रम् sram, to be weary, lengthen their vowel: ताम्य tắmya, etc.

2. Verbs in ओ o drop the ओ o before य ya; e. g. शो so, to
sharpen, श्यति syáti (cp. 136, 3).

3. भ्रंश् bhra*m*s, to fall, drops its nasal: भ्रश्य bhrásya; व्यध् vyadh,
to pierce, takes Samprasârana[1]: विध्य vídhya; जन् *g*an, to be born,
substitutes जाय *g*áya.

---

[1] The term applied by native grammarians to the contraction

Sixth or Tud Class. 1. कृत् k*rit*, to cut, खिद् khid, to vex, पिश् pi*s*, to form, मुच् mu*k*, to loosen, लिप् lip, to paint, लुप् lup, to break, विद् vid, to find, सिच् si*k*, to sprinkle, insert a nasal; e. g. सिंच sí*ñ*kā.

2. इष् ish substitutes छ *kh* for ष् sh: इच्छ ikkhā (cp. 1st cl. 2).

3. प्रछ् pra*kh*, to ask, भ्रज्ज् bhra*gg*, to fry, व्रश्च् vra*sk*, to cut, shorten र ra to ऋ *ri*: पृच्छ prikkhā, भृज्ज bhri*ggá*, वृश्च vriská.

Second Conjugation.

Second or Ad (Dvish) Class. 1. अन् an, to breathe, जक्ष् *g*aksh, to eat, रुद् rud, to weep, श्वस् *s*vas, to breathe, स्वप् svap, to sleep, insert इ i, in the present forms, before terminations beginning with consonants except य् y; but ई î or अ a before the स् s and त् t of the 2nd and 3rd sg. impf. Par.: रोदिमि ródi-mi, but रुदन्ति rud-ánti, रुद्याम् rud-yắm; impf. sg. 3. अरोदीत् árod-î-t or अरोदत् árod-a-t.

2. अस् as, to be, drops the initial अ a in the optative and all the weak forms of the pres. and impv. The 2nd sg. impv. is एधि e-dhí.

3. इ i with अधि adhi, to read, inflected in the Ātm. only, re-solves ई î in the pres. and ऐ ai (a- augm. + i) in the impf. into ईय् îy and ऐय् aiy: pr. 1. अधीये adhîyé, 2. अधीषे adhîshé; impf. 1. अध्येयि adhy-aíyi, 2. अध्येथाः adhy-aíthā*h*.

4. ईड् î*d*, to praise, and ईश् î*s*, to rule, insert इ i before termi-nations beginning with स् s and ध् dh (i. e. 2. sg. pl. pres. and impv. Ātm.); e. g. ईशिषे î*s*-i-shé, ईशिध्वे î*s*-i-dhvé; ईशिष्व î*s*-i-shvá, ईशिध्वम् î*s*-i-dhvám.

5. चकास् *k*akâs, to shine, जक्ष् *g*aksh, to eat, जागृ *g*âgri, to wake, दरिद्रा daridrâ, to be poor, शास् sâs, to rule, being treated as re-

---

of य ya, व va, र ra, ळ la, to the corresponding vowels इ i, उ u, ऋ *ri*, ऌ *li*, respectively (cp. 103, 104, foot-notes).

duplicated verbs, take अति ati and अतु atu in the 3. pl. pres. and impv., and उः uḥ instead of अन् an in 3. pl. impf.; e. g. 3. sg. दरिद्राति daridrā́-ti, 3. pl. दरिद्रति dáridr-ati. शास् sâs is changed to शिष् sish in the weak forms before consonants: 3. sg. शास्ति sâs-ti; 3. du. शिष्टः sish-táh; 3. pl. शासति sâs-ati.

6. ब्रू brû, to speak, inserts ई î in the strong forms before terminations beginning with consonants: ब्रवीमि brávîmi.

7. a. मृज् mṛig, to cleanse, takes Vriddhi instead of Guṇa: मार्ष्टि mârsh-ṭi.

b. यु yu, to join, and all other roots ending in उ u, take Vriddhi instead of Guṇa in the strong forms before terminations beginning with consonants: यौमि yaú-mi, but अयवम् áyav-am.

8. वश् vas, to desire, takes Samprasâraṇa in the weak forms: वश्मि vásmi, but उश्मः usváh.

9. विद् vid, to know, besides the regular pres. वेद्मि védmi, has also a perfect form with a pres. sense: वेद véda, pl. विद्म vidmá (Gk. οἶδα, ἴδμεν; Germ. weiss, wissen), orig. vi-veda, etc. (cp. 148).

10. शी sî, to lie down, sleep (Âtm. only), takes Guṇa in the present stem and inserts र r in the 3. pl. pres. impf. and impv.: 3. sg. शेते sé-te (Gk. κεῖται); 3. pl. शेरते séxate, शेरताम् séxatâm, अशेरत áserata.

11. हन् han (Par.), to kill, drops न् n before त् t and थ् th in the weak forms: 3. sg. हन्ति hánti, but 2. pl. हथ ha-thá. In the 3. pl. pres., impf., impv. the radical अ a is dropped and the ह h becomes घ् gh: घ्नन्ति ghnánti, घ्नन्तु ghnántu, अघ्नन् ághnan. The 2. sg. impv. is जहि ǵahí (dissimilated, like a reduplicated form, for हहि ha-hí).

Third or Hu Class. 1. दा dâ, to give, and धा dhâ, to place, use दद् dad and दध् dadh as their bases in the weak forms. दध् dadh (against 69) becomes धत् dhat before त् t and थ् th: दधामि dadhấ-mi, but दध्वः dadh-váh, धत्थः dhat-tháh. The 2. impv. Par. is देहि de-hí and धेहि dhe-hí.

2. मा mâ, to measure, and हा hâ, to run away, both Âtm., have मिमी mimî and जिही gihî as their pres. stems, dropping the ई î before vowels: pres. sg. जिहे gíh-e, जिहीषे gíhî-she, 3. pl. जिहते gíh-ate; impf. अजिहि ágih-i, अजिहीथाः ágihî-thâh, 3. pl. अजिहत ágih-ata.

हा hâ, to leave, Par., has जही gahî in weak forms, dropping the ई î before vowels and य y: जहामि gáhâmi, but 2. pl. जहीत gahî-ta, 3. pl. जहति gáh-ati; opt. जह्याम् gah-yâm; impv. 2. sg. जहीहि gahî-hi.

3. पृ pri and other verbs in which final ऋ ri is preceded by a labial change the vowel to ऊर् ûr, except where it requires Guna or Vriddhi: पिपर्मि píparmi, but 1. du. पिपूर्वः pipûrvah.

Fifth or Su Class. 1. Roots ending in vowels may drop the उ u before व् v and म् m: सुनोमि sunó-mi, but सुन्वः sun-váh or सुनुवः sunu-váh.

2. Roots ending in consonants change उ u to उव् uv before vowels: शक्नुवंति sak-nuv-ánti.

3. श्रु sru, to hear, and धू dhû, to shake, have शृणु srinu and धुनु dhunu as their pres. stems.

Seventh or Rudh Class. 1. अंज् añg, to anoint, इंध् indh, to kindle, भंज् bhañg, to break, and हिंस् hims, to kill, drop their nasal before inserting न na: भनज्मि bha-ná-gmi.

2. तृह् trih, to kill, inserts णे ne instead of ण na: तृणेह्मि trinéhmi.

Eighth or Tan Class. कृ kri, to do, has as its strong base करो karó, and as its weak base कुरु kuru, the उ u of which is dropped before म् m, य y, व् v: करोमि karó-mi, कुर्वः kur-váh, कुरुथाः kuru-tháh, कुर्याम् kur-yâm. Other verbs of this class may drop the उ u before व् v and म् m, as in the fifth. All verbs belonging to this class are both Par. and Âtm.

Ninth or Krî Class. 1. दृ dri, to tear, धू dhû, to shake, पू pû, to purify, पृ pri, to fill, लू lû, to cut, वृ vri, to choose, स्त्री strî, to cover, shorten their vowel in the pres. stem; e.g. पुनामि pu-nắ-mi.

2. ज्या *gyâ*, to grow weak, ज्ञा *gñâ*, to know, ग्रह् grah, to seize, are shortened to जि *gi*, जा *gâ*, गृह् *grih*; e.g. जानामि *gâ*-nắ-mi.

3. बंध् bandh, to bind, मंथ् manth, to shake, drop the nasal; e.g. बध्नामि badh-nắ-mi, मथ्नामि math-nắ-mi.

General or Unmodified Tenses.

145 (323). In the remaining forms—the Reduplicated Perfect, the Periphrastic Perfect, the First and Second Aorists, the Simple Future, the Periphrastic Future, the Conditional, and the Benedictive—all verbs are treated alike, the distinguishing features of the Present stem disappearing. Only the verbs of the tenth class preserve their अय aya throughout, except in the Aorist and Benedictive.

Reduplicated Perfect.

146 (313-316). **Special Rules of Reduplication.**

1. ऋ *ri*, ॠ *rî*, and ऌ *li* are represented by अ a in the replicative syllable: कृ k*ri*, to do, चकार *ka*kắra; तृ t*ri*, to cross, ततार tatắra ; कॢप् k*li*p, to be able, चकॢप *ka*kắlpa.

2. a. Initial अ a or आ â followed by *one* consonant becomes आ â : अद् ad, to eat, आद ắda ; आप् âp, to obtain, आप ắpa.

b. Initial अ a or आ â followed by *two* consonants, and initial ऋ *ri*, prefix आन् â**n** : अर्च् ar*k*, to honour, आनर्च â*nârka* ; ऋज् *rig*, to obtain, आनृजे â*nrigé*.

3. Roots beginning with इ i or उ u (not prosodically long) contract इ i + इ i and उ u + ऊ û to ई î and ऊ û ; but if the radical इ i or उ u take Guna or Vriddhi, य् y and व् v are inserted between the reduplicative syllable and the base.

इष् ish, ईषतु: îshấtu*h*, they two wished ; इयेष i-y-ésha, I wished : उच् u*k*, ऊचतु: ûkấtu*h*, they two were pleased ; उवोच u-v-óka, I was pleased.

147 (325). The reduplicated perfect may be formed from all monosyllabic roots except those beginning with any vowel prosodically long but अ a and आ â (see 146, 2). All other verbs, i. e. (1) monosyllabic roots beginning with a prosodically long vowel (except अ a or आ â), (2) polysyllabic roots, e. g. चकास् kakâs, and (3) verbs of the tenth class and derivative verbs (Causatives, Desideratives, Intensives, Denominatives), form their perfect periphrastically.

148 (326). The terminations of the reduplicated perfect are :—

PARASMAIPADA.

1.	अ a	(इ)व (i)vá	(इ)म (i)má
2.	(इ)थ (i)tha	अथु: áthu*h*	अ á
3.	अ a	अतु: átu*h*	उ: ú*h*

ÂTMANEPADA.

1.	ए é	(इ)वहे (i)váhe	(इ)महे (i)máhe
2.	(इ)षे (i)shé	आथे âthe	(इ)ध्वे (i)dhvé [1]
3.	ए é	आते âte	इरे iré

The singular Parasmai is strong.

The terminations beginning with consonants are added with the connecting vowel इ i, except in eight verbs: द्रु dru, to run, श्रु sru, to hear, स्तु stu, to praise, स्रु sru, to flow, कृ kri, to do, भृ bhri, to bear, वृ vri, to choose, सृ sri, to go, **where it must be omitted.** The 3. pl. Âtm. retains the इ i even in these verbs. The इ i is omitted in the 2. sg. Par. in those verbs which do not take इ i in the future.

Ex. चकर्थ kakártha, चकृम kakrimá, चक्रिरे kakriré.

149 (329). Roots ending in आ â (or diphthongs,=आ â, 140, 7) drop the आ â. before vowels and the intermediate इ i: दधाथ

---

[1] On the change of ध dh to द dh, cp. 158, p. 106, 5.

dadhā́-tha, दधिष dadh-i-thá, दधुः dadh-úh. These roots (except ह्वे hve, to call) also take औ au as their termination in 1. and 3. sg. Par.: धा dhâ, दधौ dadháu.

150 (327). 1. Vowels capable of Gu*n*a, take it throughout the singular if followed by *one* consonant.

इष् ish, इयेष iy-ésh-a ; बुध् budh, बुबोध bubódha; but जीव् *g*îv, जिजीव *gig*îva.

2. Final vowels take V*ri*ddhi or Gu*n*a in the first, Gu*n*a in the second, V*ri*ddhi only in the third person singular : नी nî, to lead, 1. निनाय nináya or निनय nináya, 2. निनेथ ninétha or निनयिथ nináyitha, 3. निनाय nináya.

3. Medial अ a before a single consonant is lengthened (i. e. takes V*ri*ddhi) optionally in the first and necessarily in 3. sg.; e. g. हन् han, to kill, 1. जघान *g*aghâna or जघन *g*aghána, 3. जघान *g*aghâna.

151 (328). On the other hand, the root in the weak forms is weakened in the following cases :—

1. Roots in which अ a is preceded and followed by a single consonant (e. g. पत् pat), and which in their reduplicated syllable repeat the initial consonant unchanged (this excludes roots beginning with aspirates, with gutturals, and with व् v), contract the two syllables to one with the diphthong ए e (cp. Lat. cap-io, cēp-i). This contraction takes place even in 2. sg. Par., when थ tha is added with इ i (the strong form is used when थ tha is added without इ i): पच् pa*k*, पेचिथ pe*k*i-thá, but पपक्थ papák-tha, पेचुः pe*k*úh ; तन् tan, तेनिथ ten-i-thá, तेनुः tenúh.

Note—तृ trí, to cross, फल् phal, to burst, भज् bha*g*, to enjoy, and राध् râdh (in the sense of 'killing') irregularly follow the above rule ; e. g. तृ trí, ततार tatâra, तेरुः terúh. Some others do so optionally.

2. Roots beginning with व va, also यज् ya*g*, to sacrifice, व्यध् vyadh, to pierce, and ग्रह् grah, to seize, take Samprasâra*n*a in the weak

forms. In these verbs इ i and उ u represent य ya and व va in the reduplicative syllable: वह् vah, to carry, उवाह u-váha, but ऊहिम ûhimá (= u-uh-imá); यज् yag, इयाज i-yága, but ईजिम îgimá (= i-ig-imá).

3. खन् khan, to dig, गम् gam, to go, घस् ghas, to eat, जन् gan, to be born, हन् han, to kill, drop their radical vowel in the weak forms: जगाम gagáma, जग्मुः gagmúḥ; जघास gaghása, जक्षुः ga-kshúḥ; जघान gaghána, जघ्नुः gaghnúḥ.

4. ग्रंथ् granth, to tie, दंभ् dambh, to deceive, स्रंथ् sranth, to become loose, and खंज् svañg, to embrace, optionally drop the nasal, in which case the first three follow 151, 1: जग्रंथुः gagranthúḥ or ग्रेथुः grethúḥ.

152 (330). In the weak forms, before terminations beginning with vowels, final

(1) इ i, ई î, ऋ ri, if preceded by *one* consonant, become य् y, र् r; if by more than one, इय् iy, अर् ar: नी nî, to lead, निन्युः ninyúḥ; श्रि sri, to go, शिश्रियुः sisriyúḥ; कृ kri, to do, चक्रुः ka-krúḥ; स्तृ stri, to spread, तस्तरुः tastarúḥ.

(2) उ u and ऊ û **always** become उव् uv: यु yu, to join, युयुवुः yuyuvúḥ; स्तु stu, to praise, तुष्टुवुः tushtuvúḥ.

(3) ॠ rî becomes अर् ar: कॄ krî, to scatter, चकरुः kakarúḥ.

Irregularities.

153. 1 (319). चि ki, to gather, जि gi, to conquer, हि hi, to impel, dissimilate the radical initial to a guttural: चिकाय kikáya, जिगाय gigáya, जिघाय gigháya.

2 (343, 14). भू bhû, to be, reduplicates with अ a and retains ऊ û throughout: बभूव babhûva, बभूवुः babhûvúḥ.

3. अह् ah, to say, is defective, forming only 2. sg., dual; 3. sg., du., pl.: आथ áttha, आह áha; आहथुः áháthuḥ, आहतुः áhátuḥ, आहुः áhúḥ.

Paradigms of the Reduplicated Perfect.

154 (343). 1. तुद् tud, to strike:

1. तुतोद	तुतुदिव	तुतुदिम	तुतुदे	तुतुदिवहे	तुतुदिमहे
tutóda	tutud-ivá	tutudimá	tutudé	tutudiváhe	tutudimáhe
2. तुतोदिथ	तुतुदथुः	तुतुद	तुतुदिषे	तुतुदाथे	तुतुदिध्वे
tutóditha	tutudáthuh	tutudá	tutudishé	tutudáthe	tutudidhvé
3. तुतोद	तुतुदतुः	तुतुदुः	तुतुदे	तुतुदाते	तुतुदिरे
tutóda	tutudátuh	tutudúh	tutudé	tutudáte	tutudiré

2. धा dhâ, to place: sg. 1. दधौ dadháu, 2. दधाथ dadhâtha or दधिथ dadhithá; du. 1. दधिव dadhivá; pl. 3. दधुः dadhúh; Âtm. 1. दधे dadhé, 2. दधिषे dadhishé.

3. तन् tan, to stretch: ततान tatâna or ततन tatána, तेनिथ tenithá; तेनिव tenivá; तेनुः tenúh; तेने tené, तेनिषे tenishé.

4. यज् yag, to sacrifice: इयाज iyâga or इयज iyága, इयष्ठ iyáshtha or इयजिथ iyágitha; ईजिव îgivá; ईजुः îgúh; ईजे îgé, ईजिषे îgishé.

5. हन् han, to kill: जघान gaghâna or जघन gaghána, जघंथ gaghántha or जघनिथ gaghánitha; जघ्निव gaghnivá; जघ्नुः gaghnúh; जघ्ने gaghné, जघ्निषे gaghnishé.

6. नी nî, to lead: निनाय nináya or निनय ninánya, निनेथ ninétha, निनयिथ ninányitha; निन्यिव ninyivá; निन्युः ninyúh; निन्ये ninyé, निन्यिषे ninyishé; निन्यिध्वे ninyidhvé or °ढ्वे -dhvé.

7. क्री krî, to buy: चिक्राय kikráya or चिक्रय kikráya, चिक्रेथ kikrétha or चिक्रयिथ kikráyitha; चिक्रियिव kikriyivá; चिक्रियुः kikriyúh; चिक्रिये kikriyé, चिक्रियिषे kikriyishé; चिक्रियिध्वे kikriyidhvé or °ढ्वे -dhvé.

8. कृ kri, to do: चकार kakâra or चकर kakára, चकर्थ kakártha; चकृव kakrivá; चक्रुः kakrúh; चक्रे kakré, चकृषे kakrishé; चकृध्वे kakridhvé.

9. कॄ krî, to scatter: चकार kakâra or चकर kakára, चकरिथ ka-

kárṛitha; चकरिव kakarivá; चकरु: kakarúh; चकरे kakaré; चकरिमे kakarishé; चकरिध्वे kakaridhvé or °द्वे -dhvé.

10. धृ dhri, to hold: दधार dadhára or दधर dadhára, दधर्थ dadhártha; दधिव dadhrivá; दध्रु: dadhrúh; दध्रे dadhré, दध्रिषे dadhrishé; दध्रिध्वे dadhridhvé or °द्वे -dhvé.

11. स्तृ stri, to spread: तस्तार tastára or तस्तर tastára; तस्तर्थ tastártha; तस्तरिव tastarivá; तस्तरु: tastarúh; तस्तरे tastaré, तस्तरिमे tastarishé; तस्तरिध्वे tastaridhvé or °द्वे -dhvé.

12. यु yu, to join: युयाव yuyáva or युयव yuyáva, युयविथ yuyávitha; युयुविव yuyuvivá; युयुवु: yuyuvúh; युयुवे yuyuvé, युयुविमे yuyuvishé; युयुविध्वे yuyuvidhvé or °द्वे -dhvé.

13. स्तु stu, to praise: तुष्टाव tushṭáva or तुष्टव tushṭáva, तुष्टोथ tushṭótha; तुष्टुव tushṭuvá; तुष्टुवु: tushṭuvúh; तुष्टुवे tushṭuvé, तुष्टुमे tushṭushé; तुष्टुद्वे tushṭudhvé.

14. भू bhû, to be: बभूव babhûva, बभूविथ babhûvitha; बभूविव babhûvivá; बभूवु: babhûvúh; बभूवे babhûvé, बभूविमे babhûvishé; बभूविध्वे babhûvidhvé or °द्वे -dhvé.

Periphrastic Perfect.

155 (342). Verbs which, according to 147, cannot form a reduplicated perfect, form their perfect by affixing आम् ấm (accusative of a fem. abstract noun in आ ấ) to the verbal base, and adding to this the reduplicated perfect of कृ kri, to do, भू bhû, to be, or अस् as, to be.

1. Monosyllabic roots beginning with a prosodically long vowel except अ a or आ â: उन्द् und, to wet: उन्दांचकार undấmkakára, उन्दांबभूव undấmbabhûva, उन्दामास undấmâsa.

2. Polysyllabic roots: चकास् kakâs, to shine; चकासांचकार kakâsấmkakára, °बभूव -babhûva, °आस -âsa.

3. Verbs of the tenth class and derivative verbs: बोधयांचकार bodhayấmkakára, °बभूव -babhûva, °आस -âsa.

Note—After verbs which are used in the Âtmanepada, कृ k*ri*
is conjugated as Âtm., but अस् as and भू bhû in the Parasmaipada.
Hence from एधते édhate, he grows, एधांचक्रे edhâ*mk*akre, but
एधांबभूव edhâmbabhûva and °आस -âsa. In the passive all three
auxiliary verbs follow the Âtmanepada (cp. 178).

Irregularities.

156 (326). 1. अय् ay, to go, आस् âs, to sit down, दय् day, to
pity, take the periphrastic perfect.

2. It is taken optionally:

(a) by जागृ *g*âgri, to wake (जागराम् *g*âgarâm), विद् vid, to know
(विदाम् vidâm).

(b) after reduplication, by भी bhî, to fear (बिभयाम् bibhayẫm),
भृ bhr*i*, to bear (बिभराम् bibharẫm), and हु hu, to sacrifice
(जुहवाम् *g*uhavẫm).

Aorist.

157 (346). There are two kinds of aorists in Sanskrit as in
Greek. The First is formed by inserting a sibilant between root
and termination, the Second by adding the terminations to the
base.

Both aorists take the augment (which is always accented), and
with some modifications, the terminations of the imperfect.

There are four forms of the First Aorist, three of the Second.

First Aorist.

158 (347). The first two forms of this aorist are really the same;
but the former, being peculiar to verbs which take intermediate
इ i, prefixes इ i to the sibilant, while the latter, being peculiar to
verbs which reject the इ i, attaches the sibilant directly to the
root. These two are the only forms of the aorist which take
Gu*n*a or V*ri*ddhi. They have V*ri*ddhi in the Parasmaipada (in
the first form a medial vowel takes Gu*n*a only) and Gu*n*a in the

Âtmanepada (a medial vowel, as well as final श्रृ *ri*, remains unchanged in the second form).

First Form.

लू *lû*, to cut. **Parasmaipada.**

1. अलाविषम् *álâv-isham* अलाविष्व *álâv-ishva* अलाविष्म *álâv-ishma*
2. अलावी: *álâv-îh* अलाविष्टम् *álâv-ishtam* अलाविष्ट *álâv-ishta*
3. अलावीत् *álâv-ît* अलाविष्टाम् *álâv-ishtâm* अलाविषु: *álâv-ishuh*

Âtmanepada.

1. अलविषि *álav-ishi* अलविष्वहि *álav-ishvahi* अलविष्महि *álav-ishmahi*
2. अलविष्टा: *álav-ishthâh* अलविषाथाम् *álav-ishâthâm* अलविध्वम् *álav-idhvam*
3. अलविष्ट *álav-ishta* अलविषाताम् *álav-ishâtâm* अलविषत *álav-ishata*.

बुध् budh, to perceive, as it ends in a consonant, takes only Guṇa.
Par. sg. 1. अबोधिषम् *ábodhisham*; Âtm. अबोधिषि *ábodhishi*.
Note—ग्रह् grah, to seize, does not take Vṛddhi. Other roots with अ *a* followed by a single consonant take it optionally.

Second Form.

क्षिप् kship, to throw. **Parasmaipada.**

1. अक्षैप्सम् *ákshaip-sam* अक्षैप्स्व *ákshaip-sva* अक्षैप्स्म *ákshaip-sma*
2. अक्षैप्सी: *ákshaip-sîh* अक्षैप्तम् *ákshaip-tam* अक्षैप्त *ákshaip-ta*
3. अक्षैप्सीत् *ákshaip-sît* अक्षैप्ताम् *ákshaip-tâm* अक्षैप्सु: *ákshaip-suh*

Âtmanepada.

1. अक्षिप्सि *ákship-si* अक्षिप्स्वहि *ákship-svahi* अक्षिप्स्महि *ákship-smahi*
2. अक्षिप्था: *ákship-thâh* अक्षिप्साथाम् *ákship-sâthâm* अक्षिभ्म्वम् *ákshib-dhvam*
3. अक्षिप्त *ákship-ta* अक्षिप्साताम् *ákship-sâtâm* अक्षिप्सत *ákship-sata*

नी nî, to lead (final vowel): Par. अनैषम् *ánaisham*; Âtm. अनेषि *áneshi*, 2. pl. अनेद्वम् *ánedhvam*.

कृ kri, to do (final श्रृ ri): Par. अकार्षम् *ákârsham*; Âtm. अकृषि *ákrishi*, 2. अकृथा: *ákrithâh*, 3. अकृत *ákrita*.

Irregularities.

1. Terminations beginning with स्त् st or स्थ् sth drop their स् s if the base ends in a short vowel or in a consonant except nasals : अक्षैप्त ákshaip-ta, अकृथाः ákri-thâh ; but अमंस्त ámamsta, from मन् man, to think.

2. दा dâ, to give, धा dhâ, to place, स्था sthâ, to stand, change their vowels to इ i before the terminations of the Âtmanepada. These verbs take the second aorist in the Parasmaipada (163).

3. दृश् dris, to see, सृज् srig, to create, स्पृश् spris, to touch, take Vriddhi with metathesis in the Par.: सृज् srig, असार्क्षम् ásrâksham ; du. 2. असार्ष्टम् ásrâshtam ; Âtm. असृक्षि ásrikshi, असृष्टाः ásri-shthâh, असृष्ट ásrishta ; du. असृक्ष्वहि ásrikshvahi ; pl. 2. असृड्ढ्वम् ásriddhvam.

4. The aor. of दह् dah, to burn, is difficult (cp. 60 and 69) : अधाक्षम् ádhâksham ; du. 2. अदाग्धम् ádâgdham ; pl. 2. अदाग्ध ádâgdha ; Âtm. अधक्षि ádhakshi, 2. अदग्धाः ádagdhâh, अदग्ध ádagdha ; pl. 2. अधग्ध्वम् ádhagdhvam (69, note).

5. The termination ध्वम् dhvam of 2. pl. Âtm. becomes ढ्वम् dhvam when immediately attached to a root ending in any other vowel than आ â ; optionally after intermediate इ i preceded by a semi-vowel or ह् h : अकृढ्वम् ákridhvam ; but अलविध्वम् álavidhvam or °ढ्वम् -dhvam. The ध्वे dhve of the perf. Âtm. 2. pl. under the same conditions becomes ढ्वे dhve.

Third Form.

159 (357). This is conjugated in the Par. only. The terminations are the same as in the first form, but with an स् s prefixed to them. Most verbs taking this form end in आ â or in diphthongs (which take आ â as their substitute). In the Âtm. these verbs take the second form.

या yâ, *to go.* **Parasmaipada.**

1. अयासिषम् áyâsisham   अयासिष्व áyâsishva   अयासिष्म áyâsishma
2. अयासी: áyâsî*h*   अयासिष्टम् áyâsish*t*am   अयासिष्ट áyâsish*t*a
3. अयासीत् áyâsît   अयासिष्टाम् áyâsish*t*âm   अयासिषु: áyâsishu*h*

Fourth Form.

160 (360). The roots which take this form must end in a sibilant or ह h, preceded by any vowel but अ a or आ â. Their radical
vowel remains unchanged. The terminations are those of the
imperf. of the first conjugation (cp. 161), while the first three
forms (cp. especially the second form) have the terminations of the
second. This form corresponds to the Greek first aorist ($\check{\epsilon}$-τυπ-σα).

1. दिश् dis, *to show.* **Parasmaipada.**

1. अदिक्षम् ádik-sham   अदिक्षाव ádikshâva   अदिक्षाम ádikshâma
2. अदिक्ष: ádik-sha*h*   अदिक्षतम् ádikshatam   अदिक्षत ádikshata
3. अदिक्षत् ádik-shat   अदिक्षताम् ádikshatâm   अदिक्षन् ádikshan

Âtmanepada.

1. अदिक्षि ádikshi   अदिक्षावहि ádikshâvahi   अदिक्षामहि ádikshâmahi
2. अदिक्षथा: ádikshathâ*h*   अदिक्षाथाम् ádikshâthâm   अदिक्षध्वम् ádikshadhvam
3. अदिक्षत ádikshata   अदिक्षाताम् ádikshâtâm   अदिक्षंत ádikshanta

2. गुह् guh, *to hide.* **Parasmaipada.**

1. अघुक्षम् ághuksham   अघुक्षाव ághukshâva   अघुक्षाम ághukshâma

Âtmanepada.

1. अघुक्षि
   ághukshi   अघुक्षावहि or अगुह्वहि   अघुक्षामहि
   ághukshâvahi or ághuhvahi ághukshâmahi
2. अघुक्षथा: or अगूढा:   अघुक्षाथाम्   अघुक्षध्वम् [1]
   ághukshathâ*h* or ág**û**dhâ*h* ághukshâthâm   ághukshadhvam
3. अघुक्षत or अगूढ   अघुक्षाताम्   अघुक्षंत
   ághukshata or ag**û**d*h*a ághukshâtâm   ághukshanta

---

[1] Or अगूढ्वम् ág**û**d*h*vam.

3. लिह् lih, to smear: Par. अलिक्षम् áliksham; Âtm. अलिक्षि álik-shi, अलिक्षथाः álikshathâh or अलीढाः áliḍhâh(79), अलिक्षत álikshata or अलीढ áliḍha; अलिक्षध्वम् álikshadhvam or अलीढ्वम् áliḍhvam.

4. दुह् duh, to milk: अधुक्षम् ádhuksham; अधुक्षि ádhukshi.

5. दिह् dih, to anoint: अधिक्षम् ádhiksham; अधिक्षि ádhikshi.

Second Aorist.
First Form.

161 (363). This form is like an imperfect of the sixth class, the terminations of the first conjugation being attached to the unmodified root. It corresponds to the second aorist of the first conjugation in Greek (ἔ-τυπ-ον).

सिच् sik, to sprinkle. **Parasmaipada.**

1.असिचम् ásik-am	असिचाव ásikâva	असिचाम ásikâma
2.असिच: ásik-ah	असिचतम् ásikatam	असिचत ásikata
3.असिचत् ásik-at	असिचताम् ásikatâm	असिचन् ásikan

Âtmanepada.

1.असिचे ásike	असिचावहि ásikâvahi	असिचामहि ásikâmahi
2.असिचथाः ásikathâh	असिचेथाम् ásikethâm	असिचध्वम् ásikadhvam
3.असिचत ásikata	असिचेताम् ásiketâm	असिचंत ásikanta

Irregularities.

162 (364). 1. ख्या khyâ, to tell, श्वि svi, to swell, ह्वे hve, to call, take this aorist by substituting a base ending in अ a: अख्यम् ákhyam, अश्वम् ásvam, अह्वम् áhvam.

2. दृश् dris, to see, takes Guna: अदर्शम् ádarsam.

3. अस् as, to throw, and शास् sâs, to command, are irregular: आस्थम् ástham, अशिषम् ásisham (cp. 144, cl. ii, 5).

4 (366). वच् vak, to speak, पत् pat, to fall, नश् nas, to destroy, form contracted reduplicated aorists: अवोचम् ávokam (= á-va-vak-am, cp. Gk. εἶπον = ἐϝεϝεπον), अपप्तम् ápaptam (= ápapatam), अनेशम् ánesam (= ánanasam, cp. 151).

Second Form.

163 (368). The imperfect terminations of the second conjugation are attached to the root. This form corresponds to the second aorist of the second conjugation in Greek, e. g. ἔ-θη-ν = अधाम् á-dhâ-m. A few verbs ending in आ â take this form; also भू bhû, to be. The आ â is retained throughout, except before उः uh of 3. pl., when it is rejected. There is no Âtmanepada (cp. p. 106, note 2).

दा dâ, to give.   **Parasmaipada.**

1. अदाम् ádâm   अदाव ádâva   अदाम ádâma
2. अदाः ádâh   अदातम् ádâtam   अदात ádâta
3. अदात् ádât   अदाताम् ádâtâm   अदुः áduh

भू bhû, to be.

1. अभूवम् ábhûvam   अभूव ábhûva   अभूम ábhûma
2. अभूः ábhûh   अभूतम् ábhûtam   अभूत ábhûta
3. अभूत् ábhût   अभूताम् ábhûtâm   अभूवन् ábhûvan

Third or Reduplicated Form.

164 (370). Excepting a few primitive verbs, this form of the aorist is limited to verbs in अय aya (tenth class, denominatives, and causatives). The base, after dropping अय aya, is reduplicated, and takes the terminations of the imperfect (of the first conjugation).

The primitive verbs which take this form are: कम् kam, to love, द्रु dru, to run, श्रि sri, to go: अदुद्रुवत् ádudruvat, he ran; अशिश्रियत् ásisriyat, he went.

165 (372). a. The derivative verbs, after dropping अ aya, reduce their Guna and Vriddhi vowels to the original simple vowels (20).

b (374). All roots in which the shortened vowel is not long by position, lengthen the vowel of the reduplicative syllable (ámûmudat). Those in which the vowel is long by position, leave the vowel of the reduplicative syllable short (áraraksshat).

c. Where, as in roots beginning with double consonants, the vowel of the reduplicative syllable is necessarily long by position, it is not changed to the long vowel (ákuḱyutat, not ákûḱyutat).

In other words, the reduplicated base, with the augment, is either ∪ – ∪ or ∪ ∪ –. In roots beginning and ending with two consonants, this metrical rhythm is necessarily broken: áḱaskandat.

Special Rule of Reduplication.

166 (375). अ a, इ i, उ u, ऋ ri are represented in the reduplicative syllable by
अ a or इ i, इ i, उ u, इ i, which are all lengthened
if necessary.

I. ∪ – ∪.

जन् ɡan, to beget: अजीजनत् áɡîɡanat; मुच् muḱ, to release: अमूमुचत् ámûmuḱat; वृध् vridh, to grow: अवीवृधत् ávîvridhat; ज्ञप्य ɡñap-aya, caus. of ज्ञा ɡñâ, to know: अजिज्ञपत् áɡiɡñapat.

2. ∪ ∪ –.

दीप् dîp, to shine: अदिदीपत् ádidîpat.

Irregularity.

167 (379). The causal aorist of स्था sthâ, to stand, is slightly irregular: अतिष्ठिपत् átishṭhipat (for átishṭhapat).

Simple Future.

168 (381). The future is formed by adding to the base स्य sya, or, with intermediate इ i, इष्य ishya, to which are attached the terminations of the present of the first conjugation (cp. 142).

1. Final ए e, ऐ ai, ओ o are changed to आ â: गै gai, to sing: गास्यामि gâsyâmi.

2. Final vowels and prosodically short medial vowels take Guṇa: जि ɡi, to conquer: जेष्यामि ɡeshyâmi; दृश् dris, to see: द्रक्ष्यामि drakshyâmi; बुध् budh, to perceive: भोत्स्ये bhotsyé; भिद् bhid,

to cleave: भेत्स्यामि bhetsyāmi; वच् va*k*, to speak: वक्ष्यामि vakshyāmi.

चुर् *k*ur, to steal, forms its future चोरयिष्यामि *k*orayishyāmi.

बुध् budh, to know: Par. बोधिष्यामि bodhishyāmi, बोधिष्यसि bodhishyāsi, बोधिष्यति bodhishyáti, etc. Âtm. बोधिष्ये bodhishyé, बोधिष्यसे bodhishyáse, बोधिष्यते bodhishyáte.

इ i, to go: Par. एष्यामि eshyāmi, एष्यसि eshyási, एष्यति eshyáti, etc. Âtm. एष्ये eshyé, एष्यसे eshyáse, एष्यते eshyáte, etc.

Periphrastic Future.

169 (384). It is formed by adding the present of the verb अस् as, to be, to the nom. masc. of a base in तृ *tri* (cp. 112). The nom. sg. is used in all forms except the third persons dual and plural, in which the nom. dual and pl. are used. The auxiliary is omitted in the third persons.

तृ *tri* is added, with or without the intermediate इ i, to the root, which takes Gu*n*a: कृ k*ri*, कर्तृ kart*ri*; भू bhû, भवितृ bhavit*ri*.

बुध् budh, to know. **Parasmaipada.**

1. बोधितास्मि bodhitāsmi बोधितास्व: -tāsva*h* बोधितास्म: -tāsma*h*
2. बोधितासि bodhitāsi बोधितास्थ: -tāstha*h* बोधितास्थ -tāstha
3. बोधिता bodhitā́ बोधितारौ -tā́rau बोधितार: -tā́ra*h*

Âtmanepada.

1. बोधिताहे bodhitā́he बोधितास्वहे -tāsvahe बोधितास्महे -tāsmahe
2. बोधितासे bodhitāse बोधितासाथे -tāsāthe बोधिताध्वे -tādhve
3. बोधिता bodhitā́ बोधितारौ -tā́rau बोधितार: -tā́ra*h*

इ i, to go. **Parasmaipada.**

1. एतास्मि etāsmi एतास्व: etāsva*h* एतास्म: etāsma*h*
2. एतासि etāsi एतास्थ: etāstha*h* एतास्थ etāstha
3. एता etā́ एतारौ etā́rau एतार: etā́ra*h*

Âtmanepada.

1. एताहे etấhe	एतास्वहे etấsvahe	एतास्महे etấsmahe
2. एतासे etấse	एतासाथे etấsâthe	एताध्वे etấdhve
3. एता etấ	एतारौ etấrau	एतार: etấra*h*

Conditional.

170 (383). It is formed by turning the simple future into an imperfect.

बुध् budh: Fut. बोधिष्यामि bodhishyấmi; Cond. अबोधिष्यम् ábodhishyam, अबोधिष्य: ábodhishya*h*, अबोधिष्यत् ábodhishyat, etc.; Âtm. अबोधिष्ये ábodhishye, etc.

इ i, to go: Fut. एष्यामि eshyấmi; Cond. ऐष्यम् aíshyam, ऐष्य: aíshya*h*, ऐष्यत् aíshyat, etc.; Âtm. ऐष्ये aíshye.

Benedictive (Precative).

171 (385). This mood is formed in close analogy to the optative, being really an aorist optative. It differs from the optative in not being formed from the present base, and by inserting स् s before the personal terminations. In the Parasmaipada this स् s stands between the या yâ of the optative and the actual signs of the persons, being lost, however, in the 2nd and 3rd sing.

Note 1. The termination of the Optative (याम् yâm, etc.) is an ancient second aorist of या yâ, to go, while that of the Benedictive (यासम् yâsam, etc.) is the first aorist of the same root. या: yâ*h*, यात् yât in the Ben. stand for यास् yâss and यास्त् yâst (cp. 29).

In the Âtm.[1] the स् s stands *before* the terminations of the opt.; e. g. सीय sîyá instead of ईय îyá. Besides this, the personal terminations originally beginning with त् t, थ् th, take an additional स् s.

---

[1] The Âtm. occurs hardly at all, and the Par. very rarely, in classical Sanskrit.

Note 2. The सय aya of the tenth class and of derivative verbs is dropped in the Par.: चोर्यासम् *k*oryâsam, but Âtm. चोरयिषीय *k*orayishîyá.

172 (387). 1. The Ben. Par. weakens the root, while the Âtm. strengthens it; from चित् *k*it, Par. चित्यासम् *k*ityâsam ; Âtm. चेतिषीय *k*etishîyá.

2. The Ben. Par. never takes intermediate इ i, while the Âtm. generally takes it.

3. Before the या yâ of the Ben. Par. the base undergoes exactly the same changes as before the य ya of the Passive (175).

बुध् budh, to know. **Parasmaipada.**

1. बुध्यासम् budhyâsam	बुध्यास्व budhyâsva	बुध्यास्म budhyâsma
2. बुध्याः budhyâ*h*	बुध्यास्तम् budhyâstam	बुध्यास्त budhyâsta
3. बुध्यात् budhyât	बुध्यास्ताम् budhyâstâm	बुध्यासुः budhyâsu*h*

Âtmanepada.

1. बोधिषीय -shîyá	°षीवहि -shîváhi	°षीमहि -shîmáhi
2. बोधिषीष्ठाः -shîsh*thâh*	°षीयास्थाम् -shîyâsthâm	°षीध्वम् -shîdhvám
3. बोधिषीष्ट -shîsh*t*á	°षीयास्ताम् -shîyâstâm	°षीरन् -shîrán

Passive.

173 (397). The Passive takes the terminations of the Âtmanepada.

Special Forms.

174 (398). The pres., impf., opt., impv. of the Passive are formed by adding य ya to the root. The Passive differs from the Âtm. of verbs of the fourth class in accent only : नह्यते náhyate, he binds ; नह्यते nahyáte, he is bound.

Note—सय aya is dropped before the य ya of the Passive : बोधय bodháya, to make known ; बोध्यते bodhyáte, it is made known.

175 (390). Before adding य ya, the base undergoes the following changes :—

1. Final **आ** â or diphthongs become either **आ** â or **ई** î: **पा** pâ, to protect, **पायते** pâyáte; **पा** pâ, to drink, **पीयते** pîyáte; **गै** gai, to sing, **गीयते** gîyáte.

2. Final **इ** i and **उ** u are lengthened: **इ** i, to go, **ईयते** îyáte; **चि** ki, to collect, **चीयते** kîyáte; **श्रु** sru, to hear, **श्रूयते** srûyáte.

3. Final **ऋ** ri after a single consonant becomes **रि** ri, after two consonants it becomes **अर्** ar: **कृ** kri, to do, **क्रियते** kriyáte; **स्मृ** smri, **स्मर्यते** smaryáte.

4. Final **ॠ** rî is changed to **ईर्** îr, and, after labials, to **ऊर्** ûr: **स्तृ** stri, to stretch, **स्तीर्यते** stîryáte; **पृ** pri, **पूर्यते** pûryáte.

5. **खन्** khan, to dig, has either **खन्यते** khanyáte or **खायते** khâyáte; **जन्** gan, to beget, **जन्यते** ganyáte (**जायते** gáyate is Âtm., cl. iv; cp. 174).

6. Roots ending in consonants preceded by a nasal lose the nasal: **रञ्ज्** rañg, to tinge, **रज्यते** ragyáte.

7. Roots liable to Samprasarana (151, 2) take it: **यज्** yag, **इज्यते** igyáte; **वच्** vak, **उच्यते** ukyáte; **ग्रह्** grah, **गृह्यते** grihyáte.

8. **शास्** sâs makes **शिष्यते** sishyáte (cp. 144, cl. ii, 5); **ह्वे** hve, **हूयते** hûyáte; **वे** ve, to weave, **ऊयते** ûyáte; **व्ये** vye, to envelope, **वीयते** vîyáte.

176 (400).   Passive.

Pres.	**भूये** bhûyé	**भूयसे** bhûyáse	**भूयते** bhûyáte, etc.
Impf.	**अभूये** ábhûye	**अभूयथाः** ábhûyathâh	**अभूयते** ábhûyate, etc.
Opt.	**भूयेय** bhûyéya	**भूयेथाः** bhûyéthâh	**भूयेत** bhûyéta, etc.
Impv.	**भूयै** bhûyaí	**भूयस्व** bhûyásva	**भूयताम्** bhûyátâm, etc.

General Forms of the Passive.

177 (401). As the general forms of the Passive drop the **य** ya, they do not differ, except in the periphrastic perfect and the aorist, from the general forms of the Âtmanepada.

Periphrastic Perfect.

178. This tense is the same as in the Âtmanepada, only the **auxiliary verbs** सस् as and भू bhû, as well as कृ kri, **must be conjugated in the Âtmanepada.**

Aorist.

179 (402). The Âtm. of this tense (158, 160, 161) supplies the place of the Passive **except in the third person singular,** which has a special form.

180 (403). The 3rd sing. adds to the root the suffix इ i, which requires Vriddhi of final and Guna of medial vowels (but स a is lengthened) followed by *one* consonant: लू lû, अलावि álâv-i; बुध् budh, अबोधि ábodh-i; क्षिप् kship, अक्षेपि ákshep-i; नी nî, अनायि ánây-i; कृ kri, अकारि ákâr-i; स्तृ strî, अस्तारि ástâr-i; सृज् srig, असर्जि ásarg-i; दह् dah, अदाहि ádâh-i.

Note—Verbs in अय aya drop the suffix before the passive इ i: चोरय koráya, अचोरि ákor-i.

Irregularities.

181. 1. दा dâ and other roots in आ â insert य् y before the इ i: अदायि ádây-i.

2. A few verbs with medial स a are irregular in inserting a nasal or in not lengthening the स a: रभ् rabh, to desire, अरंभि árambh-i; जन् gan, अजनि ágan-i. हन् han has अघानि ághân-i or अवधि ávadh-i.

PARTICIPLES, GERUNDS, AND INFINITIVE.
I. Active Participles.

182 (414). The base of the **present** and **future** participles Par. is formed with the suffix अत् at. The strong base is obtained by dropping the इ i of the 3rd pl. pres. and fut. Par.: hence **verbs of the third class and other reduplicated verbs** (144, cl. ii, 5; 203) **have no nasal** in the strong base of the **pres.** part., while the **fut.** part. **always** has अंत ant as its strong base. Thus:—

Root.	Pres. part. (strong base).	Fut. part. (strong base).
भू bhû (1)	भवंत् bhávant	भविष्यंत् bhavishyánt
क्री krî (9)	क्रीणंत् krînánt	क्रेष्यंत् kreshyánt
हु hu (3)	जुह्वत् *g*úhvat	होष्यंत् hoshyánt

Note—The pres. part. of अस् as, to be, is सत् sat, that of हन् han is घ्नत् ghnat. (On the decl. of participles in अत् at, see 97.)

183 (416). The **reduplicated perfect** participle is formed with वस् vas (101). It is most easily formed by taking the 3rd pl. Par., with which the weakest base is identical; only that the स् s, being here always followed by a vowel, is changed to ष् sh. In forming the middle and strong bases from this, it must be remembered—

1. That roots ending in a vowel restore that vowel, which, before उ: u*h*, had been naturally changed to a semivowel.

2. That all verbs which, without counting the उ: u*h*, are monosyllabic in the 3rd pl., insert इ i.

3rd plur.	Weakest Base.	Strong Base.	Middle Base.
बभूवुः	बभूवुषा	बभूवांसम्	बभूवद्भिः
babhûvú*h*	babhûvúsh-â	babhûvá*m*s-am	babhûvád-bhi*h*
चोरयामासुः	चोरयामासुषा	चोरयामासिवांसम्	चोरयामासिवद्भिः
*k*orayâmâsú*h*	-yâmâsúsh-â	-yâmâs-i-vá*m*s-am	-yâmâs-i-vád-bhi*h*
तेनुः	तेनुषा	तेनिवांसम्	तेनिवद्भिः
tenú*h*	tenúsh-â	ten-i-vá*m*s-am	ten-i-vád-bhi*h*
ईजुः	ईजुषा	ईजिवांसम्	ईजिवद्भिः
î*g*ú*h*	î*g*úsh-â	î*g*-i-vá*m*s-am	î*g*-i-vád-bhi*h*

Note—The present perfect वेद véda does not insert इ i: विदुषा vidúsh-â, विद्वांसम् vid-vá*m*sam, विद्वद्भिः vidvád-bhi*h*.

Âtmanepada and Passive Participles.

184 (419–421). **Present** and **Future** participles Âtmanepada and Passive are formed with the suffix मान mâna, which is added

after dropping the 3rd pl. termination °न्ते -nte : भवमान bháva-
mâna, भविष्यमान bhavishyá-mâna ; भूयमान bhûyá-mâna.

Verbs of the **second conjugation** take आन **âna** instead of
मान mâna in the **pres. Âtm.** : होष्यमाण hoshyá-mâna, हूयमान
hûyá-mâna, but जुह्वान gúhv-**âna.**

185 (418). The **Perfect Âtm.** is formed with, the suffix आन
âna, which is added after dropping इरे ire, the termination of
the 3rd pl. Âtm. : बभूविरे babhûv-iré, बभूवान babhûv-âná ; तेनिरे
ten-iré, तेनान ten-âná.

186 (422). The **Perfect Passive** Participle is formed with
the suffixes त **tá** and न **ná.** The latter is attached immediately
to the root : लू lû, लून lû-ná ; the former either immediately : जि
gi, जित gi-tá, or with intermediate इ i : पत् pat, पतित pat-i-tá.
The number of verbs taking इ i is, however, very small.

The suffixes being accented, the root has a tendency to be
weakened in the usual way.

1 (442). Most verbs in ई î and ऊ û, and those in ऋ rí (which
becomes ईर् îr, or ऊर् ûr after labials) and in द d, take the suffix
न ná : ली lî, to cling, लीन lî-ná ; लू lû, लून lû-ná ; स्तृ strí, स्तीर्ण
stîr-ná ; पृ prí, पूर्ण pûr-ná ; भिद् bhid, भिन्न bhin-ná.

Note—नुद् nud, to push, विद् vid, to find, and उन्द् und, to wet,
optionally take त tá : नुन्न nun-ná or नुत्त nut-tá.

2. Other verbs, with a few exceptions, take त tá. Causative
verbs form this participle with intermediate इ i after rejecting अय
aya : कारय kâr-áya, from कृ krí, to do, कारित kâr-i-tá.

Note—By adding the possessive suffix वत् vat to the past pass.
part. a new participle of very common occurrence is formed, being
in fact a **perfect active** participle. Thus कृत krí-tá, done, becomes कृतवान् kritá-vân, one who has done, but generally used as
a finite verb : स तत् कृतवान् sá tát kritávân, he has done it ; सा
तत् कृतवती sấ tát kritávatî, she has done it (cp. 101, note 2).

187 (453). The **Future Passive** Participle is formed with the suffixes तव्य **távya**, अनीय **aníya**, and य **ya** (yá, yã, ya), which correspond to the Latin participles in -ndus : कर्तव्यः kar-távya*h*, करणीयः kar-aní*ya*h, कार्यः kâr-ya*h*, faciendus.

I (454). The participle in तव्य távya is most easily formed by taking the periphrastic future (169) and substituting तव्य távya for ता tá : दा dâ, दाता dâ-tá, दातव्य dâ-távya ; जि *g*i, जेता *g*e-tá, जेतव्य *g*e-távya.

II (455). अनीय aníya is generally added to the root as it appears before तव्य távya, intermediate इ i being omitted. Gu*n*a vowels of course change their final element to the corresponding semi-vowel : जि *g*i, जेतव्य *g*e-távya, जयनीय *g*ay-aníya.

The अय áya of the causative is rejected : भावय bhâv-áya, भाव-नीय bhâv-aníya.

III (456). In order to form the participle in य ya, it is generally sufficient to take the form in अनीय aníya and to cut off अनी aní. Thus भवनीय bhav-aní-ya becomes भव्य bháv-ya ; चेतनीय *k*et-aní-ya, चेत्य *k*et-ya ; जयनीय *g*ay-aní-ya, जेय *g*e-ya.

The following are a few special rules :—

1. Final आ â and diphthongs become ए e : दा dâ, देय dé-ya ; गै gai, गेय ge-ya.

2. Final ऋ ri and ॠ rí take Vriddhi instead of Gu*n*a : कृ kri, कार्य kâr-ya (but करणीय kar-aníya).

3. Penultimate ऋ ri generally remains unchanged : दृश्य drí*s*-ya (but दर्शनीय dar*s*-aníya) ; penultimate ॠ rí becomes ईर îr.

4. Penultimate अ a, prosodically short, is lengthened, unless the final consonant is a labial : हस् has, हास्य hâs-ya, but लभ् labh, लभ्य labh-ya. It remains short in शक्य *s*ak-ya, from शक् *s*ak, to be able, in सह्य sah-ya, from सह् sah, to bear, and in some other verbs.

हन् han forms वध्य **vadh**-ya and घात्य **ghât**-ya.

188 (423). The **indeclinable participle** or **Gerund** is formed with the suffixes त्वा tvằ (य ya, त्य tya) and अम् am.

त्वा tvằ may, as a rule, be substituted for the त tá of the passive participle: कृ kri, to do, कृत kri-tá, done, कृत्वा kri-tvằ, having done; वच् vak, to speak, उक्त uk-tá, spoken, उक्त्वा uk-tvằ, having spoken. The suffix अय aya, however, is retained (cp. 186, 2) before त्वा tvằ, which in this case is always added with intermediate इ i: चुर् kur, चोरयित्वा koray-i-tvằ.

189 (445). Verbs compounded with prepositions take य ya (unaccented) instead of त्वा tvằ: भूत्वा bhû-tvằ, but संभूय sam-bhû́-ya; उक्त्वा uk-tvằ, but प्रोच्य pra-úk-ya; from तृ tri, to cross, अवतीर्य ava-tî́r-ya, having descended; पृ pri, संपूर्य sam-pûr-ya.

The अय aya of causatives is retained (the final अ a being dropped) before य ya, if the radical vowel is short: संगमय sam-gam-áya, to cause to assemble, संगम्य sam-gam-áy-ya; but विचारय vi-kâr-áya, to consider (caus. of चर् kar, to move), विचार्य vi-kâr-ya.

त्य **tya** is added, instead of य ya, to compound verbs ending in—

a. A short vowel: जित्वा gǐ-tvằ, but विजित्य vi-gí-tya.

b. न् n, which is dropped (in some cases only optionally): हन् han, °हत्य -há-tya; मन् man, °मत्य -má-tya or °मन्य -mán-ya. खन् khan has °खाय -khằ-ya.

c. म् m, if it is dropped (which is optional): गम् gam, आगत्य â-gá-tya or आगम्य â-gám-ya; नम् nam, प्रणत्य pra-ná-tya or प्रणम्य pra-nám-ya.

190 (460). The indeclinable participle in अम् am (unaccented) is most easily formed by adding the suffix to that form which the verb assumes before the इ i of the 3rd sg. aor. pass. (180): भुज् bhug, अभोजि á-bhog-i, it was eaten, भोजम् bhóg-am, having eaten; पा pâ, to drink, अपायि á-pây-i, पायम् pây-am.

Infinitive.

191 (459). The infinitive (=Lat. supine) is formed by adding तुम् tum (unaccented) to the form which the verb assumes before

the ता tấ of the periphrastic future or the तव्य távya of the fut. part.
pass.: बुध् budh, बोधितुम् bódh-i-tum; भू bhû, भवितुम् bháv-i-tum;
कृ kri, कर्तुम् kár-tum; दृश् dris, द्रष्टुम् drásh-tum; चुर् kur, चोरयितुम्
kor-áy-i-tum.

Derivative Verbs.

I. Causatives.

192 (461). These verbs are formed in the same way as those of
the tenth class (136, 4): नी nî, to lead, नायय nây-áya, to cause
to lead; कृ kri, to make, कारय kâr-áya, to cause to make; विद्
vid, to know, वेदय ved-áya, to cause to know; सद् sad, to sit,
सादय sâd-áya, to set.

Note—Most verbs in अम् am do not lengthen their vowel:
गम् gam, गमय gam-áya.

193 (463). Nearly all verbs in आ â, and most of those in ए e,
ऐ ai, ओ o (which become आ â), insert प् p before the causative
suffix: दा dâ, to give, दापय dâ-páya, to cause to give; दो do, to
cut, दापय dâ-páya, to cause to cut.

Irregularities.

194 (463, II). इ i with अधि adhi, to read, अध्यापय adhy-âpáya,
to teach; ऋ ri, to go, अर्पय ar-páya, to place; जि gi, ज्ञापय
gâpáya; ज्ञा gñâ, ज्ञापय gñâ-páya or ज्ञपय gñâ-páya; धू dhû, to
shake, धूनय dhûnáya; पा pâ, to protect, पालय pâláya, to protect;
प्री prî, to love, प्रीणय prînáya, to delight; भी bhî, to fear, भीषय
bhîsháya or भायय bhâyáya, to frighten; रुह् ruh, to grow, रोहय
roháya or रोपय ropáya; लभ् labh, लंभय lambháya; शद् sad, to fall,
शातय sátáya, to fell; सिध् sidh, to succeed, साधय sâdháya, to perform,
सेधय sedháya, to perform sacred rites; हन् han, घातय ghâtáya.

195 (464). Like the verbs of the tenth class, causatives retain
अय áya throughout, except in the reduplicated aorist and the
Benedictive Par.

196 (465). If a causative is to be used in the passive, सय áya
is dropped, but the root remains the same as it would have been
with सय áya. Hence कार्यते kâr-yáte, he is made to do; रोप्यते
rop-yáte, he is made to grow. In the general tenses, however,
where the य ya of the passive disappears, the causative सय áya
may or may not reappear: there are thus two forms throughout,
e.g. Fut. भावयिष्यते bhâvay-ishyáte or भाविष्यते bhâv-ishyáte.

II. Desideratives.

197 (467). Desiderative bases are formed by reduplication of a
peculiar kind and by adding स s to the root, with or without intermediate इ i. Thus from भू bhû, to be, बुभूष bú-bhû-sh, to wish
to be. These new bases are conjugated like verbs of the first
conjugation. The accent is on the reduplicative syllable.

Special Rules of Reduplication.

198 (473-7). 1. All vowels, except उ u or ऊ û, are represented
by इ i in the reduplicative syllable; उ u or ऊ û (also when ऋ ûr
stands for ऋ ri or ॠ rî after labials) is regularly represented
by उ u.

Ex. पच् pak, पिपक्षति pí-pak-sha-ti; स्था sthâ, तिष्ठासति tí-
shṭhâ-sa-ti; वृत् vrit, to turn, विवृत्सति ví-vrit-sa-ti. But तुद् tud,
तुतुत्सति tú-tut-sati; मृ mri, मुमूर्षति mú-mûr-shati.

2. Roots beginning with a vowel have a peculiar kind of internal
reduplication with इ i.

Ex. अश् as: अशिशिषति as-ís-ishati; अक्ष् aksh: अचिक्षिषति
ak-íksh-ishati; उक्ष् ukkh: उचिक्षिषति uk-íkkh-ishati. आप् âp,
to obtain, forms (by contraction) ईप्सति íp-sati.

If the root ends in a double consonant, the first letter of which
is न् n, द् d, or र् r, the second letter is reduplicated: अर्क् ark:
अर्चिक्षिषति ark-ík-ishati; उन्द् und: उन्दिदिषति und-íd-ishati.

Irregularities.

199 (471). गम् gam: जिगांसति *gí*-gâm-sati or जिगमिषति *gí*-gam-i-shati; कृ *kri*: चिकीर्षति *kí*-kîr-shati; ग्रह् grah: जिघृक्षति *gí*-ghr*ik*-shati; जि *gi*: जिगीषति *gí*-gî-shati; दुह् duh: दुधुक्षति dú-dhuk-shati; पत् pat: पिपतिषति pí-pat-i-shati or पिप्सति pít-sati; प्रछ् pra*kh*: पिपृच्छिषति pí-pri*kkh*-i-shati; लभ् labh: लिप्सते líp-sate; शक् sak: शिक्षते *sík*-shate; स्वप् svap: सुषुप्सति sú-shup-sati; हन् han: जिघांसति *gí*-ghâm-sati.

III. Intensives (Frequentatives).

200 (478). These bases are meant to convey an intenseness or frequent repetition of the action expressed by the simple verb.

Only verbs beginning with a consonant and consisting of one syllable are liable to be turned into intensive bases. Verbs of the tenth class therefore cannot be changed into intensive verbs.

201 (480). Intensives are formed by a peculiar reduplication. There are two kinds: the one adds य yá (accented) to the reduplicated base and is conjugated in the Âtmanepada only; the other adds the personal terminations immediately to the reduplicated base (the first syllable of which is accented) and is conjugated in the Parasmaipada only.

भू bhû accordingly forms बोभूयते bo-bhû-yá-te and बोभोति bó-bho-ti. Roots ending in vowels retain the य ya of the intensive base in the general tenses, roots ending in consonants drop it. Hence Fut. बोभूयिता bobhûy-i-tâ, but सोसूचिता so-sû*k*-i-tâ.

202 (481). When य yá is added the effect on the base is the same as in the Passive (175) and Bened. Par. (172); only ऋ *ri*, when following a simple consonant, is changed to री rî, not रि ri: कृ *kri*, चेक्रीयते *ke*-krî-yáte.

203 (482). Intensives in य ya are conjugated like the fourth class in the Âtmanepada, while those which do not take य ya are

treated like bases of the third class, the radical syllable taking Guṇa in the strong forms. The reduplicated syllable, of course, has Guṇa throughout.

In the second form, ई î may be optionally inserted before the personal terminations in the sg. pres., 2. and 3. sg. impf., and 3. sg. impv. Bases ending in consonants do not take Guṇa before this ई î nor before terminations beginning with vowels; e. g. विद् vid: वेवेसि vé-ved-mi or वेविदीमि vé-vid-î-mi, वेविदानि vé-vid-âni; but बोभवानि bó-bhav-âni.

Special Rules of Reduplication.

204 (484). 1. Regular intensives take Guṇa and lengthen अ a to आ â in the reduplicative syllable.

In the second form, ऋ ri is reduplicated with अर् ar; ऋ rí with आ â (अर् ar being considered the base): कृ krí, चर्कर्ति kár-kar-ti; पृ prí, पापर्ति pắ-par-ti.

2 (486). Roots ending in a nasal preceded by अ a, repeat the nasal in the reduplicative syllable. The repeated nasal is treated like म् m, and the vowel being long by position, is not lengthened.

Ex. गम् gam: जंगम्यते gaṅ-gam-yá-te, जंगमीति gáṅ-gam-îti; हन् han: जंघन्यते gaṅ-ghan-yáte, जंघनीति gáṅ-ghan-îti.

Irregularities.

205 (487-490). 1. A few verbs insert a nasal in the reduplicative syllable: जप् gap, to recite, जंजप्यते gañ-gapyáte; दह् dah, दंदह्यते dan-dahyáte.

2. Some roots insert नी nî between the reduplicative syllable and the root: पत् pat, पनीपत्यते pa-nî-patyáte, पनीपतीति pá-nî-patîti.

3. Roots with penultimate ऋ ri and, in the second form, those ending in ऋ ri, insert री rî after the reduplicative syllable: दृश् dris, दरीदृश्यते da-rî-drisyáte; मृ mri, मरीमर्ति má-rî-marti.

IV. Denominatives.

206 (493). These verbs are formed with श्वय áya, य yá, and स्य syá, or without any suffix from nominal bases, and express some relation of the subject to the nouns from which they are derived. They are inflected like verbs of the first conjugatioň, partly in the Par., partly in the Âtm.

1 (503). Without a derivative suffix: from कृष्ण krishna, कृष्णति krishna-ti, he behaves like Kríshna; from पितृ pitrí, father, पितरति pitár-ati, he behaves like a father.

2, a (494). Denominatives in य yá, Parasmaipada, are formed by adding य yá to the base of a noun, and express—

a. A wish: from गो go, cow, गव्यति gav-yáti, he wishes for cows. These are a kind of nominal desideratives, but never govern an accusative.

β. Looking upon or treating something like the object expressed by the noun: from पुत्र pútra, son, पुत्रीयति putrí-yáti, he treats like a son.

b (497). Denominatives in य yá, Âtmanepada, mean behaving like, or becoming like, or actually doing what is expressed by the noun. Final श्व a, इ i, उ u are lengthened: from श्येन syená, hawk, श्येनायते syenâ-yáte, he behaves like a hawk; शुचि súki, pure, शुचीयते sukî-yáte, he becomes pure.

Note (501)—Denominatives in य yá retain the य y in the general tenses, unless it is preceded by a consonant, when it may or may not be dropped: Fut. पुत्रीयिता putríy-itắ only, but समिध्यिता samidhy-itắ or समिधिता samidh-itắ.

3 (502). Denominatives in श्वय áya, which are treated like verbs of the tenth class and are conjugated in the Parasmaipada and Âtmanepada, express the act implied by the nominal base: शब्द sábda, sound, शब्दयति sabdáyati, he makes a sound; मिश्र misrá, mixed, मिश्रयति misráyati, he mixes.

4 (499). Denominatives in स्य sya express a wish : क्षीर kshîrá,
milk, क्षीरस्यति kshîra-syáti, the child longs for milk.

CHAPTER V.

INDECLINABLE WORDS.

Prepositions.

207 (504). The following prepositions may be joined with verbs,
while the first ten may be used separately governing cases :—

a. अति áti, beyond ; अधि ádhi, over (sometimes धि dhi); अनु
ánu, after ; अप ápa, off ; अपि ápi (sometimes पि pi), upon ; अभि
abhí, towards ; आ á̃, near to ; उप úpa, upon, next, below ; परि
pári, round ; प्रति práti, back.

b. अव áva (sometimes व va), down ; उद् úd, up ; दु: duḥ, ill ;
नि ní, into, downwards ; नि: níḥ, without ; परा párâ, back, away ;
प्र prá, before ; वि ví, apart ; सम् sám, together ; सु sú, well.

208 (506). Prepositions are usually placed **after**[1] the case they
govern: Only three, अनु ánu, आ á̃, प्रति práti, are in common
use as independent prepositions.

a. The **accusative** is governed by अति áti, अनु ánu, अभि
abhí, उप úpa, परि pári, प्रति práti.

b. The **ablative** by अप ápa, आ á̃, परि pári, प्रति práti.

c. The **locative** by उप úpa and अधि ádhi.

Thus three of the above ten prepositions govern two cases
परि pári and प्रति práti the acc. and abl. ; उप úpa, acc. and loc.

209 (507). Several adverbs are used like prepositions governing
a case :—

a. **Acc.:** अंतर् antár, between ; अंतरा antarâ, अंतरेण ántarena

---

[1] Greek prepositions preserve their original position and accen
tuation in the so-called anastrophe : πέρι, πάρα (cp. Benfey, Vedic
und Linguistica, pp. 112-114).

without, regarding; **अंतिकम्** antikám, near (also abl., gen.);
अभितः abhítah, around; **उपरि** upári, above, over (also gen.);
उभयतः ubhayátah, on both sides; **ऋते** rité, without (also abl.);
तिरः tiráh, across (also loc.); **निकषा** nikashâ, near; **विना** vínâ
(also instr., abl.)

b. **Instr.:** **अलम्** álam, enough (also dat.); **समम्** samám, **सह**
sahá, **साधँम्** sârdhám, together with.

c. **Abl.:** **अनंतरम्** anantarám, after; **आरभ्य** ârábhya, beginning
from; **ऊर्ध्वम्** ûrdhvám; **परम्** páram, after; **प्रभृति** prábhriti, from;
बहिः bahíh, outside.

d. **Gen.:** **अग्रे** ágre, before; **अध:** adháh, below (also gen.); **अवः**
aváh, below; **कृते** krité, for the sake of; **पश्चात्** paskât, after;
पुरः puráh, **पुरस्तात्** purástât, before; **समक्षम्** samakshám, in the
presence of.

Conjunctions and other Particles.

210 (508). **अति** áti, commonly prefixed to adjectives and adverbs in the sense of 'very:' **अतिसत्वरम्** atisatvaram, very quickly.
It is sometimes used in the sense of 'going beyond' with *nouns*
to form adjectives: **अतिस्त्रिः** atistrih, going beyond (= excelling)
a woman.

अथ átha: 1. in narration, 'then,' 'afterwards;' 2. connecting
parts of a sentence = and, also, moreover; 3. in the headings of
books, chapters, etc., now = here begins (opposed to **इति** iti, here
ends); 4. if: **अथ तान्नानुगच्छामि गमिष्यामि यमक्षयम्** atha tân
na anugakkhâmi, gamishyâmi yamakshayam, if I do not follow
them, I shall go to Yama's abode.

अथ किम् atha kim, what else = it is so, certainly, yes.

अथ वा atha vâ: 1. or; 2. or rather, correcting a previous statement; 3. for indeed: **अथ वा साधिवदमुच्यते** atha vâ sâdhu idam
ukyate, for it is indeed well said.

अधिकृत्य adhikritya, a gerund governing the acc., is used like a prep. = regarding, with respect to, with reference to : शकुंतलाम्-धिकृत्य ब्रवीमि sakuntalâm adhikritya bravîmi, I speak with reference to Sakuntalâ (cp. उद्दिश्य uddísya).

अपि ápi : 1. like च ka, connecting parts of a sentence : moreover, and (अपि ápi—अपि ápi, both—and); 2. also : दमनकोऽपि निर्जगाम damanako×pi nirgagâma, Damanaka also (on his part) went away; 3. even, though : बालोऽपि bâlo×pi, even a child; एकाक्यपि ekâki api, though alone; 4. 'all,' with numerals : चतुर्णा-मपि वर्णानाम् katurnâm api varnânâm, of all the four castes.

Besides these four senses, in which it always follows the word it belongs to, अपि ápi is used at the beginning of sentences as an interrogative particle : अपि तपो वर्धते api tapo vardhate, is your penance prospering ?

आ â, prefixed to adjectives and participles, means : somewhat, a little, scarcely : आपक्व âpakva, a little cooked (half-cooked); आरक्त ârakta, somewhat red, reddish; आलक्ष्य âlakshya, scarcely, only just, visible. (There is also a preposition and an interjection आ â.)

इति íti, thus, 1. is placed at the end of the exact words of quotations. With verbs of saying it supplies the place of inverted commas and of the indirect construction in English : तवाज्ञां करिष्यामीति स मामुवाच tava âgñâm karishyâmi iti sa mâm uvâka, he said to me, 'I will do thy bidding,' or, he said to me that he would do my bidding.

It is similarly used to quote thoughts, intentions, knowledge, though not uttered : बालोऽपि नावमंतव्यो मनुष्य इति भूमिपः bâlo×pi na avamantavyo manushya iti bhûmipah, one should not despise a king, though a child, because (= saying to oneself) he is a mere human being; न धर्मशास्त्रं पठतीति कारणम् na dharmasâstram pathatîti kâranam, (the knowledge) that he reads the book of the law, is not a cause; दातव्यमिति यद्दानं दीयते dâtavyam iti yad dânam dîyate, a gift which is presented from a sense of duty.

2. = here ends, at the end of books, chapters, etc.: इति तृती- यो ऽ ड्कः iti tritîyo-ṅkaḥ, here ends the third act.

3. In the capacity of, as far as, as regards, as for: शीघ्रमिति सुकरं निभृतमिति चिंतनीयं भवेत् sîghram iti sukaram nibhritam iti kintanîyam bhavet, as for doing it quickly, it is easy; as for doing it secretly, it must be thought of.

किमिति kimiti, why indeed? तथेति tathâ_iti, yes.

इव iva, enclitic: 1. like: अयं चोर इवाभाति ayam kora iva_âbhâti, this man looks like a thief; 2. as if, as it were: साक्षात् पश्यामीव पिनाकिनम् sâkshât pasyâmîva pinâkinam, I see, as it were, Siva himself; 3. indeed, possibly (German wohl), with interroga- tives: किमिव मधुराणां मंडनं नाकृतीनाम् kim iva madhurânâm mandanam na_âkritînâm, what indeed is not an ornament to lovely figures?

उद्दिश्य uddísya, a gerund, lit. pointing towards, is used like a prep. governing the acc., = with reference to, towards: स्वपुरमुद्दिश्य प्रतस्थे svapuram uddisya pratasthe, he set out towards his town.

एव evá, just, only, exactly, quite, gives emphasis to the pre- ceding word. It must be rendered in various ways, sometimes merely by stress: एक एव eka eva, quite alone; वसुधैव vasudhâ_eva, the whole earth; मृत्युरेव mrityur eva, sure death. तथैव tathâ_eva, also; तदेव tad eva, this very, the same; नैव na_eva, by no means; चैव ka_eva, and also.

एवम् evám, thus, so: एवमस्तु evam astu, so be it; मैवम् mâ_evam, not so!

कच्चित् kákkit, = I hope, implies a question, to which the answer expected is 'yes' (= Lat. nonne): कच्चिद्दृष्टा त्वया राजन् दमयंती kakkid drishtâ tvayâ râgan damayantî, I hope you have seen Damayantî, O king? With a negative = I hope not (Lat. num):

कच्चित् नापराधं ते कृतवानस्मि ka*kk*it tu na‿aparâdham te k*ri*tavâ*n* asmi, I have not done you any injury, I hope?

कामम् kấmam, 1. gladly: कामम् kâmam—न तु na tu, rather—than (cp. वरम् varam—न na); 2. indeed, certainly, forsooth; 3. granted, supposing: generally followed by तु tu, but, or तथापि tathâpi, nevertheless.

क्व kvá, where, if repeated with another question, expresses great difference, incongruity or incompatibility: तप: क्व वत्से क्व च तावकं वपु: tapa*h* kva, vatse, kva *k*a tâvaka*m* vapu*h*, how great is the incompatibility between (the tenderness of) thy body and (the hardship of) penance, O girl!

किम् kím, 1. what; 2. why, wherefore; 3. whether, in dependent clauses, followed by ' or :' वा vâ, उत utá, आहो ấho, or आहोस्वित् ấhosvit; 4. bad, when prefixed to nouns: किंराजा ki*m*râ*g*â, a bad king.

किमु kim u, किमुत kim uta, or किं पुन: ki*m* puna*h*, how much more, how much less: एकैकमप्यनर्थाय किमु यत्र चतुष्टयम् ekai-kam api‿anarthâya kimu yatra *k*atush*t*ayam, even one of these (taken singly) causes ruin, how much more the four together!

किल kíla (quidem) follows the word to which it belongs, 1. indeed, to be sure, or merely emphatic: अर्हति किल कितव उपद्रवम् arhati kila kitava upadravam, to be sure the rogue deserves annoyance; एकस्मिन् दिने व्याघ्र आजगाम किल ekasmin dine vyâghra â*g*agâma kila, one day a tiger *did* come; 2. as is well known, they say: बभूव योगी किल कार्तवीर्य: babhûva yogî kila kârtavîrya*h*, there lived, as is well known, a Yogi Kârtavîrya.

केवलम् kévalam, 1. adj. mere, absolute; 2. adv. only, merely: केवलं स्वपिति kevalam svapiti, he sleeps only. न केवलम् na ke-valam—अपि api, किंतु kintu, or प्रत्युत pratyuta (on the contrary), not only—but.

खलु khálu, 1. indeed, often merely emphasizing the preceding word; 2. pray, please, in entreaties: देहि खलु मे प्रतिवचनम् dehi khalu me prativakanam, please give me an answer (German *doch*); 3. = do not, with gerund: खलु रुदित्वा khalu ruditvâ, do not weep (cp. अलम् álam, 230, III, 3). न खलु na khalu, certainly not, I hope not.

च *ka*, enclitic (= τε, que), and, also: गोविंदो रामश्च govindo râma*s* ka, Govinda and Râma. When more than two words are connected, the conjunction is commonly used with the last only, as in English.

च *ka*—च *ka*, 1. both—and; 2. on the one hand—on the other hand, though—yet; 3. no sooner—than.

चेत् *két*, if, never begins a sentence like यदि yádi, if. न चेत् na *ket* or नो चेत् no *ket*, otherwise, lest: सर्वं विमृश्य कर्तव्यं नो चेत् पश्चात्तापं व्रजिष्यसि sarva*m* vim*r*isya kartavyam no *ket* pa*sk*âttâpa*m* vra*g*ishyasi, everything should be done after deliberation, otherwise (lit. if not), you will (or, lest you) come to repentance.

ततः tátah, 1. from that place, thence; 2. after that, then. ततस्ततः tatastata*h* = what next, go on, proceed; said by one listening to a narration.

तथा táthâ, 1. in that manner, so, accordingly; 2. and, as well as (= च ka); 3. yes, it is so, it shall be done.

तथापि tathâ api, nevertheless.

तद् tád, 1. pron. that; 2. adv. then, therefore: राजपुत्रा वयं तद्विग्रहं श्रोतुं नः कुतूहलमस्ति râ*g*aputrâ vaya*m* tad vigraha*m* *s*rotu*m* na*h* kutûhalam asti, we are princes; therefore we have a curiosity to hear of war.

तु tú, never at the beginning of a sentence: but, however. किं तु ki*m* tu has the same meaning.

तावत् tâvat, 1. so long: correl. यावत् yâvat, how long; 2. at once, in the first place, first of all = before doing anything else: इतस्तावदागम्यताम् itas tâvad âgamyatâm, come here first; 3. mean-

while, on one's part; 4. it is true, certainly (concessive): अस्ति
देव तावदयं महान् भयहेतुः—किंतु asti, deva, tâvad ayam mahân bha-
ya-hetuh—kintu, Sire, this is certainly a great cause of fear—but;
5. indeed, as for, as regards (emphatic): आवयोस्तावदेकमुदरम् âva-
yos tâvad ekam udaram, as for us two, we have only one belly.
न तावत् na tâvat, not yet.

न ná, not; with indef. pron. = no; न कोऽपि नरः na ko×pi
narah, no (= not any) man. न na—न na sometimes = an emphatic positive.

ननु nanú (na+nu), 1. with questions, why, surely, indeed, pray:
ननु भवानग्रतो मे वर्तते nanu bhavân agrato me vartate, why, you
yourself are before me; ननु को भवान् nanu ko bhavân, pray who
are you? 2. with imperatives, pray: ननूच्यताम् nanu ukyatâm, pray
tell; 3. with vocatives, oh, ah, well: ननु मानव nanu, mânava,
well, man! 4. in arguments = it may be objected; followed by
अत्रोच्यते atra ukyate, to this we reply.

नाम nâma, 1. by name: नलो नाम nalo nâma, Nala by name;
2. indeed, certainly, to be sure: मया नाम जितम् mayâ nâma gitam,
I have indeed conquered; 3. pray, with interrogatives: को नाम
राज्ञां प्रियः ko nâma râgñâm priyah, who, pray, is a favourite with
kings? 4. perhaps: पूर्वं दृष्टस्त्वया कश्चिदिमैश्रो नाम pûrvam dri-
shtas tvayâ kaskid dharmagño nâma, you have, perhaps, seen before
a righteous man; 5. granted, with imperatives: स धनी भवतु नाम
sa dhanî bhavatu nâma, granted he is rich.

अपि नाम api nâma, (at the beginning of a sentence) perhaps;
मा नाम mâ nâma, perhaps (= I hope not); ननु नाम nanu nâma,
surely: ननु नामाहमिश किल तव nanu nâma aham ishtâ kila
tava, surely I am dear to thee.

नु nú, now, pray, in questions; expresses doubt or uncertainty
when repeated: अयं भीमो नु धर्मो नु ayam bhîmo nu dharmo nu,
can this be Bhîma or Dharma?

प्राय: práyaḥ, प्रायश: práyasaḥ, प्रायेण práyeṇa, 1. for the most part, generally, as a general rule; 2. in all probability.

पुन: púnaḥ, 1. again; 2. but, on the other hand.

पुन: पुन: punaḥ punaḥ, again and again, repeatedly.

मुहु: múhuḥ, often, repeatedly; generally मुहुर्मुहु: muhur muhuḥ.

मुहु: muhuḥ—मुहु: muhuḥ, now—now; at one time—at another time.

यत: yátaḥ, 1. whence; often = यस्मात् yasmât, from whom; sometimes used for 'where' and 'whither;' 2. for, because, since; frequently introduces a verse supporting a previous statement.

यथा yáthâ, 1. as, in the manner that: यथाज्ञापयति देव: yathâ âgñâpayati devaḥ, as your Majesty commands; 2. like, as (= इव iva); 3. as, for instance; 4. in order that, so that (in this sense येन yena = íva is often used instead): अहं तथा करिष्ये यथा स वधं करिष्यति aham tathâ karishye yathâ sa vadham karishyati, I shall so manage that he will slay him; 5. that, introducing (like यद् yad) a direct assertion, with or without इति iti: त्वयोक्तं मे यथा— tvayâ uktam me yathâ—, you told me that—. यथा यथा yathâ yathâ—तथा तथा tathâ tathâ is used, like the Lat. quo—eo, with comparatives.

यद् yád, 1. that: किं यन्न वेत्सि त्वम् kim yan na vetsi tvam, how is it that you do not know? 2. that, introducing direct assertions (like Gk. ὅτι) with or without इति iti at the end: वक्तव्यं यदिह मया हता प्रियेति vaktavyam yad iha mayâ hatâ priyâ iti, you must say, 'I have slain my beloved here:' 3. because, since; 4. in order that: किं शक्यं कर्तुं यन्न क्रुध्यते नृप: kim sakyam kartum yan na krudhyate nripaḥ, what can be done, in order that the king be not angry?

यावत् yâvat, 1. as far as, till, for, with acc., like a prep., of time and space: वर्षं यावत् varsham yâvat, for a year; आगमनं यावत् âgamanam yâvat, till the arrival; 2. just; expressing the will to do an action at once: यावदिमां छायामाश्रित्य प्रतिपालयामि ताम् yâ-vad imam *khâyâm âsritya pratipâlayâmi tâm, having resorted to this shade, I will just wait for her; 3. with correl. तावत् tâvat, as long as—so long; no sooner—than; scarcely—when; when—then.

वत् vat, like, used at the end of adv. compounds, = इव iva or यथा yathâ: मृतवत् mrita-vat, like a dead man.

वरम् váram—न ná, better—than; च ka, तु tú, or पुनः púnah being generally added after न na: वरं प्राणत्यागो न पुनरधमानामुपगमः varam prâna-tyâgo na punar adhamânâm upagamah, better death than association with the base.

वा vâ, enclitic, follows its word, 1. or; 2. pray, with interrogatives: परिवर्तिनि संसारे मृतः को वा न जायते parivartini samsâre mritah ko vâ na gâyate, in the revolving world, who, pray, that is dead is not born again?

हि hí, never at the beginning of a sentence; 1. for, because; 2. indeed, surely, verily: त्वं हि तस्य प्रियवयस्यः tvam hi tasya priya-vayasyah, thou art indeed his dear friend; 3. pray, with interr.: कथं हि देवाज्ञानीयाम् katham hi devâñ gânîyâm, how, pray, shall I know the gods?

Interjections.

211 (509). अयि ayi, with vocative or supplying its place, = friend, prythee: अयि मकरोद्यानं गच्छावः ayi makara udyânam gakkhâvah, prythee let us go to the garden of love.

अहह ahaha, exclamation of joy, amazement, or sorrow: अहह महापंके पतितोऽस्मि ahaha mahâpanke patito*smi, alas! I have fallen into a deep quagmire.

अहो aho expresses astonishment, joy, sorrow, anger, praise, or blame: अहो गीतस्य माधुर्यम् aho gîtasya mâdhuryam, Oh the sweetness of the song! अहो हिरण्यक श्लाघ्योऽसि aho hiranyaka, slâghyo*si, Ah, Hiranyaka, you are praiseworthy.

आ â is used when something is recollected: आ एवं किल तत् â evam kila tat, Ah, so indeed it was!

आः âh, excl. of joy, pain, or indignation : आः शीतम् âh sîtam, Oh, how cold it is !

दिष्ट्या dishtyâ (instr. of दिष्टि dishti, good luck), happily, thank heaven ! दिष्ट्या प्रतिहतं दुर्ग्रातम् dishtyâ pratihatam durgâtam, thank heaven, the evil is averted ; with वृध् vridh, to increase = a person (nom.) is to be congratulated upon (instr. of thing): दिष्ट्या महाराजो विजयेन वर्धते dishtyâ mahârâgo vigayena vardhate, your Majesty is to be congratulated upon your victory.

धिक् dhik, excl. of dissatisfaction or reproach, with acc.: धिक्त्वामस्तु dhik tvâm astu, shame on you !

वत vata, 1. sorrow: alas, woe; 2. joy or surprise: oh ! 3. a simple voc. particle: एहि वत सखे ehi vata sakhe, ho ! friend, come.

साधु sâdhú, well ! bravo !

स्वस्ति svastí, hail ! adieu !

हंत hánta, excl. of joy or sorrow: Oh, alas ! हंत धिङ् मामधन्यम् hanta dhiṅ mâm adhanyam, alas, fie upon me, a wretch !

हा hâ, हाहा hâ hâ, expresses grief (alas ! woe !) or astonishment, and is sometimes used with an accusative.

CHAPTER VI.

COMPOUND WORDS.

212 (510). The power of forming two or more words into one, which belongs to all Âryan languages, has been so largely developed in Sanskrit and enters to so considerable an extent into its syntax, that the general rules of composition claim a place even in an elementary grammar. All words making up a compound, except the last, appear in that form which is called their base, and when they have more than one, their middle base (84). Hence देवदासः deva-dâsah, a servant of a god, or of the gods.

213 (512). Compounds are most conveniently divided into

Determinative, Copulative, and **Possessive.** The first are called determinative compounds, because in them the first word determines (limits) the meaning of the last. There are two kinds of Determinatives: **Dependent** and **Descriptive.**

214 (513). I. a. A **Dependent** determinative (by native grammarians called **Tatpurusha**) is a compound in which the first word depends on the last. The relation of the former to the latter, if the compound were resolved, would be expressed by an oblique case, e. g. तत्पुरुष: tat-purusha*h*, the man of him, his man. The last word may be a substantive or a participle, or an adjective if capable of governing a noun.

Dependent compounds in which the first noun would be in the—

1. **Acc.:** वर्षभोग्य varsha-bhogya, m. f. n. to be enjoyed a year long; ग्रामप्राप्त grâma-prâpta, m. f. n. having reached the village. The latter kind of compound, however, generally has the past participle at the beginning (प्राप्तग्राम prâpta-grâma), in which case it is a possessive compound (lit. having a reached village; cp. 218).

2. **Instr.:** धान्यार्थ: dhânya arthah, m. wealth (artha*h*) (acquired) by grain (dhânyena); देवदत्त: deva-dattah, given by the gods, commonly used as a proper name with an auspicious sense (Dieudonné).

3. **Dat.:** यूपदारु yûpa-dâru, n. wood for a sacrificial stake.

4. **Abl.:** स्वर्गपतित svarga-patita, m. f. n. fallen from heaven.

5. **Gen.:** राजपुरुष: râga-purusha*h*, m. the king's man.

6. **Loc.:** उरोज uro-ga, m. f. n. produced on the breast.

Note 1. A few dependent compounds retain the case-terminations in the governed noun: धनंजय dhanam-gaya, m. gaining spoil, proper name (Arguna); परस्मैपदम् parasmai-padam, a word for the sake of another, i. e. the transitive form of verbs; वाचस्पति: vâkas-pati*h*, lord of speech; युधिष्ठिर: yudhi-sh*th*irah, firm in battle, proper name.

Note 2. If the last part of a dependent compound is a verbal base, no change takes place, except that diphthongs, as usual, are changed to आ â, and bases ending in short vowels take a final त् t : विश्वजित् visva-*gít*, all-conquering, from जि *gi*, to conquer.

215 (517). I. b. **Descriptive** determinative compounds (by native grammarians called **Karmadhâraya**) are those in which the first word, either a noun (in apposition), or an adjective, or an adverb (particle), describes the second.

1. Nominally descriptive (appositional): राजर्षि râga_*ṛi*shi, king-sage = royal sage.

When the apposition implies a comparison, it is put at the end instead of the beginning : पुरुषव्याघ्रः purusha-vyâghra*h*, a tiger-like man.

2. Adjectively : नीलोत्पलम् nîla_utpalam, blue lotus.

Those compounds in which the adjective is a **numeral,** form with the native grammarians a special class called **Dvigu.** They are generally neuters or feminines expressing aggregates, but may also form adjectives by becoming possessive compounds (218). If an aggregate compound is formed, final अ a, अन् an, or आ â is changed to ई î, fem., or अम् am, neut.: त्रिलोकी tri-lokî, the three worlds ; त्रिभुवनम् tri-bhuvanam, the three worlds ; दशकुमारी da-*sa*-kumârî, an assemblage of ten youths.

गो go, cow, and नौ nau, ship, are changed to गव gava and नाव nâva : पंचगवम् pa*ñk*a-gavam, an aggregate of five cows, but पंचगुः pa*ñk*a-gu*h*, adj., worth five cows.

रात्रि râtri, f. night, always becomes रात्र râtra, m. (n.), e. g. द्वि-रात्रः dvi-râtra*h*, two nights.

3. Adverbially (including particles and prepositions): सुकृत su-k*ṛi*ta, well done; अज्ञात a-*gñ*âta, unknown; अधिस्त्री adhi-strî, chief woman. Some compounds of this kind are used adverbially in the accusative neuter, forming a special class, called **Avyayî-bhâva,** with the native grammarians : निर्मक्षिकम् nir-makshikam,

flylessly; अनुरूपम् ánu-rûpam, after the form, i. e. accordingly; यथाशक्ति yathâ-sakti, according to one's ability; सविनयम् sa-vina-yam, politely.

Note—At the beginning of a descriptive compound महत् mahat, great, becomes महा mahâ: महाराज: mahâ-râ*g*á*h*; while at the end, राजन् râ*g*an, king, अहन् áhan, n. day, सखि sákhi, friend, become राज râ*g*a, अह aha, m. (n.) (sometimes अह्न ahna, m.), सख sakha: परमाह: parama ahah, m. the highest day; प्रियसख: priya-sakha*h*, m. a dear friend.

II. Copulative (Dvandva) Compounds.

216. The parts of these compounds are connected in sense by 'and.' The terminations are dual or plural, according to the sense, or else singular neuter: हस्त्यश्वौ hasty-asvau, an elephant and a horse; हस्त्यश्वा: hasty-asvâ*h*, elephants and horses; हस्त्यश्वम् hasty-asvam, the elephants and horses (in an army, collectively).

217. a. Adjectives are sometimes compounded into Dvandvas: शुक्लकृष्णौ sukla-k*rish*nau, white and black.

b. Words ending in ऋ ri, expressive of relationship or sacred titles, forming the first member of a compound and being followed by another word ending in ऋ ri or by पुत्र putrá, son, change their ऋ ri to आ â: मातापितरौ mâtâ-pitárau, mother and father; पितापुत्रौ pitâ-putrau, father and son; होतापोतारौ hotâ-potârau, the Hotri and Potri priests.

c. When the names of certain deities are compounded, the first sometimes lengthens its final vowel: मित्रावरुणौ mitrâ-várunau, Mitra and Varuna; अग्नीषोमौ agnî-shómau, Agni and Soma.

III. Possessive (Bahuvrîhi) Compounds.

218. These are always predicates referring to a subject expressed or understood, and are in fact determinatives ending in

nouns (which, as a rule, undergo no further change than that of
accent and of being inflected in the three genders) used as adjectives. Thus नीलोत्पलम् nîlotpalam, a blue lotus, becomes a
possessive adjective in नीलोत्पलं सरः nîlotpala*m* sárah, a lake
possessed of blue lotuses. The accent is, as a rule, that of the
first member of the compound. Possessives often come to be
used as appellatives or proper names: सुहृत् su-hr*i*t, m. f. n. having
a good heart, becomes masc., a friend; वीरसेन vîra-sena, m. f. n.
having an army (sénâ) of heroes (vîrá), becomes Vîrasena, m.
(proper name).

Note—Possessives may contain other compounds: राजपुरुष-
कार्य râ*g*a-purusha-kârya, having the business of (a king's man);
नीलोत्पलसरस्तीरः nîla_utpala-saras-tîra*h*, possessing {the bank
of a [(blue-lotus) lake]}: in the latter case, the whole compound,
before becoming an adjective, was a genitive dependent; nîlotpala-
sara*h* is a dependent, nîlotpala a descriptive compound. In
नीलोज्ज्वलवपुः nîla_u*gg*vala-vapu*h*, having a blue and resplendent
body, the first two words form a copulative, the whole a descriptive, which finally becomes a possessive compound.

219. a. Words meaning 'hand' are placed at the end of possessive compounds: शस्त्रपाणि *s*astra-pâni, having a weapon in one's
hand; तृणहस्त tr*i*na-hasta, having grass in one's hand.

b. अक्षि ákshi, eye, गंध gandhá, smell, धनुः dhánu*h*, bow, and
पाद pâda, foot, at the end of possessives become in most cases अक्ष
aksha, गंधि gandhi, धन्वन् dhanvan, पाद् pâd.

c. At the end of possessives :—

a. आदि âdi, beginning, आद्य âdya, first, प्रभृति prábhr*i*ti, beginning, = et cetera: देवा इंद्रादयः devâ indra_âdaya*h*, the gods Indra
and the rest, lit. the gods having Indra as first. The qualified
noun is often omitted: इंद्रादयः indrâdaya*h*, Indra and the rest.

β. मात्र mâtra, n. measure = only, merely: जलमात्रम् *g*ala-mâtram,
water alone, lit. that which has water for its measure, limit.

γ. संतर antara, n. difference = different, another: देशांतरम् de-sa antaram, another country, lit. that which has a difference of country.

δ. अर्थ artha, aim, object, = for the sake of (commonly acc., dat., or loc. sing.): दमयंत्यर्थम् damayanty-artham, for the sake of Dama-yantî, lit. that which has Damayantî for an object.

d. क ka is added to words in ऋ ri, to feminines in ई î (like नदी nadî), and in the fem. to words in इन् in : बहुभर्तृक bahu-bhartrika, having many husbands; बहुकुमारीक bahu-kumârîka; बहुखामिका bahu-svâmikâ, having many masters (खामिन् svâmín). Most other words optionally add क ka.

CHAPTER VII.

OUTLINES OF SYNTAX.

220. Owing to the great bulk of the literature consisting of poetry, Sanskrit style is naturally in a crude state as compared with that of Latin or Greek. Its chief characteristics are the pre-dominance of co-ordination, the use of the locative absolute, a fondness for long compounds and indeclinable participles supply-ing the place of subordinate clauses, the frequent employment of the past participle instead of the finite verb, a predilection for passive forms, and the absence of the indirect construction and of the subjunctive mood. For the latter reason the use of the tenses and moods is comparatively simple ; on the other hand, the use of the cases, being much less definite than in Latin and Greek, presents some difficulties.

The Order of Words.

221. The usual arrangement of words in a Sanskrit sentence is: first, the subject with its adjuncts (the genitive preceding its nomi-native); second, the object with its adjuncts ; and lastly, the pre-

dicate. Adverbs or extensions of the predicate are usually placed near the beginning, after the subject or object, not at the end; e. g. जनकः सत्वरं खीयं नगरं जगाम *ganaka*h *satvaram svîyam nagaram gag*âma, Ganaka went in haste to his city.

222. Just as the determining word comes first in compounds, so a relative and subordinate clause precedes the principal, which regularly begins with a correlative word; e. g. यस्य धनं तस्य बलम् yasya dhana*m* tasya balam, lit. of whom there is wealth, of him there is power, i. e. he who has wealth has power. Similarly: यदा yâdâ—तदा tâdâ, यावत् yâvat—तावत् tâvat, etc.

The Article.

223. There is properly neither an indefinite nor a definite article in Sanskrit; but एक éka, one, and कश्चित् ká*skit*, some one, are frequently used = a certain, and स sá, सा sấ, तद् tád (ó, ή, τό), he, she, it or that, sometimes = the; e. g. स राजा sá rấg*â*, the king; generally, that king.

Number.

224. a. Singular collective words are sometimes used at the end of compounds to form a plural; e. g. सखीजनः sakhî-*gana*h, female friends; जन *g*ana = kind in mankind (men).

b. The dual number is in regular use. It is invariably employed with the names of things occurring in pairs, such as parts of the body; e. g. हस्तौ पादौ च hástau pâdau *k*a, the hands and the feet. A masc. dual is sometimes used to express a male and a female of the same class; e. g. जगतः पितरौ *g*ágata*h* pitárau, the parents of the universe (पितृ pit*rí*, father).

c. The plural sometimes marks respect; e. g. इति श्रीशंकराचार्याः iti srîsankara *âkâryâh*, thus says the revered Sankarâ*k*ârya.

The 1st pers. pl. is sometimes used simply instead of the sing.:

वयमपि भवत्यौ किमपि पृच्छामः vayam api bhavatyau kimapi prikkhâmah, we (=I) too ask you something.

Names of countries (which are really the names of the people) are plural: विदेहेषु videhéshu, in Videha; मगधेषु magádheshu, in Magadha.

Compounds ending in words meaning country, such as देश desá, विषय vishaya, etc., are of course singular.

Concord.

225. The rules of concord between verbs, adjectives, relatives and their substantive are the same as in other inflectional languages; but the following points may be noted:—

a. The verb is in the sing. after sing. collective nouns, and in the dual after two sing. nouns connected by च ka, and: त्वमहं च गच्छावः tvam aham ka gakkhâvah, you and I go.

b. When a dual or plur. verb refers to two or more subjects, the first person is preferred to the second or third, and the second to the third.

c. A dual or plur. adjective agreeing with masc. and fem. nouns is put in the masc., but in the **neuter** when agreeing with a masc. and a neut., or a fem. and a neut.

d. A verb or adjective often agrees with the nearest noun.

Pronouns.

226. A. Personal Pronouns. These, unless emphatic, are not used as subjects of verbs, being inherent in finite verbal forms.

The unaccented forms of अहम् ahám and त्वम् tvám (cp. 121), viz. मा mâ, मे me; त्वा tvâ, ते te; वाम् vâm, वः vah, are used neither at the beginning of a sentence or pâda (cp. Appendix II), nor before the particles च ka, वा vâ, एव evá, and ह ha, nor after vocatives; e. g. मम मित्रम् mama (not मे me) mitram, my friend; तस्य मम वा गृहम् tasya mama vâ griham, his house or mine; देवास्मान् पाहि deva asmân (not नः nah) pâhi, O God, protect us.

भवत् bhávat, Your Honour, the polite form of त्वम् tvám, takes
the verb in the 3rd pers.: किमाह भवान् kim âha bhavân, what
does your Honour say? आगच्छंतु भवंत: âga*kkh*antu bhavanta*h*,
may you come.

B. Demonstrative Pronouns: इदम् idám or एतद् etád, this; तद्
tád, that; अद: adá*h*, this or that.

इदम् idám and एतद् etád, agreeing with a subject in the 1st or
3rd pers., often = here: अयमस्मि ayam asmi, here I am; अयमा-
गतस्तव पुच्र: ayam âgatas tava putra*h*, here comes your son.

तद् tád (like Lat. ille) often = well-known, celebrated : सा रम्या
नगरी sâ ramyâ nagarî, that well-known charming city.

तद् tád with एव evá = the very, the same: तदेव नाम tad eva
nâma, the name is the same.

तद् tád, when repeated, means various, several: तानि तानि शा-
स्त्राण्यध्यैत tâni tâni sâstrâni adhyaita, he read several sâstras.

THE CASES.
Nominative.

227. The nominative is far less frequently used in Sanskrit as
the subject of a sentence than in English. Its place is very commonly supplied by the instrumental of the agent with a passive
verb ; e. g. तेनोक्तम् tena uktam, he said, lit. it was said by him.

The nom. is used after verbs meaning to be, to become, appear,
seem ; also after the passive of verbs of making, calling, considering, sending, appointing, etc.; e. g. तेन मुनिना कुक्कुरो व्याघ्र: कृत:
tena muninâ kukkuro vyâghra*h* k*ri*ta*h*, the dog was turned into
a tiger by the sage.

Note—The nom. with the particle इति iti may be used instead
of the acc. after the *active* of verbs of calling, considering, etc.;
e. g. इमं वयस्य इति मन्ये imam vayasya iti manye, I consider this
person my friend.

Accusative.

228. The accusative, besides expressing the object of most transitive verbs, is employed—

1. With verbs of motion; e. g. **स ग्राममगच्छत्** sa grâmam aga*kkh*at, he went to a village.

Note—Verbs of going, like **गम्** gam and **या** yâ, are very commonly joined with an abstract noun, where we should use either the corresponding adjective with 'to become,' or merely an intransitive verb: **स कीर्तिं याति** sa kîrti*m* yâti, he becomes famous; **पंचत्वं गच्छति** pañ*k*atva*m* ga*kkh*ati, he dies, lit. goes to death.

2. To express duration of time and distance in space: **मासमधीते** mâsam adhîte, he learns for a month; **क्रोशं गच्छति** krosa*m* ga*kkh*ati, he goes (the distance of) a kos.

Double Accusative.

229. 1. Verbs of calling, making, appointing, choosing, considering, knowing, take two accusatives: **जानामि त्वां प्रकृतिपुरुषम्** *g*ânâmi tvâ*m* prakr*i*ti-purusham, I know thee (to be) the chief person.

2. Verbs of asking (**प्रछ्** pra*kh*), begging (**याच्** yâ*k*), telling (**ब्रू** brû, **वच्** va*k*), and instructing (**शास्** sâs) govern two accusatives; e. g. **बलिं याचते वसुधाम्** bali*m* yâ*k*ate vasudhâm, he asks Bali for the earth.

Note—In the passive construction the nom. takes the place of the direct acc., while the indirect acc. remains: **बलिर्याच्यते वसुधाम्** balir yâ*k*yate vasudhâm, Bali is asked for the earth.

3. Causative verbs usually govern two accusatives; but sometimes the instrumental is employed instead of the direct accusative (the agent): **रामं वेदमध्यापयति** râma*m* vedam adhyâpayati, he causes Râma to learn the Veda; but **भृत्येन भारं नाययति** bhr*i*tyena bhâra*m* nâyayati, he causes the servant to carry the load (= he causes the load to be carried by the servant).

Note—In the passive construction, the nom. takes the place of the direct acc. (the agent): रामो वेदमध्याप्यते râmo vedam adhyâpyate, Râma is taught the Veda.

Instrumental.

230. The instrumental case primarily expresses either the **agent** or the **instrument** (means) by which an action is performed: तेनोक्तम् tena uktam, it was said by him = he said; स खड्गेन व्यापादित: sa khadgena vyâpâditah, he was killed with a sword.

I. From the above are developed the following secondary senses:—

1. **Accompaniment,** with सह sahá, साकम् sâkám, सार्धम् sârdhám, समम् samám; e. g. पुत्रेण सह पिता गत: putrena saha pitâ gatah, the father went with his son; or its opposite, **separation,** with or without the above words; e. g. पित्रा वियोगं न सहते pitrâ viyogam na sahate, he cannot endure separation from his father.

2. **Cause, reason, motive:** on account of, through, etc.: भवतोऽनुग्रहेण bhavato-nugrahena, through your favour; तेनापराधेन त्वां दंडयामि tena aparâdhena tvâm dandayâmi, I punish you for that fault.

Note—The instr. of बुद्धि buddhi, thought, and भ्रांति bhrânti, error, is used = 'under the impression' and 'under the erroneous impression;' e. g. व्याघ्रबुद्ध्या vyâghra-buddhyâ, thinking that it was a tiger.

3. **Manner:** तौ दंपती महता स्नेहेन वसत: tau dampatî mahatâ snehena vasatah, that pair lives in great affection; महता सुखेन mahatâ sukhena, with great pleasure.

4. **Accordance:** स मम मतेन वर्तते sa mama matena vartate, he acts according to my opinion. So also प्रकृत्या prakrityâ, by nature; जात्या gâtyâ, by birth.

5. **Price:** आत्मानं सततं रक्षेद्दारैरपि धनैरपि âtmânam satatam rakshed dârair api dhanair api, a man should always protect himself even at the cost of his wife and of his wealth.

6. **Time** or space **within which** anything is done : द्वाद-
शैर्वर्षैर्व्याकरणं श्रूयते dvâdaśair varshair vyâkaraṇam srûyate, grammar is learnt in twelve years.

II. The instrumental is also used—

A. With **adjectives** expressing—

a. **Likeness** or **equality**: तस्य जीवितेन समा पत्नी tasya
ǵivitena samâ patnî, his wife is as dear to him as life.

b. **Possession,** or the opposite, freedom from, **destitution:**
धनेन संपन्नो विहीनो वा dhanena sampanno vihîno vâ, possessed
or destitute of wealth.

B. With **verbs** of—

a. Excelling or comparing : पूर्वान् महाभाग तयातिशेषे pûrvân
mahâ-bhâga tayâ atiśeshe, O fortunate man, you excel your ances-
tors in that (devotion).

b. Boasting or swearing : भरतेनात्मना चाहं शपे bharatena âtma-
nâ ǩa aham śape, I swear by Bharata and myself.

c. Rejoicing, being pleased, satisfied, astonished, ashamed, dis-
gusted : कापुरुषः स्वल्पेनापि तुष्यति kâ-purushah sv-alpena api tush-
yati, a low person is satisfied even with little.

d. Motion, to express the means, or the part of the body, by
which the motion is effected : वाजिना चरति vâǵinâ ǩarati, he goes
on horseback ; स श्वानं स्कंधेनोवाह sa śvânam skandhena uvâha, he
carried the dog on his shoulder.

III. Some miscellaneous uses of the instr. are the following :—

1. With words expressing a defect of body : अक्ष्णा काणः akshnâ
kânah, blind of an eye.

2. With words expressing **need** or **use,** like अर्थः arthah, प्रयो-
जनम् prayoǵanam, कृ kri, to do, with किम् kim, what : देवपादानां
सेवकैर्न प्रयोजनम् deva-pâdânâm sevakair na prayoǵanam, Your
Majesty's feet have no need of servants ; किं तया क्रियते धेन्वा kim
tayâ kriyate dhenvâ, what is to be done with that cow ?

3. With अलम् álam and कृतम् kritám, enough : कृतमभ्युत्थानेन
kritam abhyutthânena, pray do not rise; अलं शंकया alam saṅ-
kayâ, away with doubt. अलम् álam in the same sense is often used
with the gerund (which is an old instrumental), when it has the
force of a negative imperative: अलमन्यथा गृहीत्वा alam anyathâ
grihîtvâ, enough of misunderstanding = do not misunderstand.

Dative.

231. The dative case expresses either the **indirect object** of
an action, generally a person, or, predicatively, the **purpose**
of an action.

A. The dative of the indirect object is used—

1. After **transitive** verbs, with or without a direct object :—

a. Of **giving** (दा dâ, अर्पय arpaya), **owing** (धृ dhri), **pro-
mising** (प्रति° prati- or आश्रू â-sru), **telling** (कथ kath, ख्या khyâ,
चक्ष् kaksh, शंस् sams; निवेदय ni-vedaya).

Ex. विप्राय गां ददाति viprâya gâm dadâti, he gives a cow to the
Brahman; कथयामि ते भूतार्थम् kathayâmi te bhûta_artham, I tell
you the truth.

Note—यज् yag, to sacrifice, takes acc. of person and instr. of
thing: पशुना रुद्रं यजते pasunâ rudram yagate, he sacrifices a
bull to Rudra.

b. Of **sending** or **despatching** : भोगेन दूतो रघवे विसृष्ट:
bhogena dûto raghave visrishtah, a messenger was sent by Bhoga
to Raghu.

2. After **intransitive** verbs meaning to **please** (रुच् ruk), to
desire (स्पृह sprih), to **be angry with** (क्रुध् krudh), to **hate**
(द्रुह druh), to **envy** (ईर्ष्य îrshy).

Ex. किंकराय कुप्यति kimkarâya kupyati, he is angry with his servant; पुष्पेभ्य: स्पृहयति pushpebhyah sprihayati, he desires flowers.

Note—क्रुध् krudh and द्रुह druh, if preceded by prepositions,
govern the accusative.

3. With words of salutation: गणेशाय नमः ganesâya namah, salutation to Ganesa; रामाय स्वस्ति râmâya svasti, hail to Râma! also with अलम् álam = to be a match for, sufficient for: दैत्येभ्यो हरिरलम् daityebhyo harir alam, Hari is a match for the demons.

Note—प्रणम् pra-nam, to bow, takes either dat. or acc.

B. The dative of purpose is used to express either—

1. The **end for which an action is done**: मुक्तये हरिं भजति muktaye harim bhagati, he worships Hari for (= to obtain) absolution; or—

2. The **end to which an action tends,** with कृप् klip or संपद् sam-pad, to tend to, or with स्था sthâ, अस् as, भू bhû (the latter two being often omitted).

Ex. भक्तिर्ज्ञानाय कल्पते bhaktir gñânâya kalpate, piety tends to knowledge; मृताजातौ सुतौ स्वल्पदुःखाय mrita agâtau sutau svalpa-duhkhâya (sc. स्तः stah or भवतः bhavatah), a son that is dead and one that is unborn cause very little pain.

Note—A dat. is often used instead of an infinitive of purpose.

a. Instead of an infin. governing an acc.: फलेभ्यो याति phalebhyo yâti, he goes for fruit, = फलान्याहर्तुं याति phalâny âhartum yâti, he goes to get fruit.

b. The dat. of an abstract noun for the infin. from the same root: यागाय याति yâgâya yâti, he goes for sacrificing, = यष्टुं याति yashtum yâti, he goes to sacrifice.

Ablative.

232. The ablative primarily expresses the **source from which** anything proceeds; e.g. पापान्नाश उद्भवति pâpân nâsa ud-bhavati, from sin ruin results.

With this original meaning are connected the following uses:—

a. **On account of, by reason of, through**: लौभ्याद् मांसं भक्षयति laubhyâd mâmsam bhakshayati, he eats the flesh through greediness.

Note—The ablative is commonly used in this sense with abstract nouns in त्व tva, especially in commentaries: पर्वतोऽग्निमान् धूम-त्वात् parvato ≈ gnimân dhûmatvât, the mountain has fire in it, because of there being smoke.

b. With **verbs** of **fearing** and **protecting**: स्तेनाद् बिभेति stenâd bibheti, he fears the thief; पाहि मां नरकात् pâhi mâm narakât, protect me from hell.

c. With words meaning **different from** (अन्य anyá, पर pára, इतर ítara): कृष्णादन्यो गोविंद: krishnâd anyo govindah, Krishna is different from Govinda.

d. With **comparatives** or words having a comparative sense: गोविंदाद् रामो विड्वत्तर: govindâd râmo vidvattarah, Râma is more learned than Govinda; कर्मणो ज्ञानमतिरिच्यते karmano gñânam atirikyate, knowledge is superior to action.

e. With words denoting points of the compass: ग्रामात्पूर्वो गिरि: grâmât pûrvo girih, the móuntain is to the east of the village.

f. **Time within** or **after** which anything is done: सप्ताहात् sapta ahât, within seven days; बहोर्दृष्टं कालात् bahor drishtam kâlât, seen after a long time.

Genitive.

233. The primary meaning of the gen. is quasi-adjectival; the qualification of another noun which it denotes being generally expressed in English by the prep. 'of:' जगतो निर्माता gagato nirmâtâ, the Creator of the Universe.

Besides this use, the gen. is employed in various other ways :—

I. With **verbs** :—

a. To **be master of** (प्रभू pra-bhû), to **rule** (ईश् îs), to **grant, give** (दय् day), to **remember** (स्मृ smri): आत्मन: प्रभविष्यामि âtmanah prabhavishyâmi, I shall be master of myself.

b. It expresses **possession** with verbs meaning 'to be' (अस् as, भू bhû, विद् vid): मम पुस्तकं विद्यते mama pustakam vidyate, I have a book.

II. With **adjectives** :—

a. **Dear to, favourite with** : को नाम राज्ञां प्रिय: ko nâma râgñâm priya*h*, who, pray, is dear to kings?

b. **Equality** (तुल्य tulya, सदृश sadr*i*sa, सम samá): राम: कृष्णस्य तुल्य: râma*h* kr*i*shnasya tulya*h*, Râma is equal to K*r*ish*n*a.

Note 1. The **instr.** is also used with words denoting equality.

Note 2. With words expressing 'difference,' two genitives are used in the sense of 'between—and:' एतावानेवायुष्मत: शतक्रतोश्च विशेष: etâvân eva âyushmata*h* satakrato*s* *k*a viseha*h*, this is the only difference between you (the long-lived) and Indra.

III. With **passive participles** :—

a. Past participles, with a pres. sense, of roots meaning 'to think,' 'to know,' 'to worship,' take the agent in the gen.: स राज्ञां पूजित: sa râgñâm pû*g*ita*h*, he is reverenced by kings.

b. Future participles take the agent in the gen. as well as the instr.: मम (मया) सेव्यो हरि: mama (mayâ) sevyo hari*h*, Hari should be worshipped by me.

IV. With **adverbs** :—

a. Meaning **far** (दूरम् dûrám) or **near** (अंतिकम् antikám): दूरं ग्रामस्य dûra*m* grâmasya, far from the village.

Note—The **ablative** is also used with these words.

b. Adverbs in त: ta*h*, expressive of direction, and others of similar meaning (see 209): ग्रामस्य दक्षिणत: grâmasya dakshi*n*ata*h*, to the south of the village.

Note—Adverbs of direction in °एन -ena take the **acc.** as well as the **gen.**: ग्रामस्य (ग्रामं) दक्षिणेन grâmasya (grâma*m*) dakshi*n*ena.

c. The gen. of **time** is used with multiplicatives (see 120): मासस्याष्टकृत्व: mâsasya ashtakr*i*tva*h*, eight times a month.

Locative.

234. The locative denotes the **place where** an action takes place: पक्षिणस्तस्मिन् वृक्षे निवसंति pakshina*s* tasmin vr*i*kshe nivasanti, birds live in that tree.

I. It expresses the following collateral meanings :—

a. The recipient: विवरति गुरु: प्राज्ञे विद्याम् vitarati guru*h* pr*â*g*ñe* vidy*â*m, a teacher imparts knowledge to an intelligent pupil.

b. 'Towards:' प्राणिषु दयां कुर्वंति साधव: pr*â*nishu day*â*m kurvanti s*â*dhava*h*, the good show compassion towards animate beings.

c. The effect of a cause: दैवमेव हि नृणां वृद्धौ क्षये कारणम् daivam eva hi nri*n*âm vriddhau kshaye k*â*ra*n*am, Fate is the cause of the decline or prosperity of men.

d. **By reason of, with regard to :** छिद्रेषु शत्रुं हंति *k*hidreshu *s*atru*m* hanti, he slays the enemy by reason of his weak points.

e. **Amongst, of,** with superlatives: सर्वेषु पुत्रेषु रामो मम प्रियतम: sarveshu putreshu r*â*mo mama priyatama*h*, of all the sons R*â*ma is dearest to me.

Note—The **genitive** is also used in this sense.

f. **After,** of time (like abl.): अस्मिन् दिने भुक्त्वाऽयं त्र्यहे (त्र्यहात्) भोक्ता asmin dine bhuktv*â* aya*m* tryahe (tryah*â*d) bhokt*â*, having dined to-day he will dine again after (the interval of) three days.

II. The loc. is also used with—

a. Words meaning **engaged in, intent on** (आसक्त *â*sakta, तत्पर tatpara), or **skilful** (कुशल k*ú*sala, निपुण nipu*n*a, पंडित pa*n*dit*â*): रामोऽक्षद्यूते निपुण: r*â*mo·ksha-dy*û*te nipu*n*a*h*, R*â*ma is skilful in playing at dice.

b. Words meaning **attachment to** (अनुस्निह् anu-snih, अनुरंज् anu-ra*ñ*g, अभिलष् abhi-lash), **confidence in** (विश्वस् vi-*s*vas), **fitness for** (युज् yu*g*): न खलु शकुंतलायां ममाभिलाष: na khalu *s*akuntal*â*y*â*m mama abhil*â*sha*h*, my love is indeed not towards Sakuntal*â*; न मे त्वयि विश्वास: na me tvayi vi*s*v*â*sa*h*, I have no faith in you; त्रैलोक्यस्यापि प्रभुत्वं तस्मिन् युज्यते trailokyasya api prabhutvam tasmin yu*g*yate, even the sovereignty of the three worlds is fitting for him.

c. With verbs of **throwing** (अस् as, क्षिप् kship, मुच् muk): शरौ
बाणान् क्षिपति arau bânân kshipati, he darts arrows at his enemy.

d. With verbs of **taking** (कृ kri, दा dâ), **seizing** (ग्रह् grah),
or **striking**: संजीवकं सव्ये पाणौ कृत्वा (गृहीत्वा) saṅgîvakaṃ savye
pâṇau kritvâ (grihîtvâ), taking Saṅgîvaka by the left hand; केशेषु
गृहीत्वा keseshu grihîtvâ, seizing by the hair.

Note—कृ kri, दा dâ, and ग्रह् grah may take the instr. also.

Locative and Genitive Absolute.

235. The loc. and gen. absolute are used in much the same way
as the English nom., the Greek gen., and the Latin abl. absolute.

The loc. is the usual absolute case, the gen. being comparatively
seldom used in this sense.

Ex. गच्छत्सु दिनेषु gakkhatsu dineshu, as the days went by; गोषु
दुग्धासु स गतः goshu dugdhâsu sa gataḥ, the cows having been
milked, he departed; अद्य दशमो मासस्तातस्योपरतस्य adya dasamo
mâsas tâtasya upa-ratasya, to-day is the tenth month since my
father died.

Note 1. The pres. part. of अस् as, to be, may be used in agreement with other absolute participles: तथा कृते सति tathâ krite
sati, this being done.

Note 2. An indeclinable word (एवम् evám, इत्थम् itthám, तथा
táthâ, इति íti) is sometimes used in agreement with the absolute
participle: एवं गते evaṃ gate, this being the case (lit. it having
gone thus).

Note 3. The particle एव evá and मात्र mâtra (at the end of a
compound) may be used after an absolute part. to express 'no
sooner—than,' 'scarcely—when:' अप्रभातायामेव रजन्याम् aprabhâ-
tâyâm eva raganyâm, scarcely had it dawned when —; प्रविष्टमात्र
एव तत्रभवति pravishta-mâtra eva tatrabhavati, no sooner had his
honour entered than —.

Time and Distance.

236. a. The **acc.** is used to express **duration** of time and distance in space (228, 2).

b. The **instr.** expresses the time or space **within** which anything is done (230, I, 6).

c. The **abl.** expresses time **within** or **after** which anything is done (232, f).

d. The **gen.** expresses the time **in** which an action is **repeated**: द्विरह्नः dvir ahna*h*, twice a day (233, IV. c).

e. The **loc.** expresses the time (1) **at** which: अस्मिन् दिने asmin dine, on this day; (2) **after** which, like abl. (234, I. f).

Participles.

237. The **present** participle is used with आस् âs, to sit, and स्था sthâ, to stand, to express continuous action: भक्षयन्नास्ते bhakshayann âste, he keeps eating; इति विचारयन् स्थितः iti vi*k*ârayan sthita*h*, he stood thus thinking.

Past Participles.

238. The passive participle and its active form in वत् vat (but **not** the perf. part. in वस् **vas**) are very frequently used for a finite past tense; e.g. तेनेदमुक्तम् tena idam uktam, this was said by him; स इदमुक्तवान् sa idam uktavân, he said this.

In the same way the passive of intransitive verbs is used impersonally: मयात्र चिरं स्थितम् mayâ atra *k*ira*m* sthitam, I stood there for a long time.

The perf. pass. part. of intransitive verbs is used in the active sense: स गंगां गतः sa gangâ*m* gata*h*, he went to the Ganges; स पथि मृतः sa pathi m*ri*ta*h*, he died on the way.

Future Passive Participles.

239. These participles in तव्य tavya, अनीय anîya, य ya (also called verbal adjectives) express **necessity, obligation,** or **fit-**

ness. The construction is the same as in the case of the past pass. part.: मया तत्र गंतव्यम् mayâ tatra gantavyam, I must go there.

a. Sometimes this part. expresses certainty of the future: ततस्तेनापि शब्द: कर्त्तव्य: tatas tena̱ api sabdaẖ kartavyaẖ, then he also will surely make a noise.

b. Sometimes it is used for the future simply: युवयो: पक्षबलेन मयापि सुखेन गंतव्यम् yuvayoẖ paksha-balena mayâ̱ api sukhena gantavyam, I too shall go at ease by the strength of your wings.

c. भवितव्यम् bhavitâvyam and भाव्यम् bhâvyam from भू bhû, to be, are used impersonally to express necessity or high probability. The adjective or noun of the **predicate** agrees with the subject in the **instr.**: तया संनिहितया भवितव्यम् tayâ samnihitayâ bhavitavyam, she must be (= is most probably) near; असंमूढैर्भवितव्यं युष्माभि: asammûdhair bhavitavyam yushmâbhiẖ, you should be careful.

Indeclinable Participle (Gerund).

240. This participle, formed with त्वा tvâ, य ya, or त्य tya (see (187-8), expresses that an action is completed before another begins: तं प्रणम्य स गत: tam pra-namya sa gataẖ, having bowed down to him, he departed.

a. It may frequently be translated by 'in' or 'by' with the verbal noun: मां निर्धनं हत्वा किं लभेध्वम् mâm nirdhanam hatvâ kim labhedhvam, what would you gain by killing me who am destitute of wealth?

b. Some indeclinable participles are equivalent in meaning to prepositions: अधिकृत्य adhikrítya, about; आदाय âdâya, with; उद्दिश्य uddísya, towards; नीत्वा nîtvâ, with; मुक्त्वा muktvâ, except.

Infinitive.

241. The infinitive is chiefly employed to express a **purpose** (like the dat.), but is also used as the **object** of a few verbs. It

is **never** used as the **subject** of a sentence, abstract nouns
supplying its place in this case.

a. Infinitive of **purpose**: हिरण्यकश्चित्रग्रीवस्य पाशांश्छेत्तुं बहि-
रागच्छत् hiraṇyakas *k*itragrîvasya pâsâms *k*hettum bahir âga*kk*hat,
Hiraṇyaka came out to cut the bonds of *K*itragrîva ; अवसरोऽय-
मात्मानं प्रकाशयितुम् avasaro-yam âtmânam prakâsayitum, this is
the time to show yourself.

b. As the **object of verbs** meaning to be able, to be fit, to
know, to presume, to bear, to be pleased, to desire, to strive, to
begin: गंतुमिच्छामि gantum i*kk*hâmi, I wish to go ; कथयितुं शक्नोति
kathayitum saknoti, he is able to tell.

242. a. **Adjectives** meaning **fitness or ability,** and **nouns**
meaning **desire,** may also take an infin.: श्रोतुमिच्छा srotum i*kk*hâ,
a desire to hear ; लिखितमपि ललाटे प्रोज्झितुं कः समर्थः likhitam
api lalâte pra_ug*gh*itum ka*h* samarthah, who is able to avoid what is
stamped on his forehead (by fate)?

b. The 2nd and 3rd sing. ind. of अर्ह arh, to deserve, are used
imperatively = please, be pleased : भवान् मां श्रोतुमर्हति bhavân
mâm srotum arhati, will your Honour please to hear me?

c. The infin., after dropping the final म् m, is sometimes compounded with काम kâma or मनः mana*h* in the sense of having a
wish or a mind to do what the verb indicates : द्रष्टुकामः drash*tu*-
kâma*h*, desirous of seeing.

243. There being **no passive** form of the **infinitive** in Sanskrit, the verbs which govern the infin. are put in the passive in
order to give it a passive sense.

Ex. कर्तुं न युज्यते kartum na yu*g*yate, it is not fit to be done ;
न शक्यास्ते (दोषाः) समाधातुम् na sakyâs te (doshâ*h*) samâdhâtum,
those (mischiefs) cannot be repaired ; तेन मंडपः कारयितुमारब्धः
tena ma*nd*apa*h* kârayitum ârabdha*h*, a hut was begun to be erected
by him.

THE TENSES.

Present.

244. The use of this tense is much the same as in English. But the following differences should be noted:—

1. a. In narration the **historical** present is more commonly used than in English: हिरण्यको भोजनं कृत्वा बिले स्वपिति hiranyako bhoganam kritvâ bile svapiti, Hiranyaka, having taken his food, used to sleep in his hole; दमनको पृच्छति कथमेतत् damanako prikkhati katham etat, Damanaka asked, ' How was it?'

b. The present is sometimes used to express the **immediate past**: अयमागच्छामि ayam âgakkhâmi, I have just come.

Note—The particle स्म sma changes the present to a past tense: प्रतिवसति स्म prativasati sma, he dwelt.

2. The present is used for the **future**:—

a. With interrogatives and with पुरा purâ, soon, or यावत् yâvat, at once, used adverbially: तद्यावच्छत्रुघ्नं प्रेषयामि tad yâvak khatrughnam preshayâmi, therefore I will just send Satrughna; किं करोमि kim karomi, what shall I do?

b. Immediate future: तर्हि मुक्ता धनुर्गच्छामि tarhi muktvâ dhanur gakkhâmi, then leaving the bow, I am off.

c. With an exhortative sense: तर्हि गृहमेव प्रविशामः tarhi griham eva pravisâmah, then we will enter (= let us enter) the house.

Imperfect, Perfect, and Aorist.

245. These three tenses are generally found used promiscuously of past time, but their exact senses are as follow:—

a. The **imperfect** denotes a definite past, and does not refer to an action done during the current day except in questions: अगच्छत् किं स ग्रामम् agakkhat kim sa grâmam, has he gone to the village? The imperfect does not express continuous action.

b. The **perfect** is generally used in narrating events of the remote past; it never refers to events of the current day.

c. The **aorist** refers to past time generally, without reference to any particular time, and to actions of the current day. It is not a narrative tense, but is appropriate in dialogues. It is thus equivalent to the English perfect present[1]. It also expresses continuous action (like the imperfect in Latin): अदात् adât, he was giving; अददात् adadât, he gave.

Note—This tense acquires an imperative sense after the prohibitive particles मा mâ and मास्म mâsma, when it loses the augment: मा भैषी: mâ bhaishîh, do not fear (cp. 139).

Simple and Periphrastic Future.

246. The **simple** future is used of **any** future action; while the **periphrastic,** which is much less frequently employed, refers to **definite** or **remote** future time, but not to actions to take place in the course of the current day.

Imperative.

247. Special uses of the imperative are the following :—

a. With interrogatives it has the force of ' should:' किमधुना करवाम kim adhunâ karavâma, what should we do now?

b. The 1st and 3rd pers. are translated by ' let:' अहं गच्छानि aha*m* ga*kkh*âni, let me go.

c. The 2nd and 3rd pers. are sometimes used in an optative sense : पर्जन्य: कालवर्षी भवतु par*g*anya*h* kâla-varshî bhavatu, may rain pour down in season !

d. The 3rd sing. pass. is commonly used as a polite imperative instead of the 2nd pers. act.: आस्यताम् âsyatâm, please sit down.

Optative (Potential).

248. The Sanskrit optative is used in much the same senses as the Greek optative. It is commonly used to soften a statement,

---

[1] See Prof. Bhandarkar's Second Book of Sanskrit, Preface.

question, or command : **को नाम संभावयेत्** ko nâma sambhâvayet,
who would think ? **त्वमेवं कुर्याः** tvam evam kuryâ*h*, do thou act in
this manner. It often thus expresses mere futurity : **इयं कन्या
नात्र तिष्ठेत्** iyam kanyâ na atra tish*th*et, this girl will not stay here.

a. It very frequently expresses ' fitness ' in precepts : **आपदर्थं
धनं रक्षेत्** âpad-artham dhanam rakshet, one should save wealth
against calamity.

b. It is used in conditional sentences with **यदि** yádi and **चेत्** két,
in both protasis and apodosis : **यदि न स्यान्नरपतिर्विप्लवेतेह नौरिव
प्रजा** yadi na syân nara-patir viplaveta iha naur iva pra*g*â, if there
were not a king, the subjects would drift away like a boat.

Benedictive (Aorist Optative).

249. This rare mood is used to express blessings or, in the first
person, the speaker's wish : **वीरप्रसवा भूयाः** vîra-prasavâ bhûyâ*h*,
mayst thou give birth to a warrior ! **कृतार्थो भूयासम्** k*r*itârthâ bhû-
yâsam, may I become successful !

Conditional.

250. The conditional, as its form (an indicative past of the
future) well indicates, is properly used to express a past condition,
the falsity of which is implied, and is equivalent to the pluperfect
(conditional) subjunctive in Latin or English, or the aorist indicative, used conditionally, in Greek. It is employed in both protasis
and apodosis : **सुवृष्टिश्चेदभविष्यद्दुर्भिक्षं नाभविष्यत्** suv*r*ish*t*is *k*et abha-
vishyad durbhiksham na abhavishyat, if there had been plentiful
rain, there would have been no famine. The potential is employed
to express the imperfect conditional.

APPENDIX I.

LIST OF VERBS.

The order of the parts of the verb, when all are given, is : Pres., Impf., Impv., Opt.; Perf., Aor., Fut.; Pass. pres., aor., part.; Ger., Inf., Caus., aor., Desid., Intens.

The Roman numerals signify the conjugational class of the verb : P. indicates that the verb is conjugated in the Parasmai, A. that it is conjugated in the Âtmanepada.

अंच् *añk,* to go, to bend, to worship, I, P. अंचति ॥ अच्यते he is moved । संचित worshipped । अक्र bent । संचयति ॥

अंज् *añg,* to anoint, VII, P. अनक्ति । आनक् । अनक्तु । अंज्यात् ॥ आनंज । आंजीत् । अज्यते । अक्त । अंज्ञा or अक्त्वा, °अज्य । अंजयति ॥

अद् ad, to eat, II, P. अत्मि, अत्सि; अदंति । आदम्, आद:, आदत्; आदन् । अदानि, अड्डि, अत्तु; अदंतु । अद्यात् ॥ अत्स्यति । अद्यते । जग्ध (अन्न n. food) । जग्ध्वा, °जग्ध । अत्तुम् । आदयति । जिघत्सति ॥

अन् an, to breathe, II, P. अनिति । आनम्, आनी: or आन:, आनीत् or आनत् । अनानि, अनिहि । अन्यात् ॥ आन । आनिषत् । अनिष्यति । अनित । अनितुम् । आनयति ॥

अश् as, to attain, V, A. अश्नते । आश्नुवि, आश्नुथा:, आश्नुत । अश्नवै, अश्नुध्व, अश्नुताम् । अश्नुवीत ॥ आनशे, आनशिषे or आनक्षे । आक्षि, आष्ठा:, आष्ट । अष्ट ॥

अश् as, to eat, IX, P. अश्नाति । आश्नात् । अश्नानि, अशान, अश्नातु । अश्नीयात् ॥ आश । आशीत् । अशिष्यति । अश्यते । अशित । अशित्वा, °अश्य । अशितुम् । आशयति । अशिशिषति ॥

अस् as, to be, II, P. The perf. is both P. and A. The pres. A. is used to form the A. terminations of the periph. fut. अस्मि, असि, अस्ति; स्वः, स्थः, स्तः; स्मः, स्थ, संति। आसम्, आसीः, आसीत्; आस्व, आस्तम्, आस्ताम्; आस्म, आस्त, आसन्। असानि, एधि, अस्तु; असाव, स्तम्, स्ताम्; असाम, स्त, संतु। स्याम्, स्याः, स्यात्; स्याव, स्यातम्, स्याताम्; स्याम, स्यात, स्युः॥ आस, आसिथ, आस; आसिव, आसथुः, आसतुः; आसिम, आस, आसुः। A. आसे, आसिषे, आसे; आसिवहे, आसाथे, आसाते; आसिमहे, आसिध्वे, आसिरे॥

अस् as, to throw, IV, P. अस्यति॥ आस, आसिथ, etc., like अस् to be। आस्यत्। असिष्यति। अस्यते। आसि। अस्त। आसयति॥

आप् âp, to obtain, V, P. आप्नोति। आप्नोत्। आपवान्, आपुहि, आप्नोतु। आपुयात्॥ आप। आपत्। आप्स्यति; आप्त। आप्यते। आप्र। आप्त्वा, °आप्य। आपुम्। आपयति। ईप्सति॥

आस् âs, to sit, II, A. आस्ते। आस्त। आस्ताम्। आसीत॥ आसांचक्रे। आसिष्ट। आसिष्यते। आस्यते। आसित। आसीन irreg. pres. part. A.। आसितुम्॥

इ i, to go, II, P. एमि, एधि, एति; इवः; यंति। आयम्, ऐः, ऐत्; ऐव; आयन्। अयानि, इहि, एतु; अयाव; यंतु। इयात्॥ इयाय, इयेथ, इयाय; ईयिव; ईयुः। एष्यति; एता। ईयते। इत। इत्वा, °इत्य। एतुम्॥

अधी adhi_i, to read, II, A. अधीते। अध्यैत; 3. du. अध्यैयाताम्; 3. pl. अध्यैयत। अध्ययै, अधीष्व, अधीताम्; अध्ययावहै, अधीयाथाम्, अधीयाताम्; अध्ययामहै, अधीध्वम्, अधीयताम्। अधीयीत॥ अधिजगे। अध्यैष्ट; 3. du. अध्यैषाताम्; 3. pl. अध्यैषत। अध्येष्यते; अध्येता। अधीयते। अधीत। अध्यापयति॥

इध् idh or इंध् indh, to kindle, VII, A. इंद्धे। ऐंद्ध। इन्धे, इंत्स्व, इंद्धाम्। इंधीत॥ ईधे or इंधांचक्रे। ऐंधिष्ट। इंधिष्यते। इध्यते। इद्ध। इंधयति॥

इष् ish, to wish, VI, P. इच्छति। ऐच्छत्॥ इयेष, इयेषिथ, इयेष; ईषिव; ईषुः। ऐषीत्। एषिष्यति। इष्यते। इष्ट। एषुम्। एषयति॥

ईक्ष् íksh, to see, I, A. ईक्षते । ऐक्षत ॥ ईक्षांचक्रे । ऐक्षिष्ट । ईक्षिष्यते । ईक्ष्यते । ऐक्षि । ईक्षित । ईक्षितुम् । ईक्षयति ॥

उष् ush, to burn, I, P. ओषति । औषत् ॥ उवोष, उवोषिथ, उवोष; ऊषिव, etc. । औषीत् । उष्यते । उष्ट ॥

ऋ ri, to go, I, P. ऋच्छति । आर्छत् ॥ आर, आरिथ, आर; आरिव, etc. । आरत्; आरन् । अरिष्यति । ऋत । ऋत्वा, °ऋत्य । अर्पयति ॥

ऋ ri, to go, III, P. इयर्ति; इयृतः; इयृति । ऐयः or अयरत्; 3. du. ऐयृताम्; 3. pl. ऐयरुः । इयराणि, इयृहि, इयर्तु; इयराव; इयृतु ॥

ऋज् rig, to go, to gain, etc., I, A. अर्जते । आर्जत ॥ आनृजे । अर्जयति ॥

एध् edh, to grow, I, A. एधते । ऐधत । एधताम् । एधेत ॥ एधामास । एधित । एधितुम् । एधयति, °ते । एदिधिषते ॥

कम् kam, to love, I, A. कामयते ॥ कामयांचक्रे or चक्रमे । अचीकमत । कमिष्यते or कामयिष्यते । कांत । कामयते ॥

काश् kâs, to shine, I, A. काशते ॥ चकाशे । काशयति ॥

कृ kri, to do, VIII, P. A. करोमि, करोषि, करोति; कुर्वः, कुरुथः, कुरुतः; कुर्मः, कुरुथ, कुर्वंति । अकरवम्, अकरोः, अकरोत्; अकुर्व; अकुर्वन् । करवाणि, कुरु, करोतु; करवाव; कुर्वंतु ॥ चकार (å), चकर्थ, चकार; चकृव; चक्रुः । अकार्षम्, अकार्षीः, अकार्षीत्; अकार्ष्व, अकार्ष्म; अकार्ष्म, अकार्ष्ट, अकार्षुः । करिष्यति; कर्ता ॥ A. कुर्वे, कुरुषे, कुरुते; कुर्वहे; कुर्वते । अकुर्वि, अकुरुथाः, अकुरुत; अकुर्वहि; अकुर्वत । करवै, कुरुष्व, कुरुताम्; करवामहै; कुर्वताम् ॥ चक्रे, चकृषे, चक्रे; चकृवहे; चक्रिरे । अकृषि, अकृथाः, अकृत; अकृष्वहि; अकृषत । करिष्यते । क्रियते । अकारि । कृत । कृत्वा, °कृत्य । कर्तुम् । कारयति । अचीकरत् । चिकीर्षति ॥

कृत् krit, to cut, VI, P. कृंतति ॥ चकर्त । अकर्तीत् । कर्तिष्यति or कर्त्स्यति । कृत्यते । कृत्त । कर्तयति । अचीकृतत् । चिकर्तिषति ॥

कृष् krish, to drag along, to furrow, I or VI, P. कर्षति or कृषति ।

चकर्ष, चकर्षिथ, चकर्ष; चकृषिव। अकृष्तत्। कर्ह्यति। कृष्यते। कृष्ट।
कृष्ट्वा, °कृष्य। कर्ष्टुम्। कर्षयति। अचीकृषत्॥

कृ kri, to scatter, VI, P. किरति॥ चकार; चकरतुः; चकरुः। करि-
ष्यति। कीर्यते। कीर्ण। °कीर्य॥

कृत् krit, to praise, X, P. कीर्तयति॥ अचीकृतत् or अचिकीर्तत्॥

कॢप् klip, to be able, I, A. कल्पते॥ चकॢपे। कल्पिष्यते। कॢप्त।
कल्पयति। अचीकॢपत्॥

क्रम् kram, to stride, I, P. A. क्रामति, क्रमते॥ चक्राम, चक्रमे।
अक्रमीत्। क्रमिष्यति, °ते। क्रम्यते। क्रांत। क्रांत्वा, °क्रम्य। क्रमयति or
क्रामयति। चिक्रमिषति। चंक्रम्यते॥

क्री krî, to buy, IX, P. A. क्रीणाति, क्रीणीते॥ चिक्राय। क्रेष्यति,
°ते। क्रीयते। क्रीत। क्रीत्वा, °क्रीय। क्रेतुम्। चिक्रीषते॥

क्षण् kshan, to kill, VIII, P. A. क्षणोति, क्षणुते॥ क्षत॥

क्षि kshi, to destroy, V, P. क्षिणोति॥ क्षीयते। क्षित। क्षययति
or क्षपयति॥

क्षिप् kship, to throw, VI, P. A. क्षिपति, °ते। क्षिपाणि, क्षिपै॥
चिक्षेप, चिक्षिपे। क्षेप्स्यति, °ते। क्षिप्यते। क्षिप्त। क्षिप्त्वा, °क्षिप्य।
क्षेप्तुम्। क्षेपयति। चिक्षिप्सति॥

क्षुभ् kshubh, to quake, IV, P. A. क्षुभ्यति, °ते॥ चुक्षोभ, चुक्षुभे।
क्षुब्ध or क्षुभित। क्षोभयति, °ते॥

खन् khan, to dig, I, P. A. खनति, °ते॥ चखान; चख्नुः। खनि-
ष्यति। खन्यते or खायते। खात। खात्वा or खनित्वा, °खाय। खनितुम्।
खानयति॥

खाद् khâd, to eat, I, P. खादति॥ चखाद। खादिष्यते। खाद्यते।
खादित। खादयति। चिखादिषति॥

ख्या khyâ, to tell, II, P. ख्याति। ख्याहि, ख्यातु॥ चख्यौ; चख्युः।
अख्यत्। ख्यास्यति। ख्यायते। ख्यात। °ख्याय। ख्यातुम्। ख्यापयति,
°ते। चिख्यासति॥

गद् gad, to speak, I, P. गदति ॥ जगाद । गदिष्यति । गद्यते । गदित ।
गदितुम् । गादयति । जिगदिषति । जागद्यते ॥

गम् gam, to go, I, P. गच्छति ॥ जगाम, जगंथ; जग्मुः । अग-
मत् । गमिष्यति; गंता । गम्यते । गत; P. जग्मिवान् or जगन्वान् ।
गत्वा, °गम्य or °गत्य । गंतुम् । गमयति । जिगमिषति । जंगंति or
जंगम्यते ॥

गाह् gâh, to plunge, I, A. गाहते ॥ जगाहे । गाहिष्यते । गाढते ।
गाढ or गाहित । °गाह्य । गाहयति ॥

गुह् guh, to hide, I, P. A. गूहति, °ते ॥ जुगूह, जुगूहिथ or जुगोढ;
जुगुहिव; जुगुहे, जघुघ्से or जुगुहिषे । अघुक्षत् । गुह्यते । गूढ । °गुह्य ।
गूहितुम् । गूहयति ॥

गै gai, to sing, I, P. A. गायति, °ते ॥ जगौ, जगे । अगासीत् ।
गास्यति । गीयते । गीत । गीत्वा, °गाय । गातुम् । गापयति ॥

ग्रथ् grath or ग्रंथ् granth, to tie, IX, P. ग्रथ्नाति ॥ ग्रथ्यते । ग्रथित ।
°ग्रथ्य । ग्रथयति or ग्रंथयति ॥

ग्रह् grah, to take, IX, P. A. गृह्णाति, गृह्णीते । गृहाण, गृह्णातु ॥
जग्राह, जगृहे । अग्रहीत्, अग्रहीष्ट । ग्रहीष्यति, °ते; ग्रहीता ।
गृह्यते । गृहीत । गृहीत्वा, °गृह्य । ग्रहीतुम् । ग्राहयति, °ते । जि-
घृक्षति, °ते ॥

ग्लै glai, to droop, I, P. ग्लायति ॥ ग्लान । ग्लापयति or ग्लपयति ॥

घुष् ghush, to sound, I, P. A. घोषति, °ते ॥ घुष्यते । घुष्ट । °घुष्य ।
घोषयति ॥

घ्रा ghrâ, to smell, I, P. जिघ्रति ॥ जघ्रौ । घ्रायते । घ्रात । घ्रापयति ॥

चक्ष् kaksh, to speak, II, A. चष्टे, चक्षे, चष्टे; चक्ष्महे, चड्ढे, चक्षते ॥
चचक्षे । चक्ष्यते । °चक्ष्य । चष्टुम् । चक्षयति ॥

चर् kar, to move, I, P. चरति ॥ चचार, चचर्थ; चेरुः । चरिष्यति ।
चर्यते । चरित । चरित्वा, °चर्य । चरितुम् । चारयति । अचीचरत् ॥

चल् *kal*, to move, I, P. चलति ॥ चचाल ; चेलुः । चलिष्यति । चलित । चलितुम् । चलयति or चालयति । चिचलिषति ॥

चि *ki*, to collect, V, P. A. चिनोति, चिनुते ॥ चिकाय, चिक्ये । अचैषीत् । चेष्यति, °ते ; चेता । चीयते । चित । चित्वा, °चित्य । चेतुम् । चाययते । चिकीषते or चिचीषति ॥

चिंत् *kint*, to think, X, P. चिंतयति ॥ चिंतयामास । चिंत्यते । चिंतित । चिंतयित्वा, °चिंत्य ॥

चुर् *kur*, to steal, X, P. चोरयति ॥ चोरयांचकार । अचूचुरत् । चोर्यते । चोरित ॥

छिद् *khid*, to cut, VII, P. A. छिनत्ति ; छिंदंति ॥ चिच्छेद, चिच्छिदे । अच्छिदत् or अच्छैत्सीत् । छेत्स्यति, °ते । छिद्यते । छिन्न । छित्त्वा, °छिद्य । छेत्तुम् । छेदयति ॥

जन् *gan*, to beget, I, P. जनति ; to be born, IV, A. जायते ॥ जजान, जज्ञे । अजनिष्ट । जनिष्यते ; जनिता । जात । जनयति, °ते । जिजनिषते ॥

जागृ *gâgri*, to awake, II, P. (properly an intensive of गृ *gri*) जागर्ति ; जागृतः ; जाग्रति । अजागरम्, अजागः, अजागः ; अजागृताम् ; अजागहुः । जागराणि, जागृहि, जागर्तु ॥ जजागार or जागरांचकार । जागरिष्यति । जागरित । जागरयति ॥

जि *gi*, to conquer, I, P. (A. with परा and वि) जयति ॥ जिगाय ; जिगियव ; जिग्युः । अजैषीत् । जेष्यति । जीयते । जित । जित्वा, °जित्य । जेतुम् । जापयति । जिगीषति ॥

जीव् *gîv*, to live, I, P. जीवति ॥ जिजीव ; जिजीवुः । अजीवीत् । जीविष्यति । जीव्यते । जीवित । जीवित्वा, °जीव्य । जीवितुम् । जीव-यति । जिजीविषति ॥

जॄ *grî*, to grow old, IV, P. जीर्यति ॥ जजार । जीर्यते । जीर्ण । जरयति ॥

ज्ञा *gñâ*, to know, IX, P. A. जानाति, जानीते ॥ जज्ञौ, जज्ञे । अज्ञासीत् ।

ज्ञास्यति ; ज्ञाता । ज्ञायते । अज्ञायि । ज्ञात । ज्ञात्वा, °ज्ञाय । ज्ञातुम् ।
ज्ञापयति, °ते or ज्ञपयति, °ते । जिज्ञासते ॥

ज्या *gyâ,* to grow weak, IX, P. जिनाति ॥ जिज्यौ ; जिज्यिव ;
जिज्युः । अज्यासीत् । ज्यास्यति । जिज्यासति ॥

तन् *tan,* to stretch, VIII, P. A. तनोति, तनुते ॥ ततान, तेने ।
अतानीत् । तन्यते or तायते । तत । तत्वा, °तत्य or °ताय । तानयति ॥

तप् *tap,* to burn, I, P. A. तपति, °ते or IV तप्यति, °ते ॥ तताप,
तेपे । अताप्सीत् । तप्स्यति । तप्यते । तप्त । तप्त्वा, °तप्य । तप्तुम् । ताप-
यति ॥

तुद् *tud,* to strike, VI, P. A. तुदति, °ते ॥ तुतोद । तुतुदे । तुन्न । तोदयति ॥

तृप् *trip,* to be pleased, IV, P. तृप्यति ॥ ततर्प ; ततृपिव । अतृ-
पत् । तृप्त । तर्पयति । अतीतृपत् । तितृप्सति ॥

तृह् *trih,* to kill, VII, P. तृणेढि ; तृंहंति । तृणेढु ॥ ततर्ह । तृहे । तृढ ॥

तॄ *tri,* to cross, I, P. or VI, A. तरति or तिरते ॥ ततार ; तेरुः ।
अतारीत् or अतारीत् । तरिष्यति, °ते । तीर्यते । तीर्णि । तीर्त्वा, °तीर्य ।
तर्तुम्, तरितुम्, तरीतुम् । तारयति, °ते । तितीर्षति ॥

त्यज् *tyag,* to abandon, I, P. A. त्यजति, °ते ॥ तत्याज, तत्यजे ।
अत्याक्षीत् । त्यस्यति, °ते or त्यजिष्यति, °ते । त्यज्यते । त्यक्त । त्यक्त्वा,
°त्यज्य । त्याजयति । तित्यक्षति ॥

त्रस् *tras,* to tremble, I, P. or IV, P. A. त्रसति or त्रस्यति, °ते ॥
तत्रास ; तत्रसुः or त्रेसुः । अत्रासीत् । त्रस्त । त्रासयति ॥

त्वर् *tvar,* to hasten, I, A. त्वरते ॥ तत्वरे । त्वरित । त्वरयति ॥

दंश् *dams,* to bite, I, P. दशति ॥ ददंश । दशिष्यति । दश्यते । दष्ट ।
दंष्ट्रा, °दश्य । दंशयति ॥

दम् *dam,* to tame, IV, P. दाम्यति ॥ दांत । दमयति ॥

दह् *dah,* to burn, I, P. दहति ॥ देहिष or ददग्ध, ददाह । अधाक्षीत् ।
धक्ष्यति । दह्यते । दग्ध । दग्ध्वा, °दग्ध । दग्धुम् । दाहयति । दिधक्षति ॥

दा *dâ,* to give, III, P. A. ददाति, दत्ते ॥ ददौ, ददे । अदात् ; अदित,

3. pl. अदिषत । दास्यति, °ते ; दाता । दीयते । दत्त (often °न्न after prefixes: आत्त â-tta) । दत्वा, °दाय । दापयति । दित्सति ॥

दिव् div, to play, IV, P. दीव्यति ॥ दिदेव । अदेवीत् । देविष्यति । द्यूत । देवितुम् । देवयति ॥

दिश् dis, to point, VI, P. A. दिशति, °ते ॥ दिदेश, दिदिशे । अदि-क्षत् । देक्ष्यति, °ते । दिश्यते । दिष्ट । °दिश्य । देष्टुम् । देशयति । दि-दिक्षति ॥

दिह् dih, to anoint, II, P. A. देह्मि, धेक्षि, देग्धि; दिह्वः, दिग्धः, दिग्धः; दिह्नः, दिग्ध, दिहंति । दिहे, धिक्षे, दिग्धे; दिह्वहे, दिहाथे, दिहाते; दिह्महे, धिग्ध्वे, दिहते । अदेहम्, अधेक्, अधेक्; अदिह्न, अदिग्धम्, अदिग्धाम्; अदिह्न, अदिग्ध, अदिहन् । अदिदिहि, अदिग्धाः, अदिग्ध; अदिह्वहि, अदिहाथाम्, अदिहाताम्; अदिह्महि, अधिग्ध्वम्, अदिहत । देहानि, दिग्धि, देग्धु; देहाव, दिग्धम्, दिग्धाम्; देहाम, दिग्ध, दिहंतु । देहै, धिक्ष, दिग्धाम्; देहावहै, दिहाथाम्, दिहाताम्; देहामहै, धिग्ध्वम्, दिहताम् । दिह्यात्, दिहीत ॥ (दिदेह), दिदिहे । दिक्षते । दिग्ध । °दिह्म । देहयति ॥

दुह् duh, to milk, II, P. A. (like दिह्) दोग्धि । अधोक् । दोग्धु । दुह्यात् ॥ दुदोह, दुदुहे । अधुक्षत्, अधुक्षत । धोक्ष्यते । दुक्षते । दुग्ध । दुग्ध्वा । दोग्धुम् । दोहयति । अदूदुहत् । दुधुक्षति ॥

दृश् dris, to see, I, P. पश्यति ॥ ददर्श; ददृशुः । अद्राक्षीत् or अदर्शत् । द्रक्ष्यति; द्रष्टा । दृश्यते । अदर्शि । दृष्ट । दृष्ट्वा, °दृश्य । द्रष्टुम् । दर्श-यति । अदीदृशत् । दिदृक्षते ॥

द्युत् dyut, to shine, I, A. द्योतते ॥ दिद्युते । अद्युतत् । द्योतिष्यते । द्योतयति । अदिद्युतत् ॥

द्रु dru, to run, I, P. द्रवति ॥ दुद्राव, दुद्रोष; दुद्रुव । अदुद्रवत् । द्रोष्यति । द्रुत । दुत्वा, °द्रुत्य । द्रोतुम् । द्रावयति । (अदुद्रवत् or अदि-द्रवत्) ॥

दुह् druh, to hurt, IV, P. दुह्यति ॥ दुद्रोह, दुद्रोहिथ or दुद्रोग्ध or दुद्रोढ; दुदुहिव । अदुहत् । धोक्ष्यति । दुग्ध । दुधुक्षति ॥

द्विष् dvish, to hate, II, P. A. द्वेष्टि ॥ दिद्वेष । अद्विक्षत् । द्विष्ट । द्वेष्टुम् । द्वेषयति ॥

धा dhâ, to place, III, P. A. दधाति; धत्त:; दधति । धत्ते; दधाते; दधते । अदधात्; अदधाताम्; अदधु:। अधत्त; अदधाताम्; अदधत । दधानि, धेहि, दधातु; धत्ताम्; दधतु । दधै, धत्स्व, धत्ताम्; दधाताम्; दधताम् । दध्यात्, दधीत ॥ दधौ, दधे । अधात्, अधित ॥ धास्यति, °ते; धाता । धीयते । अधायि । हित । °धाय । धातुम् । धापयति । धित्सति ॥

धाव् dhâv, to run, to wash, I, P. A. धावति, °ते ॥ दधाव । अधावीत्, अधाविष्ट । धाव्यते । धावित running; धौत washed । धावयति ॥

धू dhû, to shake, V or IX, P. A. धुनोति, धुनुते or धुनाति, धुनीते ॥ दुधाव, दुधुवे । धविष्यति । धूयते । धूत । धूनयति । दोधूयते ॥

धृ dhri, to bear, I, P. A. (no present) दधार, दध्रे । धरिष्यति, °ते । ध्रियते । धृत । धृत्वा । धर्तुम् । धारयति, °ते । अदीधरत् ॥

ध्मा dhmâ, to blow, I, P. धमति ॥ दध्मौ । अध्मासीत् । धम्यते or ध्मायते । ध्मात । °ध्माय । ध्मापयति ॥

नद् nad, to hum, I, P. नदति ॥ ननाद, नेदिथ; नेदु: । नदित । नदयति or नादयति ॥

नम् nam, to bend, I, P. नमति ॥ ननाम; नेमु: । अनंसीत् । नंस्यति । नम्यते । नत । नत्वा, °नम्य । नमितुम् or नंतुम् । नमयति or नामयति । अनीनमत् । निनंसति ॥

नश् nas, to perish, IV, P. नश्यति ॥ ननाश; नेशु:।अनशत् or अने- शत् । नशिष्यति or नंक्ष्यति । नष्ट । नाशयति । अनीनशत् ॥

नह् nah, to bind, IV, P. A. नह्यति, °ते ॥ नह्यते । नद्ध । °नह्य । नाहयति ॥

नृत् nrit, to dance, IV, P. नृत्यति ॥ ननर्त; ननृतुः । नर्तिष्यति ।
नृत्यते । नृत्त । नर्तयति । निनर्तिषति । नरीनर्ति or नरीनृत्यते ॥

पच् pak, to cook, I, P. A. पचति, °ते ॥ पपाच, पेचे । पक्ष्यति;
पक्ता । पच्यते । पक्त । पक्त्वा । पाचयति । पापच्यते ॥

पत् pat, to fall, I, P. पतति ॥ पपात; पेतुः । अपप्तत् । पतिष्यति ।
पत्यते । पतित । पतितुम् । पतित्वा, °पत्य । पातयति । पिपतिषति or
पित्सति ॥

पद् pad, to go, IV, A. पद्यते ॥ पेदे । अपादि (aor. Âtm.) । पत्स्यते ।
पन्न । °पद्य । पत्तुम् । पादयति । अपीपदत् । पित्सते । पनीपद्यते ॥

पा pâ, to drink, I, P. पिवति ॥ पपौ, पपिथ or पपाथ; पपुः । अपात् ।
पास्यति । पीत । पीत्वा, °पाय । पातुम् । पीयते । अपायि । पाययति ।
पिपासति । पेपीयते ॥

पा pâ, to protect, II, P. पाति ॥ अपासीत् । पातुम् ॥

पुष् push, to thrive, IV or IX, P. पुष्यति or पुष्णाति ॥ पुपोष । पुष्यते ।
पुष्ट । पोषयति ॥

पू pû, to purify, IX, P. A. (or I, A. पवते) पुनाति, पुनीते ॥ पुपाव,
पुपुवे । अपावीत्, अपविष्ट । पूयते । पूत । पूत्वा, °पूय । पावयति ॥

पृ prî (पूर् pûr), to fill, to guard, III, P. पिपर्ति; पिप्रति ॥ (पपार),
पुपूरे । पूर्यते । पूर्त or पूर्ण । °पूर्य । पूरयति ॥

प्रछ् prakh, to ask, VI, P. पृच्छति ॥ पप्रच्छ, पप्रच्छिथ or पप्रष्ठ;
पप्रच्छुः । अप्राक्षीत्, अप्रष्ट । प्रक्ष्यति । पृच्छ्यते । पृष्ट । पृष्ट्वा, °पृच्छ्य ।
प्रष्टुम् । पिपृच्छिषति ॥

प्री prî, to please, IX, P. A. प्रीणाति, प्रीणीते ॥ (पिप्राय), पिप्रिये ।
अप्रैषीत् । प्रीयते । प्रीत । प्रीणयति ॥

फल् phal, to burst, I, P. फलति ॥ पफाल । फलित or फुल्ल । फा-
लयति ॥

बंध् bandh, to bind, IX, P. बध्नाति ॥ बबंध, बबंधिथ or बबंद्ध or
बबंध । भंत्स्यति । बध्यते । बद्ध । बद्ध्वा, °बध्य । बंद्धुम् । बंधयति ॥

बुध् budh, to perceive, I, P. A. or IV, A. बोधति, °ते or बुध्यते ॥
बुबुधे । अबुद्ध । बोत्स्यते । बुध्यते । बुद्ध । बुद्ध्वा, °बुध्य । बोद्धुम् । बोध-
यति । अबूबुधत् । बुभुत्सते ॥

ब्रू brû, to speak, II, P. A. ब्रवीमि, ब्रवीषि, ब्रवीति ; ब्रूवः, ब्रूषः,
ब्रूतः ; ब्रूमः, ब्रूथ, ब्रुवंति । ब्रूते ; ब्रुवते । अब्रवम्, अब्रवीः, अब्रवीत् ;
अब्रूताम् ; अब्रुवन् । ब्रवाणि, ब्रूहि, ब्रवीतु ; ब्रवाव, ब्रूतम्, ब्रूताम् ;
ब्रवाम, ब्रूत, ब्रुवंतु । ब्रूयात् ॥   वच् vak is used instead of ब्रू brû
in the general forms. The perfect आह âha may be used for its
present (153, 3).

भक्ष् bhaksh, to eat, devour, I, P. भक्षति ॥ भक्ष्यते । अभक्षि ।
भक्षित । भक्षितुम् । भक्षयति । अबभक्षत् ॥

भज् bhag, to divide, to enjoy, I, P. A. भजति, °ते ॥ बभाज,
बभक्थ, भेजुः ; भेजे । अभाक्षीत्, अभक्त । भजिष्यति, °ते । भज्यते । भक्त ।
भक्त्वा, °भज्य । भक्तुम् । भाजयति, °ते । भिक्षति ॥

भंज् bhang, to break, VII, P. भनक्ति । अभनक् । भनक्तु । भंज्यात् ॥
बभंज । अभांक्षीत् । भंक्ष्यति ; भंक्त्वा । भज्यते । अभाजि । भग्न । भंक्त्वा, °भज्य ॥

भा bhâ, to shine, to appear, II, P. भाति ; भांति । अभात् ; अभान्
or अभुः ॥ बभौ । भास्यति । भात ॥

भाष् bhâsh, to speak, I, A. भाषते ॥ बभाषे । अभाषिष्ट । भाषिष्यते ।
भाष्यते । भाषित । भाषित्वा, °भाष्य । भाषितुम् । भाषयति ॥

भिद् bhid, to cleave, to break, VII, P. A. भिनत्ति, भिंत्ते ॥ बिभेद,
बिभिदे । भेत्स्यति, °ते । भिद्यते । भिन्न । भित्त्वा, °भिद्य । भेत्तुम् । भेदयति ॥

भी bhî, to fear, III, P. बिभेति ; बिभ्यति । अबिभेत् ; अबिभयुः ॥
बिभाय or बिभयांचकार । अभैषीत् । भीयते । भीत । भेतुम् । भाययति
or भीषयते । बेभीयते ॥

भुज् bhug, to enjoy, VII, P. A. भुनक्ति, भुंक्ते ॥ बुभुजे । भोक्ष्यति,
°ते । भुज्यते । भुक्त । भुक्त्वा । भोक्तुम् । भोजयति, °ते । बुभुक्षति । बोभुज्यते ॥

भू bhû, to be, become, I, P. A. भवति, °ते ॥ बभूव, बभूवे । अभूत्, अभविष्ट । भविष्यति । भूयते । अभावि । भूत । भूत्वा, °भूय । भवितुम् । भावयति, °ते । बुभूषति, °ते । बोभवीति ॥

भृ bhri, to carry, III, P. A. (also I, P. A. भरति, °ते) बिभर्ति, बिभृते; बिभ्रति, बिभ्रते । बिभराणि, बिभृहि, बिभर्तु ॥ बभार, बभृषे; बभ्रुव; or बिभरांचकार । अभार्षीत्, अभृत । भरिष्यति । ध्रियते । भृत । °भृत्य । भर्तुम् । भारयति । बुभूर्षति । बरीभर्ति ॥

भ्रज्ज् bhragg, to fry, VI, P. भृज्जति ॥ भृज्ज्यते । भृष्ट । भृष्ट्वा । भर्जयति ॥

भ्रम् bhram, to wander, IV, P. or I, P. A. भ्राम्यति or भ्रमति, °ते ॥ बभ्राम; बभ्रमतुः or भ्रेमतुः । भ्रमिष्यति । भ्रांत । भ्रांत्वा, °भ्रम्य or °भ्राम्य । भ्रांतुम् or भ्रमितुम् । भ्रामयति or भ्रमयति । बंभ्रमीति, बंभ्रम्यते ॥

मज्ज् magg, to sink, I, P. मज्जति ॥ ममज्ज । मंक्ष्यति । मग्न । °मज्ज्य । मज्जितुम् । मज्जयति । मिमंक्षति ॥

मद् mad, to rejoice, IV, P. माद्यति ॥ ममाद; मेदतुः । अमादीत् । मद्यते । मन्न । मादयति or मदयति । अमीमदत् ॥

मन् man, to think, IV, A. मन्यते ॥ मेने । अमंस्त । मंस्यते । मन्यते । मत । मत्वा, °मन्य or °मत्य । मंतुम् । मानयते । मीमांसते ॥

मंथ् manth, to shake, I or IX, P. मंथति or मथ्नाति ॥ ममंथ, ममंथिथ । मंथिष्यति । मथ्यते । मथित । °मथ्य । मंथयति ॥

मा mâ, to measure, II, P. or III, A. माति or मिमीते ॥ ममौ or ममे । मीयते । अमायि । मित । मित्वा, °माय । मातुम् । मापयति । मित्सति ॥

मुच् muk, to loosen, VI, P. A. मुंचति, °ते ॥ मुमोच, मुमुचे । अमुचत्, अमुक्त । मोक्ष्यति, °ते । मुच्यते । मुक्त । मुक्त्वा, °मुच्य । मोक्तुम् । मोच-यति, °ते । अमूमुचत् । मुमुक्षति or मोक्षते ॥

मुह् muh, to be foolish, IV, P. मुह्यति ॥ मुमोह, मुमोहिथ or मुमोग्ध

or मुमोढ । अमुहत् । मोहिष्यति । मुग्ध or मूढ । मुह्यते । मोह्यति । अमूमुहत् ॥

मृ *mri*, to die, VI, P. (pres. and aor. A.) म्रियते ॥ ममार, ममर्थे ; ममिव । अमृत । मरिष्यति । म्रियते । मृत । मृत्वा । मर्तुम् । मारयति । अमीमरत् । मुमूर्षति । मरीमर्ति ॥

मृज् *mrig*, to cleanse, II, P. मार्षि ; मृष्ट: ; मृजन्ति । अमार्ट् ; अमृष्टाम् ; अमृजन् । मार्जानि, मृड्डि, माष्टु ; मृष्टाम् ; मृजन्तु । मृज्यात् ॥ ममार्ज ; ममृजु: । अमार्जीत् or अमाक्षीत् or अमृक्षत् । माक्ष्यति । मृज्यते । मृष्ट । मार्जित्वा or मृष्ट्वा, °मृज्य । मार्जयति । मरीमृज्यते ॥

म्ना *mnâ*, to study, I, P. मनति ॥ अम्नासीत् । म्नायते । म्नात ॥

म्लै *mlai*, to fade, I, P. म्लायति ॥ मम्लौ । अम्लासीत् । म्लान । म्लापयति or म्लपयति ॥

यज् *yag*, to worship, I, P. A. यजति, °ते ॥ इयाज, ईजे । अयाक्षीत्, अयष्ट । यक्ष्यति ; यष्टा । इज्यते । इष्ट । इष्ट्वा । यष्टुम् । याजयति । अयीयजत् । यियक्षति ॥

यम् *yam*, to stop, I, P. यच्छति ॥ ययाम, ययंथ or येमिथ ; येमु: । यंस्यति or यमिष्यति । यम्यते । यत । यत्वा, °यम्य or °यत्य । यंतुम् । यमयति or यामयति । यियंसति ॥

या *yâ*, to go, II, P. याति ॥ अयात् ; अयान् or अयु: । यातु । यायात् ॥ ययौ । अयासीत् । यास्यति ; याता । यायते । यात । यात्वा, °याय । यातुम् । यापयति । यियासति ॥

यु *yu*, to join, II, P. यौति ; युवन्ति । अयौत् ; अयुवन् । यौतु ; युवन्तु । युयात् । यूयते । युत । युत्वा, °युत्य । युयूषति ॥

युज् *yug*, to join, VII, P. A. युनक्ति, युंक्ते ॥ युयोज, युयुजे । अयुजत्, अयुक्त । योक्ष्यति, °ते । युज्यते । युक्त । युक्त्वा, °युज्य । योक्तुम् । योजयति, °ते । अयूयुजत् । युयुक्षति ॥

रक्ष् *raksh*, to protect, I, P. A. रक्षति, °ते ॥ ररक्ष । अरक्षीत् । रक्षिष्यति ; रक्षिता । रक्ष्यते । रक्षित । °रक्ष्य । रक्षितुम् । रक्षयति ॥

रंज् ra*ñg*, to tinge, IV, P. रज्यति ॥ रज्यते । रक्त । °रज्य । रंजयति ॥

रभ् rabh, to grasp (आरभ् â-rabh, to begin), I, A. रभते ॥ रेभे । आरब्ध । रप्स्यते । रभ्यते । आरंभि । रब्ध । °रभ्य । रब्धुम् । रंभयति, °ते । रिप्सते ॥

रम् ram, to sport, I, A. (with वि, आ, परि, उप optionally P.) रमते ॥ रेमे । आरंस्त । रंस्यते । रंतुम् । रत । रत्वा, °रम्य or °रत्य । रम्यते । रमयति । रिरंसते ॥

राज् râ*g*, to shine, I, P. A. राजति, °ते ॥ रराज, रेजे । अराजीत् । राजयति ॥

रु ru, to cry, II, P. रौति; रुतः; रुवंति ॥ रुराव; रुरुवुः । अरावीत् । रूयते । रुत । रावयति । रोरूयते ॥.

रुद् rud, to weep, II, P. रोदिति; रुदंति । अरोदम्, अरोदः or अरोदीः, अरोदत् or अरोदीत्; अरुदिव; अरुदन् । रोदानि, रुदिहि, रोदितु; रोदाव; रुदंतु । रुद्यात् ॥ रुरोद । अरुदत् । रोदिष्यति । रुद्यते । रुदित । रुदित्वा, °रुद्य । रोदितुम् । रोदयति । रुरुदिषति । रोरुद्यते ॥

रुध् rudh, to shut out, VII, P. A. रुणद्धि, रुंद्धे ॥ रुरोध, रुरुधे । अरुधत् or अरौत्सीत्; अरुद्ध । रोत्स्यति । रुध्यते । रुद्ध । रुद्धा, °रुध्य । रोद्धुम् । रोधयति । रुरुत्सति ॥

रुह् ruh, to grow, I, P. रोहति ॥ रुरोह । अरुक्षत् or अरुहत् । रोक्ष्यति । रुह्यते । रूढ । रूढ्वा, °रुह्य । रोढुम् । रोहयति or रोपयति । रुरुक्षति ॥

लभ् labh, to grasp, I, A. लभते ॥ लेभे । लप्स्यते । लभ्यते । लब्ध । लब्धा, °लभ्य । लंभयति । लिप्सते ॥

लिख् likh, to scratch, to write, VI, P. लिखति ॥ लिलेख । लिख्यते । लिखित । लिखित्वा, °लिख्य । लेखयति ॥

लू lû, to cut, IX, P. A. लुनाति, लुनीते ॥ लुलाव, लुलुवे । लून ॥

वच् va*k*, to speak, II, P. वच्मि, वक्षि, वक्ति; वच्वः, वक्यः, वक्तः;

वच्मः, वक्ष्य, वदंति । अवचम्, अवक्, अवक्; अवच्व, अवक्तम्, अव-
क्ताम्; अवच्म, अवक्त, अवदन् । वचानि, वग्धि, वक्तु; वचाव । वच्यात् ॥
उवाच; ऊचुः । अवोचत् । वक्ष्यति; वक्ता । उच्यते । अवाचि । उक्त ।
उक्त्वा, °उच्य । वक्तुम् । वाचयति । विवक्षति ॥

वद् vad, to speak, I, P. वदति ॥ उवाद, उवदिथ; ऊदुः । अवा-
दीत् । वदिष्यति । उद्यते । उदित । उदित्वा, °उद्य । वदितुम् । वादयति ।
विवदिषति ॥

वप् vap, to sow, to weave, I, P. A. वपति ॥ उवाप, उवपिथ or
उवप्थ; ऊपुः । वप्स्यति । उप्यते । उप्त । वापयति ॥

वश् vas, to desire, II, P. वश्मि, वक्षि, वष्टि; उश्मः; उशंति ।
अवशम्, अवट्, अवट्; औश्म । वशानि, उड्डि, वष्टु । उश्यात् ॥ वश-
यति ॥

वस् vas, to dwell, I, P. वसति ॥ उवास, उवसिथ or उवस्थ; ऊषिव;
ऊषुः । अवात्सीत् । वत्स्यति । उष्यते । उषित । उषित्वा, °उष्य । वस्तुम् ।
वासयति । अवीवसत् । विवत्सति ॥

वस् vas, to wear, II, A. वस्ते ॥ ववसे । अववसिष्ट । वसित । वसित्वा,
°वस्य । वसितुम् । वासयति ॥

वह् vah, to carry, I, P. A. वहति, °ते ॥ उवाह, उवहिथ or उवोढ;
ऊहिव; ऊहुः । अवाक्षीत् । वक्ष्यति; वोढा । उह्यते । ऊढ । ऊढ्वा,
°उह्य । वोढुम् । वाहयति ॥

विद् vid, to know, II, P. वेद्मि, वेत्सि, वेत्ति; विद्दः, वित्थः, वित्तः;
विद्मः, वित्थ, विदंति । अवेदम्, अवेः or अवेत्, अवेत्; अविद्द, अवित्तम्,
अविन्ताम्; अविद्म, अवित्त, अविदन् or अविदुः । वेदानि, विद्धि, वेत्तु;
वेदाव, वित्तम्, वित्ताम्; वेदाम, वित्त, विदंतु । विद्यात् ॥ विवेद or वि-
दांचकार । अवेदीत् । वेदिष्यति; वेदिता । विद्यते । विदित । विदित्वा ।
वेदितुम् । वेदयति । विविदिषति ॥ Pres. perf. वेद (οἶδα), वेत्थ (οἶσ-θα),
वेद (οἶδε); विद्द, विद्युः, विदतुः; विद्म (ἴδμεν), विद, विदुः (cp. p. 96, 9).

विद् vid, to find, VI, P. A. विंदति, °ते ॥ विवेद, विविदे । अविदत्,

अविदत् । वेत्स्यति, °ते । विद्यते (there is found, there exists, there is) । विन्न or विन्न । विल्ला, °विद्य । वेत्तुम् । वेदयति । विविदिषति ॥

विश् vis, to enter, VI, P. विशति ॥ विवेश । अविक्षत् । वेक्ष्यति । विश्यते । विष्ट । °विश्य । वेष्टुम् । वेशयति । विविक्षति ॥

वृ vri, to cover, V, P. A. वृणोति, वृणुते ॥ ववार, ववरिथ; ववृव; वव्रुः । अवारीत्, अवृत । व्रियते । वृत । वृत्वा, °वृत्य । वरितुम् or वरी- तुम् । वारयति ॥

वृ vri, to choose, IX, A. वृणीते ॥ वव्रे । अवृत । वरिष्यते । व्रियते । वृत । वृत्वा । वरीतुम् । वरयति ॥

वृत् vrit, to be, to exist, I, A. (optionally P. in aor., fut., desid.) वर्तते ॥ ववृते । अवृतत् । वर्तिष्यते or वर्त्स्यते । वृत्त । °वृत्य । वर्तितुम् । वर्तयति । अवीवृतत् । विवृत्सति ॥

वृध् vridh, to increase, I, A. (opt. P. in aor., fut., desid.) वर्धते ॥ ववृधे । अवृधत्, अवर्धिष्ट । वर्त्स्यति । वृद्ध । वर्धितुम् । वर्धयति, °ते । अवीवृधत् ॥

व्यध् vyadh, to strike, IV, P. विध्यति ॥ विव्याध; विविधुः । अव्यात्सीत् । विध्यते । विद्ध । विद्ध्वा, °विध्य । व्याधयति । विव्यत्सति ॥

व्रज् vrag, to go, I, P. व्रजति ॥ वव्राज, वव्रजिथ । अव्राजीत् । व्रजिष्यति । व्रज्यते । व्रजित । व्रजित्वा, °व्रज्य । व्रजितुम् । व्राजयति । विव्रजिषति ॥

व्रश्च् vrask, to cut, VI, P. वृश्चति ॥ वृश्च्यते । वृक्ण । वृष्ट्वा, °वृश्च्य ॥

शंस् sams, to recite, I, P. शंसति ॥ शशंस । अशंसीत् । शंसिष्यति । शस्यते । शस्त । शस्त्वा, °शस्य । शंसितुम् । शंसयति ॥

शक् sak, to be able, V, P. शक्नोति ॥ शशाक; शेकुः । अशकत् । शक्ष्यति । शक्यते । शक्त । शिक्षति ॥

शप् sap, to curse, I, P. A. शपति, °ते ॥ शशाप, शेपे । शप्स्यते । शप्यते । शप्त । शापयति ॥

शम् sam, to cease, IV, P. शाम्यति ॥ शशाम; शेमु: । अशमत् । शांत । शमयति । अशीशमत् ॥

शास् sâs, to command, II, P. शास्ति; शिष्व:; शासति । अशासम्, अशा: or अशात्, अशात्; अशिष्व; अशासु: । शासानि, शाधि, शास्तु; शासाव, शिष्टम्, शिष्टाम्; शासाम, शिष्ट, शासतु । शिष्यात् ॥ शशास । अशिषत् । शासिष्यति । शिष्यते । शिष्ट । शासित्वा । शास्तुम् ॥

शिष् sish, to distinguish, VII, P. शिनष्टि; शिंष्व:; शिंषंति । शिनषाणि, शिंड्ढि, शिनष्टु ॥ शिशेष । अशिषत् । शेक्ष्यति । शिष्यते । शिष्ट । शिष्ट्वा, °शिष्य । शेषयति ॥

शी sî, to lie down, II, A. शये, शेषे, शेते; शेवहे, शयाचे, शयाते; शेमहे, शेध्वे, शेरते । अशयि, अशेथा:, अशेत; अशेवहि, अशयाथाम्, अशयाताम्; अशेमहि, अशेध्वम्, अशेरत । शये, शेष्व, शेताम्; शयावहै, शयाथाम्, शयाताम्; शयामहै, शेध्वम्, शेरताम् । शयीत ॥ शिश्ये । अशयिष्ट । शयिष्यते । शयित । शाययति । शिशयिषते ॥

शुच् suk, to grieve, I, P. शोचति ॥ शुशोच । अशोचीत् । शोचिष्यति । शोचित्वा । शोचितुम् । शोचयति । अशूशुचत् ॥

श्रि sri, to go, I, P. A. श्रयति, °ते ॥ शिश्राय, शिश्रिये । अशिश्रियत् । अयिष्यति, °ते । श्रीयते । अश्रायि । श्रित । अयित्वा, °श्रित्य । अयितुम् ॥

श्रु sru, to hear, V, P. शृणोति; शृणुत:; शृण्वंति ॥ शुश्राव, शुश्रोष, शुश्राव; शुश्रुव; शुश्रुवु: । अश्रौषीत् । श्रोष्यति; श्रोता । श्रूयते । अश्रावि । श्रुत । श्रुत्वा, °श्रुत्य । श्रोतुम् । श्रावयति । शुश्रूषते ॥

श्वस् svas, to breathe, II, P. श्वसिति ॥ शश्वास । श्वसिष्यति । श्वस्त or श्वसित । °श्वस्य । श्वसितुम् । श्वासयति ॥

श्वि svi, to swell, I, P. श्वयति ॥ अश्वत् । शून ॥

संज् sañg, to adhere, I, P. सज्जति ॥ ससंज । असांक्षीत् । सज्यते । सक्त । °सज्य । असंजि । संजयति । सिसंक्षति ॥

सद् sad, to perish, I, P. सीदति ॥ ससाद, सेदिष or ससत्थ; सेदुः ।
असदत् । सत्स्यति । सद्यते । सन्न । °सद्य । सत्तुम् । सादयति । असी-
षदत् ॥

सह् sah, to bear, I, A. सहते ॥ असहिष्ट । सँहिष्यते; सोढा । सह्यते ।
सोढ । सोढ्वा, °सह्य । सोढुम् । साहयति ॥

सिच् sik, to sprinkle, VI, P. A. सिंचति, °ते ॥ सिषेच, सिषिचे ।
असिचत्, °त । सेक्ष्यति, °ते । सिच्यते । सिक्त । सिक्त्वा, °सिच्य । सेच-
यति, °ते ॥

सिध् sidh, to succeed, IV, P. सिध्यति ॥ सिषेध । सेत्स्यति । सिध्यते ।
सिद्ध । साधयति ॥

सु su, to distil, V, P. A. सुनोति, सुनुते ॥ सुषाव, सुषुवे । सोष्यति;
सोता । सूयते । असावि । सुत । °सुत्य । सावयति ॥

सू sû, to bear, II, A. सूते । असूत । सुवे, सूष्व, सूताम् । सुवीत ॥
सुषुवे । सविष्यते or सोष्यते । सूयते । सूत ॥

सृ sri, to go, I, P. सरति ॥ ससार, ससर्थ; ससृव; ससुः । सरिष्यति ।
सृत । सारयति । सिसीर्षति ॥

सृज् srig, to let off, VI, P. सृजति ॥ ससर्ज । अस्राक्षीत् । स्रक्ष्यति ।
सृज्यते । सृष्ट, °सृज्य । स्रष्टुम् । सर्जयति । सिसृक्षति ॥

सृप् srip, to creep, I, P. सर्पति ॥ ससर्प; ससृपिव । असृपत् । सप्स्यँति
or स्रप्स्यति । सृप्यते । सृप्त । सृप्त्वा, °सृप्य । सर्पयति । सिसृप्सति ॥

सो so, to finish, IV, P. स्यति ॥ ससौ । असात् । सीयते । सित ।
सित्वा, °साय । सातुम् । साययति ॥

स्कंद् skand, to approach, I, P. स्कंदति ॥ चस्कंद । अस्कांत्सीत् ।
स्कंत्स्यति । स्कन्न । °स्कंद्य or °स्कद्य । स्कंदयति ॥

स्तंभ् stambh, to prop, IX, P. स्तभ्नाति ॥ तस्तंभ, तस्तभान, तस्तभानु ॥
तस्तंभ । अस्तंभीत् । स्तभ्यते । स्तब्ध । स्तब्ध्वा, °स्तभ्य । स्तब्धुम् । स्तंभयति ॥

स्तु stu, to praise, II, P, A. स्तौति or स्तवीति । अस्तौत् or अस्त-

वीत् । स्तौतु or स्तवीतु । सुयात्, सुवीत ॥ तुष्टाव । अस्तावीत् or अस्तौ-
षीत् ; अस्तोष्ट । स्तोष्यति । सूयते । अस्तावि । स्तुत । स्तुत्वा, °स्तुत्य ।
स्तावयति । अतुष्टवत् । तुष्टूषति ॥

स्तृ stri, to cover, V or IX, P. A. स्तृणोति or स्तृणाति ॥ तस्तार,
तस्तरे । स्तरिष्यति । स्तीर्यते । स्तृत । स्तृत्वा, °स्तृत्य । स्तारयति । तिस्तीर्षते ॥

स्था sthâ, to stand, I, P. तिष्ठति ॥ तस्थौ । अस्थात् । स्थास्यति ।
स्थीयते । अस्थायि । स्थित । स्थित्वा, °स्थाय । स्थातुम् । स्थापयति ।
अतिष्ठिपत् । तिष्ठासति ॥

स्पृश् spris, to touch, VI, P. स्पृशति ॥ पस्पर्श । अस्प्राक्षीत् or अस्पृ-
क्षत् । स्प्रक्ष्यति । स्पृश्यते । स्पृष्ट । स्पृष्ट्वा, °स्पृश्य । स्प्रष्टुम् । स्पर्शयति ।
पिस्पृक्षति ॥

स्मि smi, to smile, I, A. स्मयते ॥ सिष्मिये । अस्मयिष्ट । स्मित ।
स्मित्वा, °स्मित्य । स्मापयति or स्माययति ॥

स्मृ smri, to remember, I, P. स्मरति ॥ सस्मार । स्मरिष्यति । स्मर्यते ।
स्मृत । स्मृत्वा, °स्मृत्य । स्मर्तुम् । स्मारयति ॥

स्यन्द् syand, to drop, I, A. स्यंदते ॥ सस्यंदे । स्यंस्यते । स्यंद्यते ।
स्यन्न । स्यंस्वा । स्यंदयति ॥

सु sru, to flow, I, P. स्रवति ॥ सुस्राव । अस्रावीत् । स्रविष्यति । स्रुत ॥

स्वंज् svañg, to embrace, I, A. स्वजते ॥ सस्वजे । स्वंक्ष्यते । स्वक्त ॥

स्वप् svap, to sleep, II, P. स्वपिति ॥ सुष्वाप ; सुष्वुपुः । अस्वाप्सीत् ।
स्वप्स्यति । सुप्यते । अस्वापि । सुप्त । सुप्त्वा । स्वप्तुम् । स्वापयति ।
सुषुप्सति ॥

हन् han, to kill, II, P. हंति ; हतः ; घ्नंति । अहन् ; अघ्नन् । हनानि,
जहि, हंतु ; घ्नंतु । हन्यात् ॥ जघान । अवधीत् । हनिष्यति । हन्यते ।
हत । हत्वा, °हत्य । हंतुम् । घातयति । जिघांसति ॥

हा hâ, to leave, III, P. जहाति ; जहति । जहानि, जहीहि, जहातु ;
जहतु ॥ जहौ, जहिथ or जहाथ । अहासीत् or अहात् । हास्यति । हीयते ।
हीन । हित्वा, °हाय । हातुम् । हापयति । जिहासति ॥

हिंस् hims, to strike, VII, P. हिनस्ति । अहिनत् ; अहिंसन् । हिनसानि,
हिंधि, हिनस्तु । हिंस्यात् ॥ जिहिंस । अहिंसीत् । हिंसिष्यति । हिंस्यते ।
हिंसित । हिंसयति । जिहिंसिषति ॥

हु hu, to sacrifice, III, P. जुहोति ॥ जुहाव or जुहवांचकार । अहौ-
षीत् । होष्यति । हूयते । हुत । हुत्वा । होतुम् । हावयति । जुहूषति ।
जोहवीति ॥

हृ hri, to take, I, P. A. हरति, °ते ॥ जहार, जहर्थ; जहुः । अहार्षीत्,
अहृत । हरिष्यति; हर्ता । ह्रियते । अहारि । हृत । हृत्वा, °हृत्य ।
हारयति । जिहीर्षति, °ते । जरीहर्ति ॥

ह्री hrî, to be ashamed, III, P. जिह्रेति; जिह्रीतः; जिह्रियति ।
अजिह्रेत् । जिह्रेतु । जिह्रीयात् ॥ जिह्राय; जिह्रियुः । ह्रीण or ह्रीत ।
ह्रेपयति । जेह्रीयते ॥

ह्वे hve, to call, I, P. A. ह्वयति, °ते ॥ जुहाव; जुहुवुः । अह्वत्, अह्वत ।
ह्वास्यते । हूयते । हूत । °हूय । ह्वाययति । जुहूषति । जोह्वीति ॥

APPENDIX II.

The versification of classical Sanskrit differs considerably from that of the Vedic hymns, being more artificial, more subject to strict rules, and showing a far greater number of varieties of metre.

Classical Sanskrit metres are divided into :—

I. Those measured by the number of syllables;

II. Those measured by the number of *morae* they contain.

All verses are divided into half-verses, while nearly all are further divided into quarter-verses (pâda).

Quantity is measured as in Latin and Greek. Vowels are long by nature or by position. Two consonants make a preceding short vowel long by position, Anusvâra and Visarga counting as full consonants. A short vowel counts as one *mora* (mâtrâ), a long vowel (by nature or position) as two.

I. Metres measured by Syllables (Aksharakkhandah).

These consist of :—

A. Two half-verses identical in structure, while the quarter-verses 1 and 3 differ from 2 and 4.

B. Four quarter-verses all identical in structure.

A. The Sloka.

The sloka (song, from sru, to hear) developed from the Vedic Anushtubh is the Epic verse, and may be considered the Indian verse *par excellence*, occurring, as it does, far more frequently than any other metre in classical Sanskrit poetry. It consists of two half-verses of 16 syllables or of four pâdas of 8 syllables.

Dividing the half-verse into four feet of four syllables, we find that only the second and the fourth foot are determined as to

quantity. The fourth is necessarily iambic (∪ − ∪ ⌣), while the
second may assume five different forms. The first and the third
foot are undetermined, except that ⌣ ∪ ∪ ⌣ is always excluded
from them. By far the commonest form of the second foot is
∪ − − ⌣ (in Nala 1442 out of 1732 half-verses).
The type of the *s*loka may therefore be represented thus :—

$$\bullet \; \bullet \; \bullet \; \bullet \; | \; \cup - - \underset{\smile}{} \; | \; \bullet \; \bullet \; \bullet \; \bullet \; | \; \cup - \cup - \; \|$$

Ex. āsīd rāgā Nălō nāmă | Vīrăsēnăsŭtō bălī |
ŭpăpannō gŭṇāīr ish*t*aī | rūpăvān a*s*văkōvĭdă*h* ||

It is only when the second foot has ∪ − − ⌣ that the first foot
may assume all its admissible forms. When the second foot has
any of the other four forms, the first foot is limited, as shown
in the following table:—

The first (typical) form is called Pathyâ ; the remaining four,
called Vipulâ, are in the above table arranged in order of
frequency of occurrence. Out of 2580 half-verses taken from
Kâlidâsa (Raghu-va*m*sa and Kumâra-sambhava), Mâgha, Bhâravi,
and Bilha*n*a, each of the five admissible forms of the *s*loka in the
above order claims the following share : 2289, 116, 89, 85, 1.

In the table a dot indicates an undetermined syllable; a comma
marks the *caesura*.

The end of a pâda coincides with the end of a word (sometimes only with the end of a word in a compound), and the whole

*s*loka contains a complete sentence. The construction does not run on into the next line. Occasionally three half-verses are found combined into a triplet.

B. All Four Pâdas identical in Form.

1. Of the numerous varieties developed from the Vedic **Trish*t*ubh** (11 syllables to the pâda), the commonest are :—

   a. Indrava*g*râ : − − ∪ | − − − ∪ | ∪ − − ∪ | − − ‖
   b. Upendrava*g*râ : ∪ − ∪ | − − − ∪ | ∪ − − ∪ | − − ‖
   c. Upa*g*âti (a mixture of the above two) :
       ⏑ − ∪ | − − − ∪ | ∪ − − ∪ | − ⏑ ‖
   d. Sâlinî : − − − | −, − − ∪ | − − − ∪ | − − ‖
   e. Rathoddhatâ : − ∪ − | ∪ ∪ ∪ | − ∪ − | ∪ − ‖

2. The commonest forms of *G*agatî (12 syllables to the pâda) are :—

   a. Va*m*sasthâ : ∪ − ∪ | − − − ∪ | ∪ − − ∪ | − ∪ − ‖
   b. Drutavilambita : ∪ ∪ ∪ | − ∪ ∪ ∪ | − ∪ ∪ ∪ | − ∪ − ‖

3. The commonest variety of *S*akvarî (14 syllables to the pâda) is :—

   Vasantatilakâ : − − ∪ | − ∪ ∪ ∪ | ∪ − ∪ | ∪ − ∪ | − ⏑ ‖

4. The commonest form of **Ati*s*akvarî** (15 syllables to the pâda) is :—

   Mâlinî : ∪ ∪ ∪ | ∪ ∪ ∪ | − −, − | ∪ − − | ∪ − ⏑ ‖

5. The commonest variety of **Atyash*t*i** (17 syllables to the pâda) is :—

   a. *S*ikhari*n*î : ∪ − − | − − −, | ∪ ∪ ∪ | ∪ ∪ − | − ∪ ∪ | ∪ − ‖
   b. Mandâkrântâ :
       − − − | −, ∪ ∪ | ∪ ∪ ∪ | −, − ∪ | − − ∪ | − ⏑ ‖

6. The commonest form of **Atidh*r*iti** (19 syllables to the pâda) is :—

   Sârdûlavikrî*d*ita :
       − − − | ∪ ∪ − | ∪ − ∪ | ∪ ∪ −, | − − ∪ | − − ∪ | ⏑ ‖

7. The commonest variety of **Prakṛti** (21 syllables to the pâda) is :—

Sragdharâ :

$$- - - \mid - \cup - \mid -, \cup \cup \mid \cup \cup \cup \mid \cup -, - \mid \cup - - \mid \cup - - \parallel$$

II. Metres measured by Morae.

A. Metres in which the sum total only of the morae is prescribed (Mâtrâkhandaḥ).

The **Vaitâlîya** contains 30 morae in the half-verse, 14 in the first pâda, 16 in the second. Each pâda may be divided into three feet, the second always consisting of a choriambus, and the third of two iambics; while the first foot in the first pâda consists of a pyrrhic, in the second pâda of an anapaest. The half-verse thus contains 21 syllables. The following is the scheme of the half-verse :

$$\cup \cup \mid - \cup \cup - \mid \cup - \cup \underset{\smile}{-} \parallel \cup \cup - \mid - \cup \cup - \mid \cup - \cup \underset{\smile}{-} \parallel$$

B. Metres in which the number of morae in each foot (gaṇa) is specified (Gaṇakkhandaḥ).

Âryâ or **Gâthâ** has $7\frac{1}{2}$ feet to the half-verse, each foot containing 4 morae (= 30 morae altogether). The 4 morae may take the form $\cup \cup \cup \cup$, $- -$, $- \cup \cup$, or $\cup \cup -$; in the 2nd and 4th they may also become $\cup - \cup$; in the 6th they appear as $\cup \cup \cup \cup$ or $\cup - \cup$. The 8th foot is always monosyllabic; the 6th of the second half-verse consists of a single short syllable. Hence the second half-verse contains only 27 morae.

SANSKRIT INDEX.

This index contains all Sanskrit words and affixes occurring in the grammar, with the exception of numerals (116–120), unless declined, and of the verbs given in Appendix I. The former, owing to their numerical order; the latter, because of their alphabetical arrangement, will easily be found. All indifferent words occurring in examples of Sandhi or of Syntax are of course excluded. The figures refer to paragraphs.

ABBREVIATIONS.

A. = adjective. **adv.**, adverb, adverbial. **af.**, affix. **aor.**, aorist. **art.**, article. **Bv.**, Bahuvrīhi. **cd.**, compound. **cj.**, conjunction. **cl.**, class. **cpv.**, comparative. **csv.**, causative. **dcl.**, declension. **dem.**, demonstrative. **den.**, denominative. **des.**, desiderative. **Dg.**, Dvigu. **Dv.**, Dvandva. **encl.**, enclitic. **f. n.**, foot-note. **ft.**, future. **grd.**, gerund. **ij.**, interjection. **indcl.**, indeclinable. **inf.**, infinitive. **ipv.**, imperative. **itrv.**, interrogative. **K.**, Karma-dhâraya. **N.**, note. **n.**, neuter. **neg.**, negative. **nm.**, numeral. **pcl.**, particle. **per.**, periphrastic. **pf.**, perfect. **pr.**, present. **prf.**, prefix. **prn.**, pronoun, pronominal. **prp.**, preposition, prepositional. **ps.**, passive. **pt.**, participle. **sf.**, suffix. **spv.**, superlative. **Tp.**, Tat-purusha. **v.**, vocative. **w.**, with.

-a, bases in, 107.
aksh, des. of, 198, 2.
akshara-*kkh*anda*h*, n. syllabic metre, App. II, 1.
ákshi, n. eye, 110, 3 ; 219 b.
agni-mát, a. having fire, 98 ; 105, 1 and 3.
agni-mátí, f., 105, 4.
agni-máth, a. fire-kindling, 89.
Agní-shómau, Dv. cd., 217 c.
ágre, adv. prp. before, 209 d.
ágho*h*, v. Sandhi of, 55.
Áṅga, strong base, 83.
a*k*, to go, bases ending in, 104.
á-*gñ*âta, a. K. cd., 215, 3.
a*ñg*, to anoint, 144, VII, 1.
-at, bases in, 97.
áti, prp. beyond, 207 a ; 208 a.

áti-, prf. very, 210.
Atidh*r*íti, f. a metre, App. II, I B, 6.
Atisakvarí, f. a metre, App. II, I B, 4.
Atyash*t*í, f. a metre, App. II, I B, 5.
átha, pcl. then, now, 210.
athavâ, cj. or, 210.
ad, to eat, type of cl. II, 138, 1 ; 144, II.
adát, pr. pt., 97.
adás, dem. prn., 124; 226. B.
ádhara, prn. a. inferior, west, 130 c.
adhás, adv. prp. below, 209 d.
ádhi, prp. over, 207 a ; 208 c.
adhi-kr*í*tya, prp. grd. regarding, 210 ; 240 b.
adhi-strí, f. K. cd. chief woman, 215, 3.
-an, bases in, 102.

an, to breathe, 144, II, 1.
ana*d*út, m. ox, 106, 3.
anantarám, adv. prp. after, 209 c.
-an'iya, pt. ps. pt., 187; 239.
ánu, prp. after, 207 a; 208; 208 a.
An-udâtta, grave accent, 18.
Anudâtta-tara, accent, 18.
ánurûpam, adv. cd. accordingly, 215, 3.
Anush*t*úbh, f. a Vedic metre, App. II, I A.
Anu-svâra, 5; 11; 17, 8; 28; 30; 3; 31; 33; 47; App. II, introd.
antár, adv. prp. within, 52, f. n.; 209 a.
ántara, pr. a. outer, 130 c.
antara, n. difference, 219 c, γ.
antará, adv. prp. without, 209 a.
ántare*n*a, adv. prp. without, 209 a.
antiká, a. near (cpv.); -m, adv., 233, IV a.
anyá, prn. a. other, 130 a.
a*n*ya-tará, prn. a. either, 130 a.
anv-á*k*, a. following, 104.
ap, f. pl. water, 106.
ápa, prp. off, 207 a; 208 b.
ápara, prn. a. other, 130 c.
ápi, pcl. w. itrv., 129; 210.
ápi, prp. upon, 207 a.
abhí, prp. towards, 207 a; 208 a.
abhí-tas, adv. prp. around, 209 a.
-am, indcl. pt. in, 188.
ambâ, f. mother, 107, f. n. 2.
ay, to go, per. pf., 156.
-áya 1. csv. sf., 192; 195; 196.
-aya 2. den. sf., 206.
ayi, v. pcl., 211.
ar*k*, to honour, 146, 2 b; 198, 2.
artha, object, at end of cd., 219 c, δ.
ardhá, prn. a. half, 130 d.
arh, to deserve, 242 b.
álam, adv. prp. enough, 209 b.
álpa, prn. a. little (cpv.), 115 d; 130 d.
áva, prp. down, 207 b.
Ava-graha, m. mark of elision of ă, 7.
ava-yâ*g*, m. Vedic priest, 90, 3, N. 2.
ávara, prn. a. posterior, 130 c.
avás, adv. prp. below, 209 d.
ávâ*k*, a. downward, 104, N.
Avyayî-bhâva, m. adv. cd., 215, 3.

a*s*, to eat, des. of, 198, 2.
ash*t*án, nm. eight, 118.
-as, bases in, 82, N. 1; 95.
as 1. to throw, aor., 162, 3.
as 2. to be, irreg. pr. forms, 144, II, 2; 178; 233, I b; 234, II c.
ás*rig*, n. blood, 90, 3.
ásthi, n. bone, 110, 3.
asmád, prn. base, 121.
ah, to say, pf., 153, 3.
áhan, n. day, 103, 2; at end of cd., 215, 3, N.
ahám, prn., I, 121; unaccented forms of, 226.
áhar, n. day, 52, f. n.
áhar-aha*h*, adv. day by day, 103, 2.
ahar-ga*n*a, m. number of days, 103, 2.
ahaha, ij., 211.
aho, ij., 211.
aho-râtra, m, day and night, 103, 2.

-â, bases in, 107; radical -â, 108.
ấ 1. prp. near, 207 a; 208; 208 b.
â 2. pcl., 210.
â 3. ij., 211.
âtmán, m. soul, 102; self, 126, 2.
Âtmane-pada, n. middle voice, 131.
â-dấ-ya, grd. = prp. with, 240 b.
âdi, m. beginning, at end of cd., 219 c, α.
âdya, a. first, 219 c, α.
-âna 1. ipv. af., 142, N. 4.
-âna 2. Âtm. pt. af., 184; 185.
âp, to ọbtain, pf., 146, 2 a; des., 198, 2.
â-rábh-ya, grd. = prp. beginning from, 209 c.
Âryâ, f. a metre, App. II, II B.
âsís, f. blessing, 95, N. 3.
âs, to sit down, pf., 156; 237.
â-sakta, pf. pt. ps. attached to, 234, II a.

-i, bases in, 109; 110.
i, to go, 138, 1; 168; 169; 170; 175, 2.
i, w. prf. adhi, to read, 144, II, 3; 194 (csv.).
i*kkh*â, f. wish, w. inf., 242 a.
ítara, prn. a. other, 130 a.

íti, pcl. thus, 210; 227, N.; 235, N. 2.
itthám, adv. thus, 235, N. 2.
idám, prn. this, 123; 226 B.
-in, bases in, 82, N. 1; 99.
Indra-vagrâ, f. a metre, App. II,
 I B, I a.
Indra âdayah, Indra and the others,
 219 c, a.
indh, to kindle, 144, VII, 1.
íyat, a. so much, 98, N. 2.
iva, encl. pcl. like, 210.
ish, to wish, 144, VI, 2; 146, 3;
 150; 241 b.
-is, bases in, 95.

-í, bases in, 111.
íd, to praise, 144, II, 4.
-íyas, cpv. bases in, 100.
írshy, to envy, 231 A, 2.
ís, to rule, 144, II, 4; 233, I a.

-u, bases in, 109.
ukh, to be pleased, 146, 3.
ukkh, des. of, 198, 2.
út-tara, prn. a. subsequent, 130 c.
úd, prp. up, 207 b.
úd-ak, a. upward, 104.
Ud-âtta, acute accent, 18.
ud-dísya, prp. grd. towards, 210;
 240 b.
und, to wet, 139; 155, 1; 186, 1,
 N.; 198, 2.
úpa, prp. upon, 207 a; 208 a and c.
Upagâti, f. a. metre, App. II, I B, I c.
Upa-dhmâníya, m. labial sibilant,
 p. 2 (table).
upári, adv. prp. above, 209 a.
upânáh, f. shoe, 94, 3 c.
Upendravagrâ, f. a metre, App. II,
 I B, I b.
ubháya, prn. a. both, 130 b.
ubhayá-tas, adv. on both sides, 209 a.
uro-ga, a. produced on the breast,
 214, 6.
Ushníh, f. a metre, 94, 3 a.
-us, bases in, 95.

-û, bases in, 111.
úrg, f. strength, 90, 3.
úrdhvám, adv. prp. after, 209 c.

-rí, bases in, 112; in Dv. cds., 217 b.
rí, to go, 139; 144, I, 2; 194.
rig, to obtain, 146, 2 b.
rité, adv. prp. without, 209 a.
ritv-íg, m. priest, 90, 3.

éka, nm. one, 117; 130 b; =art., 223.
eka-tamá, prn. a. one (of many),
 130 a.
eka-tará, prn. a. either, 130 b.
etád, dem. prn. this, 125, 2; 226 B.
edh, to grow, 155, N.
enad (encl.), prn., 125, 3.
evá, pcl. just, 210; 226; 235, N. 3.
evám, pcl. thus, 210; 235, N. 2.
eshá, m. dem. prn. this, Sandhi of, 54.

-ai, -o, -au, bases in, 113.

-ka, sf., added to Bv. cds. in -rí, -í,
 -in, 219 d.
kakúbh, f. region, 89.
kákkit, itrv. pcl. = nonne, 210.
ka-tamá, prn. a. which of many?
 130 a.
ka-tará, pr. a. which of two? 130 a.
káti, itrv. a. how many? 128, N.
kati-payá, pr. a. some, 130 d.
kánishtha, spv. of alpa, little, 115.
káníyas, cpv. of alpa, 115.
kam, to love, 144, I, 6; aor., 164.
kartrí, f. of kartrí, maker, 112, N. 4.
Karma-dhâraya, m. descriptive cd.,
 215.
kás-kit, some one = indef. art., 223.
kântá, a. beloved, 107.
kámam, adv., 210.
kím, itrv. prn., 125 B; 210.
kim-u, kim-uta, kim punah, how
 much more? 210.
kíyat, a. how much? 98, N. 2.
kíla, pcl. = quidem, 210.
kut, to sever, 140, 3.
Kúru, -û, a Kuru, 109, N. 2.
kúsala, a. skilful, 234, II a.
krí, to make, 138, 5; 144, VIII;
 146, 1; 148; 152; 154, 8; 158;
 158, 1; 175, 3; 178; 180; 186,
 2; 187; 188; 191; 192; 196.;
 199; 202; 204; to take, 234, II d.

krit, to cut, 144, VI, 1.
kri-tá, pf. pt. done, 101, N. 2.
kritá-vat, pf. pt. act. 101, N. 2 ; 186, 2, N.
krité, prp. adv. for the sake of, 209 d.
krishna, den. to behave like Krishna, 206, 1.
krí, to scatter, 136, 2 ; 152, 3 ; 154,9.
krít, to praise, 136, 4.
klip, 146, 1.
kévalam, adv. merely, 210.
kram, to step, 144, I, 1.
krí, to buy, 138, 6 ; 143 ; 154, 7 ; 182.
krúñk, m. curlew, 90, 1, N.
krósam, acc. of distance, 228, 2.
kroshtri, m. jackal, 112, N. 3.
kvá, itrv. where ? 210.
kship, to throw, 158, irreg., 1 ; 180 ; 234, II c.
kshírasyá, den. to long for milk, 206, 4.
kshudrá, a. mean, cpv. of, 115.

khan, to dig, 140, 3 ; 151, 3 ; 175, 5 ; 189 b.
khálu, pcl. indeed, 210.
khid, to vex, 144, VI, 1.
khyâ, to tell, 162.

Ganá, m. metrical foot, App. II, II B.
Gana-kkhandah, n. foot metre, App. II, II B.
gandhá, m. smell, at end of cd., 219 b.
gam, to go, 74 ; 140, 3 ; 144, I, 2 ; 151, 3 ; 189 c ; 192, N.; 199 ; 204, 2 ; 228, 1, N.
gáríyas, cpv. of gurú, heavy, 100 ; 105, 1 and 3.
gáríyasí, f., 105, 4.
gavyá, den. to wish for cows, 206, 2 a, a.
Gâthâ, f. a metre, App. II, II B.
gír, f. voice, 65 ; 92, 3.
Guná, 20.
gup, to protect, 89 ; 144, I, 6.
guh, to hide, 144, I, 1 ; 160, 2 ; a. hiding, 93.
gai, to sing, 168, 1 ; 175, 1 ; 187, III, 1.

gó, f. cow, at end of cds., 215, 2.
granth, to tie, 151, 4.
grah, to seize, 144, IX, 2 ; 151, 2 ; 158, N.; 175, 7; 199; 234, II d.
grâma-prâpta, Tp. cd. having reached the village, 214, 1.

ghas, to eat, 151, 3.
ghnát, pr. pt. of han, to kill, 182, N.
ghrâ, to smell, 144, I, 3.

ka, cj. and, 210 ; 226.
kakâs, to shine, 95, II ; 144, II, 5 ; 155, 2.
katúr, nm. four, 117.
-kana, indef. sf., 129.
kam, w. prf. â, to sip, 144, I, 1.
kar, to move, 189.
karamá, prn. a. last, 130 d.
ki, to collect, 153, 1 ; 175, 2.
kikírs, a. desirous of doing, 95, II.
-kit, indef. sf., 129.
kit, to think, 172, 1 ; 187, III.
kitra-líkh, m. painter, 88.
kur, to steal, 136, 4 ; 168, 2 ; 180, N.; 183, 2; 188; 191.
két, pcl. if, 210 ; 248 b.

gaksh, to eat, 144, II, 1 ; 144, II, 5.
Gágatí, f. a Vedic metre, App. II, I B, 2.
gagan-vás, pf. pt. act. of gam, to go, 101, N. 1.
gagmi-vás, pf. pt. act. of gam, 101, N.1.
gaghni-vás, pf. pt. act. of han, to kill, 101, N. 1.
gan, to be born, 144, IV, 3 ; 151, 3 ; 166 ; 175, 5 ; 181, 2.
gána, m. people, at end of cd., 224 a.
gap, to recite, 205.
gala-mâtram, n. water alone, 219 c, β.
gala-múk, m. cloud, 90, 1.
gâgri, to wake, 52, f. n.; 144, II, 5 ; 156, 2 a.
gâtyâ, by birth, 230, 4.
gi, to conquer, 153, 1 ; 168, 2 ; 186 ; 187, I, II, III ; 189 a ; 194 ; 199.
Gihvâ-múlíya, m. guttural sibilant, p. 2 (table).

*gí*v, to live, 150.
*gí*va-*ná*s, a. life-destroying, 94, 1 b.
*gñ*apáya, csv. of *gñ*â, to know, 166.
*gñ*â, to know, 144, IX, 2; 194; 229, 1.
*gñ*âna-vat, a. possessing knowledge, 98.
*gy*â, to grow weak, 144, IX, 2.
-tá, pf. ps. pt. sf., 186.
táksh, a. paring, 93.
tákshan, m. carpenter, 102.
tátas, adv. then, 210.
táti, a. so many, 128, N.
tat-para, a. intent on, 234, II a.
Tat-purusha, dependent cd., 214.
táthâ, adv. thus, 210; 235, N. 2.
tád, adv., 210; prn., 125; 226 B.
tan, to stretch, 138, 5; 151, 1; 154, 3; 183, 2; 185.
tántrî, f. lute, 111, 4.
tam, *to* languish, 144, IV, 1.
tarî, f. boat, 111, 4.
-távya, ft. pt. ps. sf., 187; 239.
-tas, adv. in, 233, IV b.
tasthivás, pf. pt. act. of sthâ, to stand, 101, N. 1.
tā́vat, adv. so long, 210.
tirás, prp. adv. across, 209 a.
tiry-*ák*, a. tortuous, 104.
tu, cj. but, 210.
tud, to strike, 136, 2; 154; 198.
-tum, inf. sf., 191.
tulya, a. equal, 233, II b.
tush, to be satisfied, 230, II B, c.
tri*na*-hasta, Bv. cd. having grass in one's hand, 219 a.
triprá, a. hasty, cpv. of, 115.
tr*ih*, to kill, 144, VII, 2.
tr*í*, to cross, 146, 1; 151, 1, N.; 189.
-tya, grd. sf., 188; 240.
tyád, prn. that, 125, A 1.
trayá, a. threefold, 130 d.
trí, nm. three, 117.
trítaya, a. threefold, 130 d.
tri-bhuvanam, n. Dv. cd., 215, 2.
tri-lokî, f. the three worlds, Dv. cd., 215, 2.
Trish*t*ubh, f. a Vedic metre, App. II, I B, 1.

tvá, prn. a. other, 130 a.
tvá*k*, f. skin, 90, 1.
tvád, prn. base, thou, 121.
tvám, prn. thou, 121; unaccented forms of, 226.
-tvā́, grd. sf., 188; 240.
da*m*s, to bite, 144, I, 4.
dákshi*na*, prn. a. right, south, 130 c.
dákshi*na*na, adv. 233, IV b.
dádhi, n. curds, 110, 3.
dadhr*í*sh, a. bold, 94, 2.
dam, to tame, 144, IV, 1.
Damayanty-artham, Bv. cd., 219 c, δ.
dambh, to deceive, 151, 4.
day 1. to pity, 156, 1.
day 2. to give, 233, I a.
daridrâ, to be poor, 144, II, 5.
dal, to cut, 136, 4.
dasa-kumârî, f. Dv. cd., 215, 2.
dah, to burn, 79; 158,4; 180; 205, 1.
dâ, to give, 144, III, 1; 158, irreg., 2; 163; 181, 1; 187, I and III, 1; 193; to take, 234, II d.
dā́man, f. rope, 105, 4.
div 1. to play, 65; 136, 3.
div 2. f. sky, 106, 2.
di*s*, to show, 160, 1; f. region, 94, 1 a.
dish*t*yâ, adv., 211.
dih, to anoint, 160, 5.
dîp, to shine, 166.
dîrgha-ā́yus, a. long-lived, 95.
dus, prp. ill, 207 b.
duh, to milk, 66; 69, N.; 160, 4; 199; m. milker, 60; a., 94, 3 a.
dûrám, adv. far, 233, IV a.
-dr*i*ksha, -dr*i*sa, -dr*i*s, prn. sf., 127.
dr*i*s, to see, 144, I, 5; 158, irreg., 3; 162, 2; 168, 2; 187, III, 3; 191; 205, 3; bases from, 94, 1 a.
dr*í*, to tear, 144, IX, 1.
Deva-datta, m. Tp. cd., 214, 2.
deva-dâsa, m. Tp. cd., 212.
Deva-nâgarî, character, 2; 3; letters, p, 2 (table); classification of, 5.
deve*g*, m. worshipper of the gods, 90, 3, N. 1.
desa, m. country, 224 c.
desa*_*antaram, n. Bv. cd. another country, 219 c, γ.

do, to cut, csv. of, 193.
dós, m. (n.) arm, 95, II.
dyú, f. sky, 106, 2.
dyó, f. sky, 113, N.
drash*t*u-kâma, a., 242 c.
dru, to run, 148 ; 164.
Druta-vilambita, n. a metre, App.
    II, I B, 2 b.
druh, to hate, bases from, 94, 3 b.
Dvandvá, copulative cd., 216.
dvayá, a. twofold, 130 d.
dvắr, f. door, 92, 3.
dví, nm. two, 117.
Dvigu, numerical cds., 215, 2.
dvítaya, a. twofold, 130 d.
dvi-râtrá, m. Dg. cd., 215, 2.
dvish, to hate, 66 ; 70 ; 142, N. 6 ;
    143 ; a. hating, 93.

dhanín, a. rich, 99 ; 195, 1 and 3 ;
    114.
dhaníni, f. rich, 105, 4.
dhánus, n. bow, 219 b.
dhâ, to place, 144, III, 1 ; 154, 2 ;
    158, irreg., 2 ; 163.
dhâtrí, m. providence, 112.
dhânya_artha, m. Tp. cd., 214, 2.
-dhi, ipv. sf., 142, n. 4.
dhik, ij. fie, 211.
dhí̆, f. thought, 111.
dhúr, f. yoke, 65.
dhû, to shake, 140, 2 ; 144, V, 3 ;
    144, IX, 1 ; 194.
dhûp, to warm, 144, I, 6.
dhrí, to hold, 154, 10.
dhrísh, to dare, bases from, 94, 2.
dhmâ, to blow, 144, I, 5.
-dhvam or -*dh*vam, 2. pl. aor. sf.,
    158, irreg., 5.
dhvas, to fall, bases from, 95, N. 1
    (p. 42).

-ná, pf. ps. pt. sf., 186.
na, neg. pcl. not, 210.
nadí̆, f. river, 111.
na-nú, itrv. pcl., 210.
náptrí, m. grandson, 112.
nam, to bend, 189 c.
Nala, commonest form of Śloka in,
    App. II, I A.

na*s*, to destroy, bases from, 94, 1 b ;
    162, 4.
nah, to bind, bases from, 79, N. ; 94,
    3 c ; 136, 3 ; 174.
nắma, pcl., 210.
nắman, n. name, 102.
ní, prp. into, 207 b.
nikashắ, prp. adv., 209 a.
nigá, reflex. a. own, 126, 3.
ninívás, pf. pt. act., 101, N. 1.
nipu*n*a, a. clever, 234, II a.
nir-makshikam, adv. cd., 215, 3.
nis, prp. without, 207 b.
ní, to lead, 150, 2 ; 152, 1 ; 154, 6;
    158 ; 180 ; 192.
nítvắ, grd. = prp. with, 240 b.
níla_u*gg*vala-vapu*h*, Bv. cd., 218, N.
níla_utpalam, n. K. cd., 215, 2 ; 218.
nílotpala-saras-tîra, Bv. cd., 218, N.
nú, itrv, pcl., 210.
nud, to push, 186, 1, N.
nû, to praise, 136, 2.
n*ri*, m. man, 112, N. 2.
nédish*th*a, nédîyas, spv. and cpv. of
    antiká, near, 115.
néma, prn. a, half, 130 b.
naú, f. ship, 113 ; 215, 2.
ny-ák, a. low, 104.

pa*k*, to cook, 151, 1 ; 198.
pañ*k*a-gava, n. Dg. cd,, 215, 2.
pañ*k*a-gu, a, Dg. cd., 215, 2.
pá*ñk*an, nm. five, 118.
panditá, a. learned, 234, II a.
pat, to fall, 162, 4 ; 186 ; 199 ; 205, 2.
páti, m. lord, 110.
pathín, m. path, 103.
Padá, n. middle base, 83.
pára, prn. a. subsequent, 130 c.
páram, adv. prp. after, 209 c.
parama_aha, m. the highest day,
    215, N.
Parasmai-pada, n. act. voice, 131.
parasmai-pada, n. Tp. cd., 214, N.
párâ, prp. back, 207 b.
pári, prp. round, 207 a ; 208 a ; 208 b.
pari-vrá*g*, m. mendicant, 90, 3, N. 1.
par*n*a-dhvás, a., 95, N. 1.
pa*śk*ắt, adv. prp. after, 209 d.
pâ 1. to drink, 144, I, 3 ; 175, 1 ; 190.

pâ 2. to protect, 175, 1; 194.

pắda, m. foot. 219 b; quarter-verse, Appendix II, introd.

pắdau, m. dual, the feet, 224 b.

pin*d*a-grás, a. eating a mouthful, 95.

pitára, den. to behave like a father, 206, 1.

pitárau, m. dual, parents, 224 b.

pitâ-putraú, Dv. cd., 217 b.

pit*rí*, m. father, 52, f. n.; 112, N. 1.

pipa*th*is, a. desirous of repeating, 95, N. 2.

pi*s*, to form, 144, VI, 1.

pí*v*an, a. fat, 105, 4.

pí*v*ar*î*, f. fat, 105, 4.

putrá, m. son, 217 b.

putrîyá, den. to treat like a son, 206, 2 a, β; 206, 2 b, N.

púnar, adv., 52, f. n.; 210.

púr, f. city, 92, 3.

purás, adv. prp. before, 209 d.

purástât, adv. prp. before, 209 d.

purắ, adv., 244, 2 a.

purusha-vyâghra, m. K. cd. tiger-like man, 215, 1.

puro-dắ*s*, m. a priest, 94, 1 c.

pû, to purify, 144, IX, 1.

pûrva, prn. a. prior, 130 c.

pr*î*, to fill, 175, 4; 186, 1; 189; 204, 1.

pe*k*ivás, pf. pt. act. of pa*k*, 101, N. 1.

prá, prp. before, 207 b.

Prakriti, f. a metre, App. II, I B, 7.

prak*rí*tyâ, by nature, 230, I, 4.

Prag*rí*hya vowels, 26.

pra*kkh*, to ask, 144, VI, 3; 199; 229, 2.

práti, prp. back, 207 a; 208; 208 a, b.

prati-divan, m. the sun, 105, 1, 3.

prati*kî*, f. a. behind, 105, 4.

praty-á*k*, a. behind, 84; 104; 105, 1 and 3; 114 (cpv.).

prathamá, prn. a. first, 130 d.

prábh*r*iti, adv. prp., 209 c; 219 c, a.

pra-*s*âm, a. mild, 74; 91, 4.

pra*s*ná, m. question, 71.

prâ*k*, a. eastern, 104, N.; 114 (cpv.)

prâ*kh*, a. asking, 90, 2.

prâ*ñk*, a. worshipping, 66; 90, 1, N.; 104, f. n. 3.

prâtár, adv. early, 52, f. n.

prâpta-grâma, Bv. cd., 214, 1.

prâyas, prâya*s*as, prâye*n*a, adv. generally, 210.

priyá, a. dear, 233, II a.

priya-sakha, m. K. cd., 215, N.

pr*î*, to love, csv., 194.

phal, to burst, irreg. pf., 151, 1, N.

bandh, to bind, 69; 144, IX, 3.

bahís, adv. prp. outside, 209 c.

bahu-kumârî-ka, Bv. cd., 219 d.

bahu-bhart*r*i-ka, Bv. cd., 219 d.

bahulá, a. frequent, cpv. of, 115.

Bahu-vrîhi, m. possessive cds., 218.

bahu-svâmi-kâ, Bv. cd., 219 d.

buddhi, f. thought, instr. of, 230, 2, N.

budh, to know, 136, 1; 139; 140, 1; 150, 1; 158; 168, 2; 169; 170; 172; 174, N.; 180; a. knowing, 60; 69, N.; 89.

bodháya, csv. of budh, 155, 3.

brahmán, m. n. creator, 102.

brahma-hán, a. Brahman-killing, 103, 5.

brû, to speak, 144, II, 6; 229, 2.

Bha, weakest base, 83.

bhágo*h*, v., 55.

bha*g*, to enjoy, 151, 1, N.

bha*ñg*, to break, 144, VII, 1.

bhart*rí*, m. husband, 112, N. 1.

bhávat 1. pr. pt. being, 98, N. 1; 105, 1 and 3.

bhávat 2. m. Your Honour, 98, N. 1; 226 A.

bhávatî, f., 105, 4.

bhavitávyam, ft. ps. pt. 239 c.

bhắvyam, ft. ps. pt., 239 c.

bhid, to cut, 140, 2; 168, 2; 186, 1.

bhishá*g*, m. physician, 90, 3.

bhî, to fear, 156, 2 b; 194.

bhu*g*, to eat, 190.

bhû 1. f. earth, 111.

bhû 2. to be, 136, 1; 143; 153, 2; 154, 14; 163; 169; 176; 178; 182; 183; 184; 187, II; 189; 191; 196;

197; 201; 203; 233, I b; w. prf.
pra, to be master of, 233, I a.
bh*ri*, to bear, 148; 156, 2 b.
bh*rigg*, a. roasting, 90, 3, N. I.
bhó*h*, v., 55.
bhra*ms*, to fall, 144, IV, 3.
bhra*gg*, to fry, 144, VI, 3; bases
from, 90, 3, N. I.
bhram, to wander, 144, IV, I.
bhrâg, to shine, 90, 3, N. I.
bhrânti, f. error, instr. of, 230, I, 2 N.

Magádheshu, in Magadha, 224 c.
-mat, a. sf., 98.
máti, f. thought, 109, N. I.
matimân, m. wise, cpv. and spv. of,
115.
mad, to rejoice, 144, IV, I.
-man, bases in, 102.
man, to think, 158, irreg., I; 189.
manth, to churn, 144, I, 4; 144, IX, 3.
Mandâkrântâ, f. a metre, App. II,
I B, 5 b.
mahát, a. great, 97, N.; 215, 3, N.
mahâ-râgá, m. king, 215, N.
má̆, prohibitive pcl., 139; 245, N.
mâ, to measure, 144, III, 2.
mâtá̆-pitárau, Dv. cd., 217 b.
mât*rí*, f. mother, 112, N. I.
mâtra, n. measure, 219 c, β; 235, N. 3.
má̆trâ, f. *mora*, App. II, introd.
Mâtrâ-*kh*andas, n. metre measured
by *morae*, App. II, II A.
-mâna, pt. sf., 184.
Mâlinî, f. a metre, App. II, I B, 4.
má̆sam, acc. of duration, for a month,
228, 2.
mâsma, prohibitive pcl., 245, N.
Mitrá̆-váru*n*au, Dv. cd., 217 c.
mi*sr*áya, den. to mix, 206, 3.
mí, to walk, 136, 4.
muktvá̆, grd. = prp. except, 240 b.
mu*k*, to release, 144, VI, I; 166;
234, II c.
muh, to confound, bases from, 94, 3 b.
múhus, adv. often, 210.
m*ri*, to die, 136, 2; 198, I; 205, 3.
m*rig*, to cleanse, 144, I, I; 144, II,
7 a; bases from, 90, 3, N. I.

m*ri*dú, a. soft, 109.
medhâvín, a. wise, 105, I and 3.
medhâvínî, f., 105, 4.
mnâ, to study, 144, I, 5.

-ya I. ft. pt. ps. sf., 187; 239.
-ya 2. grd. sf., 188; 240.
-ya 3. intensive sf., 201.
ya*h* ka*h*   } indef. prn. whoever, 129.
ya*h* ka*sk*it }
ya*g*, to sacrifice, 71; 151, 2; 154, 4;
175, 7; 183, 2; bases from, 90, 3, N. I.
-yat, prn. sf., 128.
yátas, adv., 210.
yáti, a. as many, 128, N.
yáthâ, cj. as, 210.
yathâ-*s*akti, adv. cd., 215, 3.
yád, relat., 125 C; cj., 210.
yádâ—tádâ, when—then, 222.
yádi, cj. if, 248 b.
yam, to restrain, 144, I, 2.
-yas, cpv. bases in, 82, N. I.
yâ, to go, 142, N. 6; 159; 228, I, N.
yâ*k*, to ask, 229, 2.
yá̆vat, cj. while, 210; adv., 244, 2 a.
yá̆vat—tá̆vat, 222.
yu, to join, 144, II, 7 b; 152, 2; 154,
12.
yu*g*, to join, 138, 3; to be fit, 234,
II b; 243.
yúvan, m. young, 103, 4.
yûpa-dâru, n. Tp. cd., 214, 3.
yo ya*h*, etc., indef. prn., 129.

ra*ñg*, to tinge, 144, I, 4; 175, 6; w.
prf. anu, 234, II b.
Rathoddhatâ, f. a metre, App. II,
I B, I e.
rabh, to desire, 181, 2.
râ*g*, to shine, 90, 3, N. I.
râ*g*an, m. king, 102; 105, I and 3;
215, N.
râ*g*a-purusha, m. king's man, Tp.
cd., 214, 5.
râ*g*apurusha-kàrya, n. Tp. cd., 218, N.
râ*g*arshi, m. K. cd., 215, I.
râ*g*ñî, f. queen, 105, 4.
rá̆tri } f. night, 103, f. n.; 215, 2.
rá̆trî }

Râmâyana, 75, N.
ri, to go, 136, 2.
rúk, f. light, 90, 1.
rúg, f. disease, 90, 3.
rud, to weep, 144, II, 1.
rudh, to obstruct, 69; 143.
rurudúshî, f. pf. pt., 105, 4.
rurud-vás, pf. pt., 101; 105, 1 and 3.
ruh, to grow, 79; 194; 196.
raí, m. wealth, 113.

Lakshmî, f. goddess of prosperity, 111, 4.
laghú, a. light, 109, N. 2.
labh, to take, 69; 187, III, 3; 194; 199.
lash, w. prp. abhi, to desire, 234, II b.
lip, to paint, 144, VI, 1.
lih, to smear, 79; 138, 1; 160, 3.
lî, to cling, 186, 1.
lup, to break, 144, VI, 1.
lû, to cut, 144, IX, 1; 158; 180; 186.

Vamsa-sthâ, f. a metre, App. II, I B, 2 a.
vak, to speak, 162, 4; 168, 2; 175, 7; 188; 189; 229, 2.
vaníg, m. merchant, 90, 3.
-vat 1. prn. sf., 128.
-vat 2. pf. pt. sf., 101, N. 2; 186, 2, N.; 238.
-vat 3. pcl. of comparison, 210.
-vat 4. a. sf., 98.
vata, ij. alas, 211.
vadh, to kill, 181, 2; 187, III, 4.
vadhû, f. woman, 111.
-van, bases in, 102.
varam—na, better—than, 210.
varsha-bhogya, Tp. cd., 214, 1.
vas, to desire, 144, II, 8.
-vas, bases in, 82, N. 1; 183; 238.
vas, to dwell, 78; 101, f. n.
Vasanta-tilakâ, f. a metre, App. II, I B, 3.
vah, to carry, 79; 151, 2.
vâ, cj. or, 210; 226.
vâgmín, a. eloquent, 105, 1, 3.
vâgmínî, f., 105, 4.
vâk, f. speech, 90, 1.

vâr, n. water, 92, 3.
vâri, n. water, 109, N. 1.
ví, prp. apart, 207 b.
vid, to know, 142, N. 6; 144, II, 9; 156, II a; 192; 203; w. prf. ni, csv. to tell, 231 A, 1 a.
vid, to find, 144, VI, 1; 186, 1, N.; ps. = to be, 233, I b.
Videhéshu, in Videha, 224 c.
vidyâvat, a. possessed of knowledge, 105, 1, 3.
vidyâvatî, f., 105, 4.
vid-vás, pf. pt. knowing, 114; 183, 2.
vínâ, adv. prp. without, 209 a.
Virâma, m., 7.
vis, a. entering, 93.
vísva, prn. a. all, 130 b.
visva-gúdh, a. all-attracting, 60.
visva-gít, a. all-conquering, 214, N. 2.
visva-pâ, a. all-protecting, 108.
vishaya, m. country, 224 c.
víshv-ak, a. all-pervading, 104.
Visargá, m., 5; 17, 6; 28; 30, 4; 33; 49-52; App. II, introd.
Vîra-sena, m. Bv. cd., 218.
vri, to choose, 148.
vrit, to turn, des., 198.
Vríddhi, f., 20.
vridh, to increase, 166
vríndâraka, a. beautiful, cpv. of, 115.
vrísk, a. cutting, 90, N.
vrî, to choose, 144, IX, 1.
ve, to weave, 175, 8.
Vaitâlîya, n. a metre, App. II, II A.
vyadh, to pierce, 136, 3; 144, IV, 3; 151, 2.
vyâghra-buddhyâ, 230, I, 2, N.
vye, to envelope, 175, 8.
vrask, to cut, 144, VI, 3.

sak, to be able, 144, V, 2; 187, III, 4; 199; 241 b.
Sákvarî, f. a Vedic metre, App. II, I B, 3.
Sankara âkâryâh, pl. of respect, 224 c.
satá, n. a hundred, 118, N. b.
sad, to fall, csv., 194.
sabdáya, den. to make a sound, 206, 3.
sam, to cease, 144, IV, 1.

*s*astra-pâ*n*i, Bv. cd., 219 a.
*S*ârdûla-vikri*d*ita, n. a metre, App. II, I B, 6.
*S*âlinî, f. a metre, App. II, I B, I d.
*s*âs, to rule, instruct, 144, II, 5 ; 162, 3 ; 175, 8 ; 229, 2.
*S*ikharinî, f. a metre, App. II, I B, 5 a.
*s*î, to lie, 144, II, 10.
*s*ukla-kri*shn*au, Dv. cd., 217 a.
*s*u*k*, to grieve, 201.
*s*ú*k*i, a. pure, 109 ; 114.
*s*u*k*iyá, den. to become pure, 206, 2 b.
*s*usru-vás,pf.pt. of *s*ru,to hear,101,N.1.
*s*o, to sharpen, 144, IV, 2.
*s*yenâyá, den., 206, 2 b.
*s*ranth, to become loose, 151, 4.
*s*ram, to be weary, 144, IV, 1.
*s*ri, to go, 152, 1 ; 164.
*s*ru, to hear, 144, V, 3 ; 148 ; 175, 2.
*S*lóka, m. epic metre, App. II, I A.
*s*ván, m. dog, 103, 3.
*s*vas, to breathe, 144, II, 1 ; w. prf. vi, to confide in, 234, II b.
*s*vi, to swell, 162.

shásh, nm. six, 70 ; 118.
sh*th*iv, to spit, 144, I, 1.

sa, m. prn. this, he, 54 ; 223.
Sa*m*skri*t*, sacred language, 1.
sákthi, n. thigh, 110, 3.
sákhi, m. friend, 110, 2 ; 215, N.
sakhî-*g*ana, m. = pl. of sakhî, 224 a.
sa*ñg*, to adhere, 144, I, 4.
sát, being, pr. pt. of as, to be, 182, N.; 235, N. 1.
sad, to sink, 144, I, 1 ; 192.
sadri*s*a, a. equal, 233, II b.
sadhryá*k*, a. accompanying, 104.
Sandhî, m. rules of, 19-79.
sám, prp. together, 207 b.
sama (encl.), prn. a. all, 130 b.
samá, a. equal, 233, II b.
samakshám, adv. prp. in the presence of, 209 d.
samám, adv. prp. together with, 209 d ; 230, I, 1.
samartha, a. able, 242 a.
samid-yá, den., 206, 2 b, N.

Samprasârana, n., 144, IV, 3, f. n.; 151, 2 ; 175, 7.
samyá*k*, a. right, 104.
samrá*g*, m. sovereign, 90, 3, N. 1.
sárva, prn. a. all, 130 b.
savinayam, adv. cd., 215, 3.
sah, to bear, 79 ; 187, III, 4.
sahá, adv. prp. together with, 209 b ; 230, I, 1.
sahásra, n. thousand, 118 b.
sâkám, adv. prp. with, 230, I, 1.
sâdhú, ij. well, 211.
sârdhám, adv. prp. together with, 209 b ; 230, I, 1.
si*k*, to sprinkle, 144, VI, 1 ; 161.
sidh, to succeed, 194.
simá, prn. a. all, 130 b.
su 1. to squeeze out, 138, 4 ; 143 ; 144, V, 1.
su 2. prp. well, 207 b.
su-kritá, a. well-done, K. cd., 215, 3.
su-gán, a. ready reckoner, 91, 2.
su-*g*yotís, a. well-lighted, 95.
su-tús, a. well-sounding, 95.
su-pís, a. well-walking, 76, f. n.; 95.
su-mánas, a. kind, 95.
su-válg, a. well-jumping, 66.
su-hí*m*s, a. striking well, 95, II.
su-hri*d*, a. friendly, 89 ; m. friend, 218.
sri, to go, 148.
sri*g*, to create, 158, irreg., 3 ; 180 ; bases from, 90, 3, N. 1.
stu, to praise, 148 ; 152, 2 ; 154, 13.
stri, to spread, 152, 1 ; 154, 11.
stri, to cover, 144, IX, 1 ; 175, 4 ; 180 ; 186, 1.
stri̇̃, f. woman, 111, N.
sthâ, to stand, 144, I, 3 ; 158, irreg., 2 ; 167 ; 198, 1 ; 237.
snih, to love, bases from, 94, 3 b ; w. prf. anu, 234, II b.
snuh, to spue, bases from, 94, 3 b.
spri*s*, to touch, 158, irreg., 3 ; bases from, 94, 1 a.
sma, pcl., 244, 1 b, N.
smri, to remember, 175, 3 ; 233, I a.
sra*m*s, to fall, bases from, 95, N. 1.
Srag-dharâ, f. a metre, App. II, I B, 7.
srá*g*, f. garland, 90, 3.

sru, to flow, 148.
sru*k*, f. ladle, 90, 1.
svá, reflex. prn. own, 126, 3 ; 130 c.
sva*ñg*, to embrace, 144, I, 4; 151, 4.
svap, to sleep, 144, II, 1 ; 199.
svayám, reflex. prn. self, 126, 1.
svár, indcl. heaven, 52, f. n.
Svarita, m. n. circumflex accent, 18.
svarga-patita, a. Tp. cd., 214, 4.
svá*sri*, f. sister, 112.
svastí, ij. hail ! 211.

ha, pcl., 226.
han, to kill, 66 ; 144, II, 11 ; 150, 3;
  151, 3; 154, 5; 181, 2; 187, III, 4;
  189 b ; 194; 199; 204, 2.

han, at end of cds., 103, 5
hánta, ij. alas ! 211.
harít, a. green, 89.
has, to laugh, 140, 3 ; 187, III, 3.
hástau, m. dual, the hands, 224 b.
hasty-asvam, -au, -*âh*, Dv. cd., 216.
hâ 1. to run away, 144, III, 2.
hâ 2. to leave, 144, III, 2.
hâ 3. ij., 211.
-hi, ipv. sf., 142, N. 4.
hí, cj. for, 210.
hi*m*s, to injure, 144, VII, 1.
hu, to sacrifice, 138, 2 ; 143 ; 156,
  2 b ; 182 ; 184.
hotâ-potârau, Dv. cd., 217 b.
hve, to call, 149; 162; 175, 8.

TIGER OF THE STRIPE

MMVIII